PRENTICE-HALL FOUNDATIONS OF MODERN POLITICAL SCIENCE SERIES
Robert A. Dahl, Editor

THE AGE OF IDEOLOGY-POLITICAL THOUGHT, 1750 TO THE PRESENT, Second Edition
by Isaac Kramnick and Frederick M. Watkins

THE AMERICAN PARTY SYSTEM AND THE AMERICAN PEOPLE, Third Edition
by Fred I. Greenstein and Frank B. Feigert

THE ANALYSIS OF INTERNATIONAL RELATIONS, Second Edition
by Karl W. Deutsch

CONGRESS AND THE PRESIDENCY, Fourth Edition
by Nelson W. Polsby

DATA ANALYSIS FOR POLITICS AND POLICY
by Edward R. Tufte

MODERN POLITICAL ANALYSIS, Fourth Edition
by Robert A. Dahl

MODERN POLITICAL ECONOMY
by Norman Frohlich and Joe A. Oppenheimer

PARTICIPATION
by Jack H. Nagel

THE POLICY-MAKING PROCESS, Second Edition
by Charles E. Lindblom

PARTICIPATION

JACK H. NAGEL
Department of Political Science
University of Pennsylvania

Prentice-Hall, Inc., Englewood Cliffs, New Jersey 07632

Library of Congress Cataloging-in-Publication Data

Nagel, Jack H.
   Participation.
  (Prentice-Hall foundations of modern political
science series)
  Includes bibliographies and index.
  1. Political participation. I. Title. II. Series.
JF2071.N34 1987   323'.042   86-25362
ISBN 0-13-651316-6

PRENTICE-HALL FOUNDATIONS OF MODERN POLITICAL SCIENCE SERIES

ROBERT A. DAHL, EDITOR

© 1987 by Prentice-Hall, Inc.
A Division of Simon & Schuster
Englewood Cliffs, New Jersey 07632

All rights reserved. No part of this book may be
reproduced, in any form or by any means,
without permission in writing from the publisher.

For

Barbara, Shen, and Ming

Printed in the United States of America

10 9 8 7 6 5 4 3 2 1

ISBN 0-13-651316-6 01

Prentice-Hall International (UK) Limited, *London*
Prentice-Hall of Australia Pty. Limited, *Sydney*
Prentice-Hall Canada Inc., *Toronto*
Prentice-Hall Hispanoamericana, S.A., *Mexico*
Prentice-Hall of India Private Limited, *New Delhi*
Prentice-Hall of Japan, Inc., *Tokyo*
Prentice-Hall of Southeast Asia Pte. Ltd., *Singapore*
Editora Prentice-Hall do Brasil, Ltda., *Rio de Janeiro*

CONTENTS

Preface xiii

Chapter 1 CONCEPTS **1**
What Do We Mean by Participation? 1
Boundaries and Fuzzy Areas 3
How This Book Is Organized 5
Notes 7

Chapter 2 VALUES **8**
Theory and Practice 9
Perspectives 10
The Case for Participation 11
Costs of Participation 15
Reconciliation? 17
Notes 20

Chapter 3 MOTIVATION **22**
Why Do People Not Participate? 23
Why Rational Egoists Sometimes Participate 26
Moral Motives for Participating 31
Notes 35

Chapter 4 CONTEXT   37
Political Culture   38
Organizational Encouragement   40
Structure   42
Policies   46
Conclusion   49
Notes   51

Chapter 5 EQUALITY   53
Extent versus Intensity   53
Representativeness and Motivation   54
Social Class   58
Responses to Inequality   60
The Dilemma Persists   64
Notes   66

Chapter 6 DEMOCRACY   69
Ideals of Direct Democracy   70
Issues in the Practice of Direct Democracy   72
Notes   82

Chapter 7 SIZE   84
The Logic of Numbers   84
Decentralization   87
Direct Legislation   90
Referendums Based on Local Assemblies   96
Indirect Elections   97
Notes   98

Chapter 8 ELECTIONS   100
Rules Matter   101
Elections Matter   109
Participation Matters   114
Notes   121

Chapter 9 PRESSURE   125
The Organization of Pressure   126
Three Types of Political Organization   129
Membership Participation in Control of Staff and Policies   135
Evaluating Participation in Pressure Politics   139
Notes   142

Chapter 10 ADMINISTRATION   145
Types of Citizen Involvement   146
Three Images of Citizen Involvement   150
Conditions Favoring Successful Coproduction   153
Notes   157

Chapter 11   WORKPLACES   **160**
    Varieties of Workplace Participation   160
    Reasons for Workplace Participation   165
    Ideology and the Future of Workplace Democracy   171
    Notes   178

Epilogue   *181*
Index   *185*

PREFACE

Texts on politics and administration usually guide your attention to the actions of leaders who specialize in making decisions: presidents, senators, generals, managers. This book will be different. The study of participation is about the rest of us, ordinary people seeking to be more than just pawns for others to direct and manipulate, striving instead to shape policies and organizations according to our own desires.

You probably already know a good deal about the most common form of participation—voting. Perhaps you have come to view it cynically, thinking that campaigns depend too much on money and media or that the sheer force of numbers dilutes the value of your ballot so much that casting it seems hardly worthwhile. I hope that reading this book will enable you to see the power as well as the problems of voting. Nevertheless, participation includes much more than voting and campaigning. In recent decades, the democratic ideal has intensified, inspiring a search for richer, less perfunctory forms of self-government. Under the banner of "participatory democracy," visionaries have claimed the right for people to share in social decisions that affect the quality and direction of their lives.

In response, scholars now recognize that methods of and occasions for popular participation are much broader than just electoral politics. Citizens also express their wishes by organizing, protesting, lobbying, litigating, meeting, and reasoning together. Settings in which people try to shape policies include many not ordinarily thought of as "political"—for instance, neighborhoods, labor unions, administrative agencies, factories, and offices. The pages that follow therefore offer an analysis that should have practical value wherever you choose to apply and test it—as a citizen, student, resident, or employee; or as a politician, organizer, planner, or executive if you want to work *with* rather than against the ordinary members of your system.

I find participation an exciting topic to teach and to write about, both because it relates so closely to personal experience and because it taps deep ideals of democracy and community. If you feel the same way, some ideas in this book may prove unsettling, though they are not meant to be antagonistic. Our subject requires a certain toughness in thought and action, for participation is easy to advocate but hard to practice. If you believe in participation, you must confront difficulties, dangers, and dilemmas that cannot be solved by mere exhortation: Most people want the right to participate, but no one consistently participates. Different forms of participation embody contradictory values and yield conflicting results. Elites, whether bureaucrats or demagogues, use participatory devices to mask their own manipulative rule. Inspired though it is by egalitarian ideals, participation often serves the interests of the privileged. Enthusiasts who encounter such obstacles unprepared all too often retreat discouraged and disillusioned. One purpose of this book is to protect you from error and paralysis by equipping you with a clearheaded appreciation of both the promise and complexity of participatory democracy.

To accomplish our task, we shall draw on three sources of enlightenment. First and most fundamental is the inventive practice of people around the world. Second are the writings of those who have observed and thought about politics: philosophers of the past, contemporary analysts or advocates, and painstaking scientific researchers. Finally, we can learn from ourselves, for the "phenomena of participation are everywhere."[1] In studying participation we may not all be expert, but we are all experienced—as citizens, neighbors, workers, and members of clubs, fraternities, sororities, and unions. We therefore can ground our thinking in our own actions as participants. With a little more reflection, we can also draw lessons from the frequent occasions when we forego chances to participate or when we are denied the opportunity. For all of us who are not politicians or officials, participation is the one topic in political analysis that enables us most directly to relate our lives to the systems that govern us—and through which we may hope to govern ourselves.

* * *

The origin of this book lies in my own youthful experiences as a participant in political events and as a student of politics trying to reflect upon what I had done and seen outside the classroom. During that period, seminars with Charles Gilbert at Swarthmore College and with Robert Dahl at Yale University had a strong effect in stimulating and structuring my thinking about

---

[1] Robert H. Salisbury, "Research on Political Participation," *American Journal of Political Science*, 19 (1975), 338.

participation. Years later, Professor Dahl again played a crucial role by encouraging me to write this book.

As a teacher myself, at the University of Pennsylvania, I learned much from my students as I developed the ideas presented here in collaboration with successive classes of graduates and undergraduates. One among them, Eva Moskowitz, deserves special thanks. Her detailed critique of the first five chapters improved those pages and influenced my approach in later chapters.

I am also grateful for the comments, suggestions, or evaluations provided by colleagues, friends, and family members who generously read part or all of the manuscript. They include Peter Bachrach, Paul D. Blanchard, Steven J. Brams, Robert A. Dahl, Joanne Gowa, Russell Hardin, Neal Herrick, Richard A. Joslyn, Edwin Koc, Stuart Langton, Jane Mansbridge, Samuel Merrill, Kevin V. Mulcahy, Ethel Nagel, Robert Nagel, William G. Nagel, Richard G. Niemi, Paul Quirk, and Patricia Bayer Richard. For typing and word-processing, I am indebted to Christine Cohen, Patricia Cook, Liz Dobson, Sandra McDermin, Elda Quinn, and especially Brigitta Howe. At various stages of the editorial process, I received patient and efficient help from Stan Wakefield, Audrey Marshall, Elizabeth O'Brien, Marjorie Turko, Barbara Bernstein, Maria Chiarino, and Dale Ramsey. Needless to say, no one who assisted me should be blamed for faults I was too stubborn or too slow-witted to correct.

My greatest debt is to the three people to whom I have dedicated the book: my wife, Barbara, and my two older children, Shen and Ming. They had to endure my preoccupation with this project for much too long; without their love and support, I might never have finished it. And, near the end, Laura arrived to give us all fresh inspiration.

CHAPTER 1

CONCEPTS

To understand participation, we must first know what it is. Generally speaking, to participate means to share or to take part in. You can participate in sports, profits, conversations, and many other activities that have nothing to do with this book. In the language of politics, the word takes on a more specialized meaning.

WHAT DO WE MEAN BY PARTICIPATION?

Participation refers to *actions through which ordinary members of a political system influence or attempt to influence outcomes.*

The key words in this definition are meant to be understood in ways reasonably compatible with both plain English and prevailing usage in political science. Nevertheless, it's worthwhile to explicate each of them in turn, both to highlight some peculiarities and to make more specific the nature and limits of our subject.

Some theorists are quite capable of defining sleep as an act, but normally, *action* connotes movement, energy, and effort. Therefore, let us exclude from the meaning of *participation* passive psychological attributes such as knowledge, beliefs, and attitudes. Focusing on activity points us directly to the problem of how to motivate effort, which, in Chapter 3, is our starting point in developing a theory of participation. What sort of acts constitute participation? Later in this chapter and throughout the book, this question is answered in more analytical fashion. For the moment let's be content with a short list of familiar examples: voting, demonstrating, canvassing, contributing money, writing letters, signing petitions, attending meetings, and joining organizations.

"*Ordinary members* of a political system" can be any persons except those who perform the activities in question as a requirement of their principal jobs. Thus, a forest ranger who presides at a public hearing on new wilderness boundaries is not a participant in our sense, but local residents who testify for and against the plan are. The ranger, in turn, participates when he attends a school board meeting. To be sure, there is a continuum here. Between the professional decision maker and the ordinary member fall such people as the part-time state representative paid to attend several legislative sessions a year, the campaign "volunteer" who will lose her city job unless she turns out voters for the mayor, and the professor who attends faculty assemblies to improve his chances for promotion. The in-between cases will not trouble us if we take as our starting point plain citizens, not bureaucrats and politicians; rank-and-file dues-payers, not union business agents; interest-group contributors, not lobbyists; and workers, not executives. Restricting participants in this way leads quickly to central difficulties of participatory action—incentives, time, information, and numbers—all quite different problems for ordinary members than for professional decision makers. Our definition also points to the intimate tie between participation and democracy, the fact that participation has to do with influence from the bottom up, not from the top down.

What then does influence mean? Participants *influence* events if their preferences concerning an issue cause outcomes they prefer to occur.[1] In other words, those with influence get what they want (or part of what they want) because they want it, rather than as a gift from benevolent rulers or a windfall from Lady Luck.

Outcome is a general term for the variety of events participants influence. Most obviously, participation can determine *who serves* in decision-making positions, as when voters elect executives or legislators. By pressuring officials or directly through referendums and meetings, participants can influence *decisions*—for instance, the passage of laws, the issuance of regulations, or the ordering of troops to war. Finally, by implementing policies through their own effort, participants can influence what is actually done, the *outputs* by which political systems are finally justified—park landscaping, safety standards enforcement, or crime prevention, for example.

Political system (or *polity* for short) I define broadly as any organized structure of power, influence, and authority. Polities include not only governments but also other organizations that control, through sanctions or legitimacy, the behavior or resources of their members. Workplaces are political in this sense, as are labor unions, pressure groups, universities, professional associations, and utopian communities. Such a broad purview is justified principally because a single body of analysis helps us understand participation in all these diverse settings.²

BOUNDARIES AND FUZZY AREAS

Broad though it is, our definition does not cover everything ordinary people do in political affairs. We can limit the concept by exploring three classes of behavior that fall on the borderline of participation.

Psychological Involvement

Many people enjoy following political events and forming opinions without engaging in action. For some political spectators politics is a form of entertainment; politicians make good copy in gossip columns, especially when romantically linked with rock singers or movie stars, and November elections enliven the dull gap between the World Series and the Super Bowl. Simply taking an interest in government—watching television news, reading newspapers, casually talking politics with friends—does not by itself influence anything; indeed, the citizen as consumer of political information is highly vulnerable to the influence of others. To be sure, the knowledge and attitudes thus acquired may be preconditions of effective action, but it is the action itself that we want to examine.

Mobilization

If psychological involvement constitutes having preferences without acting, then the converse is to engage in activity that does not depend on one's own preferences. Authorities often stimulate and control the behavior of ordinary members—turning them out for massive parades, compelling them to labor on public works projects, and inducing them to vote in single-candidate elections. Most writers in the Western world do not regard such activity as participation, preferring to call it "mobilization" instead. Others distinguish "mobilized" participation from "autonomous," or "democratic," participation. Some recognize that "virtually all political systems include a mix of mobilized and autonomous participation,"³ but American writers often dismiss mass activity in Communist systems with invidious phrases like "the pseudoparticipation of totalitarian mobilist regimes."⁴

The difference between participation and mobilization might be thought to hinge on the degree of *initiative* exercised by ordinary members. Although truly spontaneous popular action warms the heart of any good democrat, a moment's reflection shows that the people initiate little of what we normally call participation. Even the freest elections are instigated and conducted by governments. Similarly, most other acts of participation are stimulated by elites—if not by the government, then by parties, interest groups, agitators, and organizers. A second distinction might be that only *voluntary* actions constitute true participation.[5] This test also fails, for voting itself is compulsory in several democracies.

In meaningful elections, of course, citizens select among alternative candidates. Should *choice* be the decisive criterion? Almost, but not in the most obvious sense. Recall that our definition of participation requires that members influence (or attempt to influence) outcomes—that is, they cause outcomes they prefer. Certainly, a free choice among candidates or other options sets up the potential for influence. But sometimes citizens influence what happens without having any obvious choice among policies.

Consider the following fictitious, but not too farfetched, example. In a remote district of a poor country, the regional commissioner decides to enlist the people's energies in building a new airstrip. Without consulting residents, he calls a meeting, explains his plan, and asks for volunteers. The villagers, who have no desire to help the commissioner fly back and forth to the fleshpots of the capital more easily, ignore his entreaties and go back to their fields. Chagrined, the commissioner tries again. This time he proposes to build an irrigation system. Pleased by the prospect of a stable water supply, the people turn out enthusiastically. After months of labor, they complete a network of ditches that doubles farm yields in the next year. This sort of mass physical involvement in economic development is just the sort of thing many writers label mobilization. Yet the villagers' desire for one project and not the other determined the final outcome, even though they were never presented with a formal choice between alternatives. The fact that the labor was truly voluntary gave them at least the implicit choice between accomplishing each project and maintaining the status quo.

The conclusion is, then, that the existence of, or the potential for, member influence best distinguishes participation from mobilization and that although either voluntary activity or formal choice among options may be sufficient for such influence, neither is necessary.

Private Goals

When members participate, the people who will gain from successful action can range from everyone in the system to a single individual. Researchers have dignified the latter case with the technical name *particularized contacting*.[6] Examples include complaining to a caseworker about a missing welfare check and getting a member of Congress to introduce a "private bill" that will enable a relative abroad to emigrate to the United States. The accessibility of a polity to individual influence makes a big difference in the quality of life; however, the theory presented in this book depends on participants pursuing goals they share with at least some fellow citizens. Thus, while we may accept particularized contacting as a limiting form of participation, our analysis will not shed much light on that type of citizen action.[7]

HOW THIS BOOK IS ORGANIZED

Several times already, I have referred to "the theory," or "the analysis," of participation, using its relevance to justify our interest in nongovernmental systems and its inapplicability to excuse our slight attention to particularized contacting. Although some scholars question the possibility of making general statements about participation, the topic has more coherence than they recognize.[8] Accordingly, in Chapters 2 through 5, participation is treated as a unified concept, and variations in its amount are justified or explained. Chapters 6 through 10 recognize distinct forms of participation, each depending on a different basis for participants' influence, but continue to strive for broad applicability across national and organizational settings. Finally, Chapter 11 shows the vitality of participatory theory by drawing on the entire analysis to explain the worldwide movement for democracy in workplaces. Before we proceed with this plan, you may first find helpful an explanation of how the amount of participation varies and how different types of participation depend on different influence bases.

Variations in the Amount of Participation

The first fact to grasp about participation is that it fluctuates a great deal in quantity. Human beings can live without participating at all; despite the fervent claims of enthusiasts, it is not as essential to survival as breathing. Political systems also can get along without permitting participation, as autocracies have proven through the ages, although the healthfulness of such an existence—for people and for societies—may be doubted.

Participation varies along two main dimensions: extent and intensity. Participation is increasingly *extensive* as more people engage in it. In the United States, for example, the suffrage has become progressively more extensive, beginning with white male property-owners only and then broadening to include white workingmen, black men, women, and eventually people from ages eighteen to twenty. Participation is more *intensive* as its cost to the individual increases—in effort, money, or time (either duration or frequency). Holding a meeting increases the intensity of participation when compared with circulating a mail ballot; and walking in a picket line is more intensive than signing a petition.

Several other characteristics are linked to extent and intensity. Participation can be more extensive the greater the simultaneity among actions, as when hundreds of thousands vote at nearly the same instant. Participation that requires sequential acts, such as debate and discussion, must always be especially intensive.[9] Simultaneous acts, unfortunately, are likely to be low in information content when compared with intensive, costly efforts like writing a well-reasoned letter to an official.[10]

The amount of participation can be measured across individuals, groups, systems, and time. Individuals differ greatly in the intensity of their political involvement. In a 1967 survey, 22 percent of United States citizens reported no political activity at all. Another 21 percent did nothing except vote. Only 11 percent frequently engaged in the full range of activities about which people were questioned: voting, campaigning, contacting officials, and working in community organizations.[11] If individual differences in participation just reflected personal tastes or other idiosyncracies, they would be politically inconsequential. Unfortunately, tendencies to participate are closely linked with group membership: economic class, race, age, place of residence, sex, and the like. In the United States, 57 percent of highly active citizens rank in the upper third of the population in socioeconomic status; the bottom third contributes only 14 percent.[12] Participation rates also differ across systems. Variations are not confined to the obvious contrasts between repressive and free polities. A study of seven democracies found that voting rates ranged from 59 percent in India to 96 percent in Austria. Lest you think that Austrians are in all respects model citizens, note that only 9 percent of them reported involvement in community organizations, compared with 32 percent of Americans.[13] Finally, activity rates of individuals, groups, or systems can change remarkably over time. People are less likely to vote when young or very old than when middle-aged.[14] Between 1960 and 1968 in the American South, the proportion of blacks registered to vote leaped from 28 percent to 62 percent;[15] but from 1960 to 1980 the national turnout in presidential elections slid from 63 percent to 53 percent.

Does it matter how much (or how many) people participate? Are active citizens better (or better off) for their pains? Does participation invigorate or endanger a polity? In Chapter 2, we turn to these central questions of democratic political theory. Chapters 3 and 4 continue to ask questions about the amount of participation, but from an empirical (what is), rather than a normative (what ought to be), standpoint, as we try to understand why people participate and why they don't, why some systems are hotbeds of activity and others, sloughs of apathy. The conclusions we reach enable us to return, in Chapter 5, to another crucial evaluative issue: the interaction of participation and equality.

Bases of Influence

If participants succeed in bringing about outcomes they prefer, there must exist some reason for their influence—in technical terms, a power base or resource. Power, or influence, bases fall into two broad classes. First, participants themselves may possess decision-making authority. Second, when ordinary members lack such authority, they must influence those who do have the right to make decisions.

Of the later chapters in this book, three deal mainly with the first type of influence. Chapters 6 and 7 examine situations in which ordinary members themselves decide matters of policy, as in town meetings or referendums. The ancients named this "democracy," but modern writers usually call it "direct democracy," in contrast with the more familiar "indirect," or "representative democracy," which is the subject of Chapter 8. Here ordinary members have formal authority only during elections, when they decide which leaders to entrust with policymaking power.

Once authorities are in office, members still have ways to affect decisions. They can bring pressure to bear by rewarding or punishing officeholders. This is the subject of Chapter 9, where we examine how people participate through interest groups and protest movements, whose tactics can range from the mundanely respectable to the violently rebellious. Not all dealings between authorities and members are antagonistic. In Chapter 10, we look at how citizens participate in the process of administration, using several bases of influence: information, delegated power, or the giving and withholding of labor.

NOTES

1. Jack H. Nagel, *The Descriptive Analysis of Power* (New Haven: Yale University Press, 1975). See also Robert A. Dahl, *Modern Political Analysis*, 4th ed., Foundations of Modern Political Science Series (Englewood Cliffs, N.J.: Prentice-Hall, 1984), chaps. 3 and 4.

2. The study of participation is an excellent place for the interchange Herbert Kaufman advocates between political theory and organization theory, "encompassing within a single theoretical framework propositions about states . . . and propositions about other forms of human association." "Organization Theory and Political Theory," *American Political Science Review*, 58 (1964), 5–14.

3. Samuel P. Huntington and Joan M. Nelson, *No Easy Choice: Political Participation in Developing Countries* (Cambridge: Harvard University Press, 1976), p. 8.

4. David Hapgood, ed., *The Role of Popular Participation in Development* (Cambridge: MIT Press, 1969), p. 21. Other observers are less inclined toward black and white labels; for example, Jerry F. Hough, "Political Participation in the Soviet Union," *Soviet Studies*, 28 (1976), 3–20.

5. Herbert McClosky, "Political Participation," *International Encyclopedia of the Social Sciences* (New York: Collier and Macmillan, 1968), pp. 12, 252–65.

6. Sidney Verba and Norman H. Nie, *Participation in America: Political Democracy and Social Equality* (New York: Harper & Row, 1972), pp. 64–73.

7. This theoretical separateness corresponds to (and explains) Verba and Nie's empirical finding of "the absence of relationship between particularized contacting and other forms of participation." Ibid., p. 75.

8. Among the skeptics are Huntington and Nelson: "(I)f we want to understand the causes and consequences of different patterns of political participation, we cannot think of participation as a simple, homogeneous variable. 'Political participation' is *an umbrella concept*, a label for a whole set of variables; each variable fits the core definition, but each also has somewhat different causes and consequences and relates differently to social and economic trends." *No Easy Choice*, p. 14 (emphasis altered).

9. Robert A. Dahl, *After the Revolution? Authority in a Good Society* (New Haven: Yale University Press, 1970), p. 68.

10. Verba and Nie, *Participation in America*, pp. 47–48, 102–21.

11. Ibid., pp. 79–80.

12. Ibid., p. 131.

13. Sidney Verba, Norman H. Nie, and Jae-on Kim, *Participation and Political Equality: A Seven-Nation Comparison* (Cambridge: Cambridge University Press, 1978), pp. 58–59.

14. Raymond E. Wolfinger and Steven J. Rosenstone, *Who Votes?* (New Haven: Yale University Press, 1980), pp. 37–41.

15. David Campbell and Joe R. Feagin, "Black Politics in the South: A Descriptive Analysis," *Journal of Politics*, 37 (1975), 133.

CHAPTER 2

VALUES

Why should we care about participation? Do we even need to discuss this question? After all, in a democracy, doesn't everyone believe that people should take part in governing themselves?

In the modern West, especially in the United States, it is indeed hard to find anyone—scholar or plain citizen—who openly repudiates democratic government and the basic participatory rights that go with it. As we have just seen, however, the amount of participation varies widely even in democratic societies. Beliefs about the value of participation therefore affect the way people respond to highly practical questions: How much should government do to extend or protect voting rights? (Recall that most college students were once ineligible to vote.) Should we try to increase turnout rates in elections? Is it a good idea to enact laws through referendums? How readily should we join or respond to protestors? Should we compel bureaucrats to involve citizens in planning and carrying out public programs?

In nongovernmental institutions, where most of our everyday life takes place, participatory decision making remains the exception, despite the sway of democratic doctrine in the political realm. Hierarchies of managers rule most workplaces, and many other organizations offer little opportunity for effective participation. How important is it for the rank and file to insist on union democracy? Should we follow the lead of countries like Yugoslavia, West Germany, and Norway in seeking to democratize workplaces? Your personal attitudes towards participation will also be tested when you find yourself in a position of leadership in your job, club, or neighborhood. When should you govern autocratically? How much should you involve others in making decisions?

Further from home, answers to questions about the value of participation are important for policy and understanding. How tolerant should we be of "authoritarian" governments? Does the inability of people to organize cooperatively cause economic as well as political backwardness? Is it desirable to require, as Congress did in 1966, that United States foreign aid officials encourage "maximum participation" of the citizens of developing countries in promoting economic development?[1] Many communist and fascist regimes came to power with the aid of enthusiastic popular support, and most greatly expanded mass political activity. Is widespread participation therefore dangerous? Are there good and bad types of participation? Did the United States "lose" China and Vietnam because we failed to recognize the strength revolutionaries gained by using participatory techniques? Do some communist countries, as their admirers insist, practice a new type of more direct and egalitarian democracy?

THEORY AND PRACTICE

In most of this chapter, we shall be reviewing the arguments of social and political theorists. Do their debates about participation have anything to do with what really happens? Although some merely scholastic bickering does go on, this is one area where theory and practice intertwine. Occasionally, scholars strongly affect events. The research of social psychologist Kurt Lewin and his students inspired corporations to experiment with participatory decision making.[2] A University of Michigan philosopher, Arnold Kaufman, coined the phrase "participatory democracy,"[3] and his student Tom Hayden made it a slogan of a national movement in the 1960s.

More often, however, the tides of intellectual fashion follow events. In the decade after World War II, for example, American political thinkers began to doubt the value of encouraging more participation. Several developments provoked their pessimism: evidence that the votes and violence of previously apolitical segments of the German population had carried Hitler to power; surveys that showed American voters were less active, less informed, and less committed to democratic values than theorists had assumed; and the popularity of Senator Joseph McCarthy's demagogic assault on civil liberties. Thus intimidated, orthodox scholars of the 1950s and early 1960s feared efforts to intensify participation beyond the basic right to vote, condoned the apathy of average citizens under a "let sleeping dogs lie" philosophy, and looked to educated elites rather than to ordinary people for protection of democratic values.[4]

In the 1960s, this cautious doctrine suffered onslaughts from both activists and theorists. In the United States, civil rights crusaders used mass demonstrations to extend the suffrage to southern blacks; the student movement proselytized for participatory democracy on and off campus; and Congress mandated "maximum feasible participation" of the poor in the community action programs of the War on Poverty. Both stimulating and responding to this burst of activity, a new generation of scholars attacked the orthodoxy that they dubbed "democratic elitism," advocating instead a more adventurous willingness to entrust decision making to common people in government and everyday life.

In the 1970s, the participatory impulse manifested itself in somewhat different ways. New activists more often were female than nonwhite or young; the middle class turned to environmentalism and consumerism; some who once dreamed of revolution now preached neighborhood and workplace democracy; the Office of Economic Opportunity was dismantled, but Congress continued to require participation in most new programs. In the scholarly debate, some erstwhile "elitists" responded to advocates of participation with sympathetic counsel;[5] but others called for an ebbing of the participatory tide, contending that "an excess of democracy" had overburdened government with new demands while undermining the authority necessary to satisfy them.[6] In the 1980s, the Reagan administration put the latter doctrine into effect by rolling back some participatory opportunities as well as policy gains activists had won; however, the conservative ascendancy began with victories that exploited a participatory device, the referendum, to curtail local government taxing and spending, and much of the Reagan program aimed to return governmental functions to states and localities, where citizens might more easily influence decisions.

PERSPECTIVES

Within the democratic tradition, it is impossible to oppose participation across the board, but many democrats reject it in particular settings or forms. The most enthusiastic supporters of participation are inclined to make sweeping claims, but it is rare nowadays to encounter anyone who sees in participatory democracy a panacea, "the single most effective remedy for the accumulated ills of poverty, apathy, slavishness, inauthenticity, incompetence, manipulation, and, above all, powerlessness."[7] By virtue of ideology or temperament, you will have your own predisposition to favor or oppose participatory decision making. This book will not try to convert you into a friend or foe of participation; but whatever your basic attitude, I hope you will advance beyond expressing it unthinkingly. Instead you should learn to balance advantages and drawbacks from situation to situation, relating them to factors and choices that are explored throughout the book. Our shared purpose here is not to choose sides, but rather to learn to think and act with a clear head.

As we begin, a couple of basic distinctions will help straighten out claims that might otherwise seem contradictory. First, on what level of society do benefits and costs of participation fall? Consequences for individuals, groups, or the system as a whole can differ dramatically. Second, from what viewpoint is participation judged? We can evaluate it against a person's present preferences, the transformed preferences of the individual after he has experienced participation, the values of an observer, or standards drawn from some abstract ethical system.

For example, suppose a friend wants to persuade you to get involved in an off-campus political group—the National Women's Political Caucus will do. She begins with the lure that the caucus could provide a network to support the political career you've sometimes thought about (your benefit as evaluated by what she believes are your present desires). If you object that you'd rather spend your spare time at parties, she might retort that parties now seem more fun, but political activity provides deeper satisfactions that you will appreciate only after you've taken part (your benefit evaluated by your future, transformed preferences). Alternatively, your friend might argue that personal ambition and pleasure are secondary, that activism can make you a stronger, more assertive, more admirable person (an appeal from the perspective of her own values but still referring to consequences for you). Or finally, she might claim that you are morally obligated to join, because the progress of women and the nation depends on the political involvement of able people like you. (Note that arguments about ethical duties usually go hand-in-hand with appeals invoking the welfare of collectivities. Chapter 3 explains why.)

THE CASE FOR PARTICIPATION

Benefits of participation fall into three categories: instrumental, developmental, and intrinsic.[8]

Instrumental Arguments

"For most people, political participation is simply a means to other goals," say Huntington and Nelson in a succinct statement of the instrumental, or utilitarian, argument for participation.[9] What are the ends for which participation is a means? Anything participants want that they cannot achieve through purely private effort. The assumption behind this is commonsensical enough: People who act will exercise more power than people who do nothing and therefore will get more of what they want, whatever that might be. Of course, not all participants can win all the time, if only because some of them usually want incompatible things. Nevertheless, the idea that participation is a source of influence seems self-evident to most people.

If you need more convincing before agreeing to this assumption, consider the best possible situation for passive citizens: Their rulers are benevolent and want to respond to members' needs. Even such saintly authorities cannot do their jobs well unless they know what members want, understand the conditions under which the people live, and monitor whether their policies actually work. All of this requires communication from citizens to leaders, and such communication is a type of participation. To use a classic analogy, only if the customer tells where the shoe pinches can the cobbler make it fit.[10] People therefore want to be heard; they demand a voice or a say in decisions that affect their lives.

In the American political tradition, it is seldom expected that authorities will spontaneously and without additional incentives seek to please the people they are supposed to serve. Effective participation normally requires that members have the right to make decisions themselves, the authority to vote decision makers in or out of office, or the ability in other ways to reward and punish those in power. Then we can be more sure that not only will the cobbler *know how* to make good shoes, the cobbler will also *want* to make good shoes. As John Stuart Mill put it, "The rights and interests of every or any person are only secure from being disregarded, when the person interested is himself able, and habitually disposed, to stand up for them."[11]

Unfortunately, as a way of persuading people to favor universal participation, the instrumental argument suffers from major shortcomings.

First, those who make this case seldom distinguish whether the benefits of participation accrue to the individual or to the group to which the individual belongs. Consider an extreme version of Mill's lesson: Even if nations are indeed more secure when their citizens are ready to fight for them, the patriotic soldier can nevertheless end up killed in action. In fact, as will be seen in Chapter 3, groups gain if their members work for collective goals, but such effort is usually not instrumentally worthwhile for the individual.

Second, utilitarian attitudes toward participation shift in response to opportunistic calculations. Old-fashioned Democratic city organizations, for example, usually promote high turnout in statewide elections but discourage turnout in local primaries. In the first instance, they need to offset the Republican suburban and rural advantage with big margins from urban voters, but in local intraparty contests, low turnout means that uncontrolled ballots will not swamp the reliable votes of patronage-influenced loyalists. Similarly, Republicans often oppose easier voter registration, because they think that most new registrants will vote Democratic. Such dreary behavior is commonplace. One task of political philosophy, however, is to base policy positions on something more than the ancient question of *cui bono?* ("to whose advantage?").

Some writers try to make the instrumentalist framework more public-spirited by contending that participants pursuing their own interests will also advance widely shared systemic values. Chief among these are liberty and equality. As Mill implies, to protect their freedom, citizens must exercise participatory rights. Whether participation and liberty are always mutually supportive seems questionable. Some observers, doubting the commitment of common people to basic rights, welcome political activity by members of the American Civil Liberties Union but fear to rouse the less tolerant. Moreover, as we shall see in future chapters, certain forms of coercion can actually promote participation. Similarly, the contribution of participation to equality no longer seems assured. True, the poorer majority could use their votes to redistribute income through welfare spending and soak-the-rich taxes, but in Chapter 5 we'll look at reasons why this doesn't always happen. Indeed, when the affluent are more active or more effective in politics, participatory systems may protect the privileged and worsen the condition of less prosperous people.

Whenever participation is seen only as a means to other ends, commitment to it will be tentative and contingent. If the goals sought are achievable with less citizen activity, then there is no instrumental reason to extend or intensify participation. If the objectives of participation seem not worth the cost or can be secured by other means, then from the instrumental perspective, people need not participate at all.

Developmental Effects

All democrats believe that participation has some degree of instrumental value. Advocates of participatory democracy set themselves apart from so-called elitist democrats by their belief in the developmental value of participation. In the words of Arnold Kaufman, "A democracy of participation may have many beneficial consequences, but its main justifying function is and always has been . . . the contribution it can make to the development of human powers of thought, feeling, and action."[12]

Participation has developmental, or educative, effects to the extent that the process of participation itself changes participants by developing in them new values, attitudes, skills, knowledge, and beliefs. Because the individual is thus transformed by the participatory experience, advocates of the educative effects of participation rarely invoke the individual's present preferences to justify political involvement. Indeed, they usually hope that people will change by adopting more worthy values. Theorists who believe in this character-forming function of democratic participation tend to be dissatisfied with people as they are but optimistic about the possibilities for their improvement.

What are the educative effects that its advocates attribute to participation? First, they believe, people who participate will gain in political efficacy. They will learn how the system works and develop skills that enable them to affect its decisions. Second, participants, by interacting with others of diverse views, will become better democratic citizens. They will learn to accept people who differ from themselves. Seeing how they themselves are protected by rules of the democratic game, they will appreciate the need to extend rights to everyone. Hearing and understanding the needs and views of others, they will become more likely, in Rousseau's phrase, "to will the general will" rather than to push one-sidedly for their own narrow interests. Third, involvement in making decisions will elicit greater commitment to the system as a whole. As Mill wrote, "Wherever the sphere of action of human beings is artificially circumscribed, their sentiments are narrowed and dwarfed in the same proportion. The food of feeling is action.... Let a person have nothing to do for his country, and he will not care for it."[13]

Participants should also tend to accept particular decisions more readily. Having heard the pros and cons of a policy debated, members better understand its nature and justification. Having had a chance to influence a decision, participants perceive the process as fair, even when the outcome goes against their immediate interests. Group approval of a policy harnesses powerful social forces in favor of compliance. These principles have gained scientific support from a long tradition of small-group experiments and practical action stemming from the work of Kurt Lewin and his associates. Herbert Simon summarized the results of this research in the "participation hypothesis": "Significant changes in human behavior can be brought about rapidly only if the persons who are expected to change participate in deciding what the change shall be and how it shall be made."[14]

Obviously, the various educative effects of participation can greatly facilitate the smooth functioning of a polity or organization. Consequently, some managers exploit the participation hypothesis by promoting "pseudo-participation"—tricking people into feeling they have chosen something that was actually predetermined by higher authorities. Generally, just as instrumentalist arguments for participation tend to neglect personal costs of political activity that serves group interests, those who believe in the transforming power of participation too often subordinate individual wants to systemic needs. Let us therefore consider gratifications that people get directly from political action.

Intrinsic Values

Intrinsic benefits of participation are immediately and inextricably tied to the act and process of participation. Those who do not participate may not be able to imagine such rewards. As Rousseau wrote of freedom, it "is like innocence and virtue in that only those who have it are aware of its value, and when they lose it, they lose their taste for it."[15] For this reason, intrinsic benefits are often grouped with developmental effects, but the participants themselves feel gratified by intrinsic benefits, whereas developmental values may be beneficial only in the eye of the observer.

What are these intrinsic gratifications? Paradoxically, the chief among them—often experienced simultaneously—are an enhanced sense of one's own individual worth and an intensified identification with one's community. Saul Alinsky illustrates the first of these effects in the life of a poor person who joins a protesting community organization:

This man, in a demonstration at City Hall, might find himself confronting the mayor and saying, "Mr. Mayor, we have had it up to here and we are not going to take it any more." Television cameramen put their microphones in front of him and ask, "What is your name, sir?" "John Smith." Nobody ever asked him what his name was before. And then, "What do you think about this, Mr. Smith?" Nobody ever asked him what he thought about anything before. Suddenly he's alive![16]

Jack Lively puts more abstractly the importance of the pride and dignity that comes from political activity: "This idea of citizenship as a stamp denoting communal acknowledgement of individual worth has historically provided probably the strongest emotional thrust towards democracy."[17]

Of course, not every activist becomes a spokesperson on television. For most participants, perhaps the deepest gratification comes from the sense of having a purpose, of being part of a community or movement greater than oneself, identifying with a group or nation in which all may assert themselves, in which all have a share of power. Perhaps you have felt this way—at a polling place in November or marching in a demonstration or enjoying the palpable change of atmosphere when you move from an authoritarian to a participatory workplace or from a dictatorial to a democratic country.

COSTS OF PARTICIPATION

Advocates of participation group into just a few categories the benefits they believe it brings about, and they assert those values in sweeping terms. Arguments against participation comprise a more discursive list, and most are advanced not as reasons for rejecting participation across the board but as drawbacks that may prove decisive rebuttals in particular contexts, especially when the level of participation becomes too high. As Samuel Huntington puts it, "A value which is normally good in itself is not necessarily optimized when it is maximized."[18]

Time

Like any activity, participation takes time. The time required for voting is brief, but more intensive forms of participation, such as meetings and discussion, demand substantial amounts of the only resource that is inevitably fixed for all of us. In one democratic workplace studied by Jane Mansbridge, members spent an average of seven hours a week in meetings.[19] When the Chinese Communists introduced participatory government to villages as part of the land reform process in the 1940s, peasants were at first delighted, but later they become more aware of the burdens of democracy. "Under the Nationalists, too many taxes," they grumbled. "Under the Communists, too many meetings."[20] I have heard the lament echoed by many a faculty member contemplating the mixed blessings of collegial self-government.

Economic Losses

The true cost of time devoted to participation is the opportunity one forgoes to use that time for other purposes. Most people devote the largest part of their waking hours to economic production. Although there is much evidence that participation stimulates productivity, beyond some optimal point effort and time devoted to decision making must compete with material output. Probably the greatest mass political participation in history occurred during the Chinese Cultural Revolution of the 1960s, instigated by Mao Zedong. One of the chief indictments Mao's successors used in repudiating his policies was that excessive politicization of the people had curtailed Chinese economic growth. Theorists also contend that participation affects economic goals in more indirect ways. Huntington and Nelson, for example, believe that in less developed countries mobilization of the lower classes promotes economic equality at the expense of economic growth.[21]

Competence

No thornier problem exists for democratic theory and practice than the challenge raised by the limited capabilities of the ordinary citizen.[22] Can anyone seriously deny that people differ enormously both in native intellectual endowment and in expertise acquired through specialization? Antidemocrats from Plato onwards have based their philosophies on this premise. H. L. Mencken (quoting Lecky) wrote, "Nothing in ancient alchemy was more irrational than the notion that . . . the best way to improve the world and secure rational progress is to place government more and more under the control of the least enlightened classes."[23] Joseph Schumpeter, one of the fathers of the elitist theory of democracy, compounds the insult: "The typical citizen drops down to a lower level of mental performance as soon as he enters the political field."[24]

How indeed is the average citizen to participate sensibly in such technical decisions as the licensing of nuclear power plants or the regulation of experiments with recombinant DNA? Yet, history shows that experts—like leaders generally—have biases and interests of their own that give us no guarantee they will use their superior knowledge to select policies beneficial to the people. Moreover, expertise does not always correspond to hierarchical authority. Combining knowledge with power and competence with correct motivation remain ever-present problems not only for advocates of participation but also for their critics.

Diseducative Effects

Although supporters of participation tout its developmental effects, skeptics can point to instances where political activity has undesirable impact on citizens. These "diseducative" effects, as we might call them, are parallel but opposite to their favorable counterparts. Instead of becoming more conscious of their efficacy, some activists end up cynical, exhausted, "burnt out." Instead of learning to tolerate differences, some participants become fanatically partisan, even to the point of wanting to kill their opponents. As Plato wrote, "All goes wrong when, starved for lack of anything good in their own lives, men turn to public affairs hoping to snatch . . . the happiness they hunger for. They set about fighting for power, and this internecine conflict ruins them and their country."[25] Even elections, intended to replace force in settling disputes, can lead to disorder, as normal political competition escalates into violence. Although participation is supposed to legitimize the system that permits it, highly politicized persons sometimes abandon legal means or turn on the system itself. Failure to win can produce intolerable frustration, as when pro-life activists resorted to bombing abortion clinics after legal efforts to close them proved unavailing. Ironically, in other instances, frustration stems from success that lifts expectations faster than they can be met. This seems to have been the case with leaders of the Student Nonviolent Coordinating Committee who became Black Power radicals despite the triumphs of the civil rights movement during the mid-1960s.

System Strain

Critics of excessive participation contend that intense popular involvement weakens polities in several other important ways besides the danger of too much conflict.[26] Authorities faced with myriad pressures from a mobilized populace become overloaded with too many decisions to make, too many inconsistent demands to reconcile. Even after policies are decided, these critics fear, officials will have trouble getting them accepted if citizens, thinking themselves the source of all legitimacy, become less willing to defer to authorities. Although leaders are less trusted in an overly participatory system, so this argument runs, active citizens demand that their government do more and more for them. Consequently, the tangible resources of the polity are stretched too thin, resulting in inadequate performance, economic inflation, and diversion of effort from really essential tasks.

RECONCILIATION?

At many points, the predictions and evaluations of "participatory" democrats and their "elitist" opponents clash so sharply that we must wonder whether they are using the same words to talk about different things. Are there any ways to reconcile views that seem so opposed?

Transitions

Proponents of participation are seldom so rash as to claim that their remedy will produce instantaneous cures, rendering overnight the apathetic efficacious, the ignorant competent, the bigoted tolerant, and the selfish public-spirited. They admit that the developmental effects they foresee require time and experience. This produces what Arnold Kaufman calls "the paradox of participatory democracy":

> Participation must begin by being unsuccessful if it is to fulfill its principal function. For, by hypothesis, participation is typically an essential condition of making men competent and responsible. But individuals who are incompetent and irresponsible will not make good decisions. They will be neither effective nor wise. Therefore, before participatory decisions can become sound, they will be unsound—necessarily.[27]

Or, as Lively, citing Tocqueville, writes, "It is never a good argument against giving a group power that it is irresponsible in its attitudes, since it can never learn to be responsible if it is excluded."[28]

On this point, then, friends and foes of participation differ not so much in their predictions about its effects (though many critics are less optimistic even about the long term) as in their tolerance for a period of disruption while the formerly passive or powerless become socialized into the skills and attitudes democracy requires. And, we may reasonably assume, even the most enthusiastic supporter of participation must sometimes hesitate at empowering the masses when high immediate costs of failure or short time horizons make the slow process of citizen education appear too risky.

Success and Failure

Which is it? Does participation foster efficacy or cynicism? The obvious answer from common sense and basic psychology alike is that it may do either, depending on whether participants' efforts are rewarded or fruitless (or worse yet, punished). Political scientists too often treat the sense of political efficacy as though it were a personality trait, fixed by early childhood experiences. While people no doubt differ along these lines, evidence abounds in both everyday observation and in scholarly research that individuals and groups respond strongly to the results of their participation.[29] Sometimes, as when expectations rise faster than accomplishments, effects of participation feed back to influence future efforts in counterintuitive ways. Generally, however, those who succeed, or who are at least partially reinforced, will try again when conditions are right, whereas those who consistently fail will steer clear of political struggle. The effect of political action on subsequent attitudes therefore depends on factors affecting the success and failure of participation—the responsiveness of authorities, the power resources and skill of participants, the strength of their opponents, and the vicissitudes of fortune.

Extent of Conflict

Another cause of success and failure is the extent of underlying conflict. When all participants' goals are basically compatible, everyone can win. But when conflicts are irreconcilable, enmity can become so severe that everyone loses—as when Samson, captive and blinded, pulled down the house of the Philistines (an early example of system destabilization). Those who preach the gospel of participation are often faulted for assuming away conflict. Rather than debate assumptions, we should recognize (as Chapter 6 will explain) that conflictful situations demand a different type of participatory decision making. And, when the clash of wills becomes truly extreme, participation simply may not work.

Making Decisions versus Making Demands

People who support participation for its developmental or intrinsic benefits usually have in mind (though not always explicitly) direct decision making in a small-scale setting such as a town meeting. Forced to think not only of desired new programs but also of whether to raise taxes to pay for them, citizens learn responsibility. Thrown together with others whose interests and beliefs differ, citizens learn tolerance. Having a direct opportunity to share in deciding public questions, citizens become committed to the choices made. Seeing themselves as part of government rather than government as something apart, citizens feel that the system deserves their allegiance.

As we shall see in Chapter 7, direct participatory decision making works only in tiny polities. Proponents of "democratic elitism" are more often concerned with large systems, in which ordinary members can seldom take part directly in making policies. Instead, citizens must act through partial associations—parties or pressure groups—that assert particular demands but do not always share responsibility for decisions. It is questionable whether participation of this sort provides all the educative benefits that enthusiasts tout. Indeed, Rousseau, perhaps the most influential theorist of participation, specifically warned against partial associations.[30] Instead of learning responsibility, members of demand-asserting systems of participation typically try to secure their own interests while foisting costs off on everyone else. Instead of developing tolerance, they interact with like-minded others who reinforce and accentuate their differences from opponents, thus sharpening conflict. Instead of identifying with the system, individuals learn loyalty to subgroups—racial, religious, economic, geographic, or whatever. Even the opportunity to affect policy through interest-group activity may not foster much acceptance of decisions when final choices are made in remote centers of power.

To a great extent, then, advocates and critics of expanded participation are talking about two distinct patterns of popular involvement. Though we use a single umbrella term to cover both types we must keep aware of the differences between them.[31]

Basic Attitudes

We can thus bridge part of the gap between elitist and participatory democrats by realizing that they are thinking about dissimilar types of participation, taking different time perspectives, or assuming less or more favorable circumstances. Nevertheless, the two camps remain apart, separated by fundamental disagreements. Those who advocate a participatory society are more optimistic about people and their potential for improvement, more concerned with human character and relationships than with the satisfaction of material wants, and more willing to risk or endure conflict. Rooted partly in personality and basic attitudes toward life, differences of this sort have no doubt existed as long as humans have tried to govern themselves. For an extreme contrast, compare the policies of Solon and Peisistratus, two early leaders of Athens:

> Solon—observing that the state was often plunged in dissensions, while a number of its citizens acquiesced in any turn of events, because they were too indolent to do otherwise—enacted a law expressly intended to deal with such persons. This law disfranchised, and deprived of civic rights, all who failed, in a time of civic dissension, to take up arms on either of the two sides. . . .
>
> Peisistratus . . . pursued a policy of advancing money to the poor to give them employment and to enable them to make a living by farming. [One reason] for this policy . . . was to ensure (by giving them a moderate competence and some business to engage their attention) that they should have neither the desire nor the leisure to concern themselves with public affairs.[32]

NOTES

1. David Hapgood, ed., *The Role of Popular Participation in Development* (Cambridge: MIT Press, 1969).

2. Alfred J. Marrow, *The Practical Theorist: The Life and Work of Kurt Lewin* (New York: Basic Books, 1969), ch. 14.

3. According to Jane J. Mansbridge, *Beyond Adversary Democracy* (New York: Basic Books, 1980), p. 376n.

4. Peter Bachrach, *The Theory of Democratic Elitism: A Critique* (Boston: Little, Brown & Co. 1967), chaps. 3 and 4.

5. Notably Robert A. Dahl, *After the Revolution? Authority in a Good Society* (New Haven: Yale University Press, 1970).

6. Michel J. Crozier, Samuel P. Huntington, and Joji Watanuki, *The Crisis of Democracy: Report on the Governability of Democracies to the Trilateral Commission* (New York: New York University Press, 1975).

7. Arnold S. Kaufman, "Participatory Democracy: Ten Years Later," in *The Bias of Pluralism*, ed. William E. Connolly (New York: Atherton, 1969), p. 203. Kaufman does not subscribe to this view but offers those who do some friendly advice.

8. Most writers use "educative" in place of "developmental"; I owe the latter term to William M. Lafferty, "Political Participation in the Social-Democratic State" (paper presented at the annual meeting of the American Political Science Association, 1981). Lafferty is also one of the few authors who distinguishes intrinsic benefits, though he calls them "expressive."

9. Samuel P. Huntington and Joan M. Nelson, *No Easy Choice: Political Participation in Developing Countries* (Cambridge: Harvard University Press, 1976), p. 51.

10. A. D. Lindsay, *The Modern Democratic State* (New York: Oxford University Press, Galaxy edition, 1962; originally 1943), pp. 269–73.

11. John Stuart Mill, "Representative Government," *Three Essays*, The World's Classics Series (London: Oxford University Press, 1960), p. 186.

12. "Human Nature and Participatory Democracy," in Connolly, ed., *The Bias of Pluralism*, p. 184.

13. "Representative Government," p. 181.

14. Quoted in Sidney Verba, *Small Groups and Political Behavior: A Study of Leadership* (Princeton: Princeton University Press, 1961), p. 206. Chapters 9 and 10 of this book are an excellent discussion of the participation hypothesis.

15. Jean-Jacques Rousseau, "Discourse on the Origin and Basis of Inequality Among Men," in *The Essential Rousseau*, trans. Lowell Bair (New York: Mentor Books, 1974), p. 189.

16. *Rules for Radicals: A Pragmatic Primer for Realistic Radicals* (New York: Random House, Vintage Books, 1971), p. 121.

17. *Democracy* (New York: St. Martin's Press, 1975), pp. 134–35.

18. "The United States," in *The Crisis of Democracy*, ed. Crozier et al., p. 115.

19. *Beyond Adversary Democracy*, p. 234.

20. William Hinton, *Fanshen: A Documentary of Revolution in a Chinese Village* (New York: Monthly Review Press, 1966), p. 222. Copyright © 1966 by William Hinton. Reprinted by permission of Monthly Review Foundation.

21. *No Easy Choice*, chap. 3.

22. Dahl, *After the Revolution?* pp. 28–40.

23. *Notes on Democracy* (New York: Farrar, Straus & Giroux, 1977; originally 1926), pp. 56–57.

24. *Capitalism, Socialism and Democracy*, 3rd. ed. (New York: Harper & Row, 1950), p. 262.

25. *The Republic*, trans. Francis MacDonald Cornford (New York: Oxford University Press, 1945), p. 235.

26. Avoidance of conflict is the major theme in the classic argument of Bernard Berelson, Paul Lazarsfeld, and William McPhee, *Voting* (Chicago: University of Chicago Press, 1954), pp. 305–23. Strain on authorities and resources is emphasized by Huntington, "The United States."

27. "Participatory Democracy: Ten Years Later," p. 207.

28. *Democracy*, p. 86.

29. For a persuasive general theory of how efficacy is learned, see Martin E. P. Seligman, *Helplessness: On Depression, Development, and Death* (San Francisco: W. H. Freeman & Co., 1975).

30. *The Social Contract*, trans. Willmoore Kendall (Chicago: Henry Regnery Co., 1954), bk. Two, chap. III.

31. For similar arguments, see Lively on "constitutional" versus "mass" participation, *Democracy*, pp. 86, 143; and Lawrence A. Scaff on "participation as interaction" versus "participation as instrumental action" in "Two Concepts of Political Participation," *Western Political Quarterly*, 28, 1975, 447–62.

32. Aristotle, "On the Constitution of Athens," Appendix IV in Ernest Barker, trans., *The Politics of Aristotle* (New York: Oxford University Press, 1962), p. 377.

CHAPTER 3

MOTIVATION

Theorists' debates over whether to encourage or discourage participation have an air of unreality about them, for both sides usually assume that people want to participate. Yet in practice, nothing could be more evident than the fact that most people seldom use the chances offered them to influence decisions. United States presidential elections attract to the polls barely half the number entitled to vote. Primaries and state and local elections are generally ignored by the great majority of potential voters. Union local meetings normally draw only 5 to 10 percent of members.[1] As for interest groups, the following lament from a Sierra Club chapter is typical:

> Increasing apathy, endemic to the environmental movement in recent years, has reached epidemic proportions on Long Island. Responses to the Group's survey of member interest can be counted on two hands. Less than 2% of the Group's Nassau and western Suffolk County members attended the first of the Group's monthly meetings this September.[2]

In response to such inactivity, editorialists and agitators scold citizens for lacking patriotism and foolishly throwing away the power that democracy gives them. The politically disaffected put the blame on elite rule, meaningless choices, and fear of repression (claims that may be on target in some settings, as will be seen in the next chapter). The most common reaction, as in the quotation above, is distressed and puzzled handwringing about "apathy." *Apa-*

thy means "indifference, lack of concern." Seldom does it occur to those who want more people to participate that the inactive may be both genuinely concerned and perfectly sensible.

Unfortunately, mainstream political science sheds little useful light on this problem. Unable to see beyond the beam cast by their favorite searchlight, survey research, investigators lavish attention on psychological and social characteristics of individuals in order to explain why they differ in political activity. Thus we learn that those who participate most feel more efficacious, have a stronger sense of civic duty, are less cynical about politics, are better educated, and so on.[3] While much of this information is instructive and even, for some purposes, important, it fails to enlighten us in a really basic way about why people participate or, more often, do not participate.

WHY DO PEOPLE NOT PARTICIPATE?

To gain that understanding, we must look not at how people differ but at what they have in common. We must explain first not why they act but why they more often do nothing. We shall then appreciate that political effort must be motivated and that individual attitudes, beliefs, and social characteristics are secondary in explaining what motivates people politically. We shall see instead that if we want to influence participation its most important determinants are laws, organizations, and other properties of the social context in which individuals find themselves.

Olson's Pessimistic Logic

As we have noted, political theorists traditionally assumed that if given the chance, people will try to influence decisions that affect their lives. They regarded failures to live up to this expectation as abnormalities, signs of individual or systemic pathology. In 1965, the economist Mancur Olson published a fundamentally important book, *The Logic of Collective Action*.[4] In it he established a new baseline expectation: that rational individuals in large groups will ordinarily *not* participate without external inducement.

By "collective action," Olson means effort to further common interests. His logic therefore encompasses almost all acts of participation—any that are aimed at goals shared by a group of people. When citizens try to elect a candidate or block a proposed expressway, everyone who wants the goal benefits if the effort proves victorious. Economists call objectives of this sort "collective goods."[5] They are distinguished from private consumer goods partly by the fact that the benefits they bestow are *nonexcludable*—that is, everyone within a specified group or "public" can enjoy them, regardless of whether he or she helped provide them. If environmentalists compel the government to clean up the air, I enjoy blue skies whether or not I demonstrated on Earth Day. If gun control laws are blocked in Congress, I can keep a pistol under my pillow even if I never sent a check to the National Rifle Association. Because inactive people cannot be excluded from sharing collective goods, members are greatly tempted to become *free riders*, to reap the benefits others have sowed without themselves joining the collective effort.

The free-rider effect alone does not suffice to establish Olson's argument. After all, it must occur to would-be free riders to ask, "If everyone does nothing, won't our shared goal be lost? Will there be any ride to hitch?" Olson therefore needs a second premise: that in large groups anybody who asks such questions will recognize *the imperceptibility of individual effects*. What can one person do? How likely is it that the election will turn on a single vote? Will my twenty-five-dollar check enable Handgun Control, Inc., to push through the legislation I desire? Even if you become a full-time organizer, how much can you do to eliminate unemployment in your country?

The Participant's Dilemma

To oversimplify somewhat, the individual can think of two possibilities, and in either case a rational self-interested calculation recommends inactivity as the best policy. If others participate in sufficient numbers, the individual saves time, money, or effort by taking a free ride. Or, if few others act, it is improbable in large-scale situations that one person's decision to join them will make any noticeable difference, so again the cost required would be wasted. Consequently, as the saying goes, everybody's business is nobody's business.

It may be easier to visualize this choice if we borrow from game theorists the diagram known as a payoff matrix. Consider the plight of Jo College, a typical student struggling, with her parents' help, to pay outrageous tuition bills. A group of campus politicos establish an organization called HIT (Halt Increased Tuition).[6] The goal of HIT is to persuade the University president and trustees to rescind a planned thousand-dollar boost in annual tuition. Because Jo's parents have reached the bottom of their bank account, HIT's success or failure will determine whether she must take a part-time job next year to finance the extra thousand dollars. Having to work would wipe out her social life, so Jo has a real stake in the outcome. The organizers of HIT ask all students to write letters to trustees, to demonstrate in front of the president's office, and to contribute money to defray publicity costs. They are confident that if 3,000 students heed their call, the administration will roll back the tuition hike.

The total cost to Jo of joining HIT will be about ten dollars in cash and five hours of time. Since this is much less than she will sacrifice next year if tuition rises, we might expect her to enlist eagerly. Perhaps she will, but let's see what happens if she calculates more carefully. The rows of the payoff matrix in Figure 3–1 depict Jo's two choices: to participate or not to participate with HIT. The columns indicate (in a simplification) two possibilities about the actions of other students: Three thousand angry protesters descend on College Hall, or no one shows up except HIT's self-appointed leaders. The cells of

MOTIVATION 25

	Action of Others	
	Many Participate	Few Participate
Participate (Jo's Choices)	Outcome: Save $1,000 — Cost: $10 and 5 Hours A	Outcome: Pay $1,000 — Cost: $10 and 5 Hours C
Not Participate	Outcome: Save $1,000 — Cost: Nothing B	Outcome: Pay $1,000 — Cost: Nothing D

FIGURE 3–1 Collective Action as a Prisoner's Dilemma

the matrix represent Jo's payoff for each combination of choice and contingency.

Jo benefits significantly from collective success; the cost of contributing to it is minor. Nevertheless, no matter what other students do, Jo is better off ignoring HIT's appeal. Payoff B is better than payoff A, and D is better than C. Not participating is therefore what game theorists call a dominant strategy, a choice that gives preferable results under all contingencies. There is only one problem: If most other students make the same calculation, outcome D will result; but Jo and her peers would much rather have A than D. Their *individually rational choices add up to a collectively irrational outcome.*

This pattern of payoffs—B 〉 (preferred to) A 〉 D 〉 C— defines the game known as the Prisoner's Dilemma. (The name comes from one of the early scenarios, or stories, associated with the payoff structure—a prosecutor imposes the dilemma on two prisoners in order to get them to testify against each other.) Prisoner's Dilemmas are part of a broader group of choice situations in which individually optimal decisions result in social outcomes that are decidedly less than optimal. Such payoff patterns are pervasive in everyday life and help account for the existence of many political and social ills.[7] Collective action is a Prisoner's Dilemma.[8] Its logic explains why citizens so seldom participate at the rates observers think best for the healthy functioning of democracy. As Olson puts it,

> Even if all of the individuals in a large group are rational and self-interested, and would gain if, as a group, they acted to achieve their common interest or objective, they will still not voluntarily act to achieve that common or group interest.[9]

Olson's pessimistic conclusion established a new and more realistic starting point for thinking about participation. Instead of expecting people to participate as democratic theory says they should, Olson tells us to expect that rational individuals will *not* participate. How, then, does any political action ever occur?

WHY RATIONAL EGOISTS SOMETIMES PARTICIPATE

Before looking at answers that Olson and others have given to that question, it will help to have in mind a general framework in which we can place various considerations affecting the decision to participate.

The Calculus of Participation

We can find such a schema in an expanded version of William Riker and Peter Ordeshook's calculus of participation.[10] Let us suppose that people behave as if the following comparison must be satisfied before they will participate in collective action.

$$P(B_i + B_g) + S + D - C > 0.$$

Not everyone likes ideas expressed in mathematical shorthand, but we shall often refer to the calculus, so it is worthwhile to pay close attention to this inequality and the symbols in it, which represent the following subjective quantities:

> P = the individual's power to affect the collective outcome, which can range from 0 (no power) to 1 (complete power); for example, the probability that his vote will decide an election;
>
> B_i = the value to the individual of the collective good; for example, how much she personally will benefit from the policies of her preferred candidate;
>
> B_g = the value the individual places on the benefit other people receive from the collective goal; for example, his empathy for the unemployed who he expects will get jobs if his candidate wins;
>
> S = the value of any personal or selective incentives that depend on the individual's participation; for example, the worth to her of the patronage job she will lose if she fails to vote;
>
> D = the strength of the individual's sense of duty or responsibility to participate;
>
> C = the cost the individual incurs in participating; for example, the time and trouble of registering to vote and going to the polls.

Because all these quantities are subjective, we cannot measure or calculate them in any strict sense. But the formula does give us an idea of how people weigh various considerations in deciding whether or not to participate. Thus, even if a citizen's B_i is great (he cares strongly about an election), he may not vote if that value is discounted by a tiny P (he feels he cannot affect the result) and offset by a large C (he must give up an hour's pay because lines at the polling place are long).

Using the calculus of participation, let us look for situations where a rational egoist—a calculating person who considers primarily her own welfare—might find it worthwhile to contribute to a collective goal. The first three answers are those provided by Olson.

Small Numbers

Olson draws a strong distinction between small and large groups of potential participants. He believes that rational individuals will rarely act spontaneously to advance goals shared by large numbers of people, who are likely to remain latent—unorganized and inactive. In contrast, people in small groups more often act to further common ends.[11] There are several reasons for this difference.

First, Olson argues, small groups are more likely to be "privileged" in the sense that one or more members find it individually worthwhile to take action that benefits everyone. This follows because *individuals can often perceptibly and significantly affect small-scale situations.* (In terms of the calculus, P is larger when the group is small.) For example, residents of single city blocks often agitate to get traffic lights installed at their corners; seldom do residents of an entire section of a city petition for a change in overall traffic patterns. The likelihood of privilege is further increased if one member has a disproportionate stake in the goal or unusual power to accomplish it. If we look more closely at active blocks, we may find a parent with six children or a party worker who knows someone in the streets department. Either might find it individually worthwhile to initiate action that pleases everyone else on the block.

Second, small groups are less costly to organize than large groups. Anyone who has ever tried to schedule a mutually convenient meeting time knows that the difficulty of such tasks increases exponentially with the number of people involved.

Third, Olson contends, "social incentives are important mainly only in the small group."[12] People care about the opinions of others who know them personally, and in a face-to-face situation, members of the group know who shirks work and who takes a fair share of common burdens. Intangible interpersonal rewards and punishments, ranging from high status to ostracism, are effective in small groups. Indeed, a great deal of social-psychological research as well as everyday observation shows that such pressures can be extremely powerful.

Unfortunately, groups that have a stake in most state and national decisions typically consist of thousands or millions of persons, not a dozen or a score. Although large numbers are a source of democratic legitimacy, they produce political weakness by inhibiting individual action and collective organization. Olson does, however, see two ways for large groups to overcome their tendency toward latency.

Federation

The analysis of small groups, Olson says, suggests that large numbers might be able to sustain action if they organize themselves into federations of small groups. In fact, many large, enduring organizations do depend on small-group dynamics for much of their solidarity. Examples include Communist parties with their cells, and armies with their platoons and squads. However, without some stronger glue to keep the entire organization together, collective action problems will arise in the relations among small-group units, if not in the behavior of individual members. This was the case with the New Left in the 1960s and with the women's movement in the early 1970s. National organizations had trouble organizing coherent large-scale efforts, because they depended excessively on voluntary cooperation among hundreds of local chapters and "affinity groups."[13] For a stronger source of unity and persistence in large-scale political action, we must look to Olson's theory of selective incentives.

Selective Incentives

As we have seen, Olson contends the collective goods that are the ostensible goals of political action cannot effectively motivate individuals. Instead, he believes large-scale collective action depends on selective incentives—rewards and punishments that can be given or withheld contingent on the member's contribution (S in the calculus). Thus, Olson contends, interest groups, political parties, and nations motivate their members to participate reliably only through coercion or positive inducements.[14] Examples consistent with his theory are easy to supply. Political "machines", the most durable party units in American politics, are simply organizations that motivate their workers with selective material incentives, including cash, jobs, contracts, and favors. American labor unions did not gain large, stable memberships until the Wagner Act legalized the union shop contract, which provides that workers who do not join the union lose their jobs. Business and professional lobbying organizations typically finance their political efforts with surpluses generated by selling their members publications, insurance, technical assistance, and the like.

Together, Olson's small-group, federation, and selective incentive theories explain much about participation in American politics. He accounts for the usual dominance of the pressure group system by economic lobbies, often representing single large firms or small numbers of firms.[15] He renders less surprising the frequent passivity or highly imperfect mobilization of ordinary citizens, even when they have a substantial stake in government decisions. He gives reasons for the strength of some organizations that do manage to sustain the effort of numerous members.

Nevertheless, Olson's logic falls short of explaining some important instances of participation. He helps us understand why so many people fail to vote, but he does not adequately explain why a majority vote at least some of the time. Olson tells why only a fraction of the sympathizers of most political movements ever demonstrate, contribute, or canvass, but he cannot account for the hundreds of thousands who engage in such actions. In particular, his theory handles poorly the great upsurge of participation that began just about the time his book was published: the mass movements for civil rights, peace in Vietnam, and equality between men and women; the influential member-sustained organizations that promote "public-interest" causes; and the domination of political parties by zealous volunteers apparently stirred more by causes than by personal rewards. Prompted by this challenge from reality, theorists started looking for additional explanations. Some of these supplement Olson's logic of rational behavior. Others are more at odds with his basic assumptions about human nature.

Perceptible Effects

Must members of a large group always feel they contribute insignificantly to a collective goal? Is P always small when many people are involved? Even aside from the individual's realization that "every little bit counts," there are circumstances in which participants can reasonably feel that their actions really matter.

Sometimes, large groups are "privileged" in the sense that a member finds it personally worthwhile to do something that benefits all. The little Dutch boy who stuck his finger in the dike saved himself from drowning, but by doing so he also saved everyone else in Amsterdam. Modern societies are so highly organized that collective action often takes forms other than the simple accumulation of each person's drop in the bucket. This is especially likely when an individual uses mass media to communicate information that profoundly affects others. Examples include the influential participation of public-interest advocates and well-publicized "whistle-blowers."[16]

Individuals are more likely to feel that they count when they believe that a collective effort is on the threshold of an all-or-nothing victory or defeat. Some collective goods are just the sum of countless individual contributions—for example, the air becomes a little cleaner for every auto that is fitted with an antipollution device. In politics, however, achievement of goals frequently involves sudden leaps.[17] A priori, the voter's chance of casting the decisive ballot is indeed vanishingly small; but if people expect the election will be close, more citizens turn out, thinking that their votes may be critical after all. For this reason, every campaign manager must convince the faithful that their candidate is neither a hopeless cause nor a shoo-in, regardless of what polls say.[18] Because of this sort of calculation, participation may surge and dwindle not because underlying concern about an issue fluctuates but because people change their estimates of what difference they can make as a struggle becomes more evenly matched or as a decisive stage approaches.

The Chinese have a saying, "A journey of ten thousand *li* begins with a single step." Those who fix their eyes only on a distant destination easily grow discouraged, but those who concentrate on the step just taken and the one about to come feel more satisfied and more competent. Skilled political organizers know that sustaining large-scale, long-term participation requires realistic intermediate goals. Although grand objectives and ideologies give coherence and direction to political movements, motivation of participants depends on a rewarding series of secondary achievements, especially on a scale small enough that individuals can see the impact of their own efforts.

An important instance of this principle is the effect of each person's action on the participation of others. Olson's logic treats people as atomized, each deciding in isolation from others whether or not to participate (except when influenced by small-group pressures). But a political canvasser, to take one example, influences many votes besides her own; each voter she converts or gets to the polls not only increases her candidate's chance of victory but also directly reinforces the canvasser's own efforts. Our actions are multiplied in less deliberate ways as well. If I decide not to attend a faculty meeting, my colleagues in adjoining offices will be less likely to go, and so will their neighbors and their neighbors' neighbors. If I am aware of the ripple effects of my decision, my inclination to participate will increase.[19]

Efficacious Subgroups

Olson's concept of a privileged group depends on one or more members' deciding separately that contributing to a collective goal will be individually worthwhile. If this is not true for anyone and the group is large, he expects it to remain latent. However, the superior organizing power of small groups can be combined with an expanded notion of privilege to suggest another way collective action occurs in large groups. This possibility arises when the members of a small subgroup feel individually better off if they act together to share costs in a way that serves the entire population.[20]

For example, in my Philadelphia neighborhood, thousands of people (and dogs) benefit from our local public park, but we enjoy it more when it is not littered with trash. If I alone tried to keep the park clean, I would have to work full-time at the job—an absurd sacrifice. If I put in a reasonable two or three hours on litter patrol, my puny effort would be overwhelmed by nine acres of hamburger wrappers and beer bottles. But if twenty or thirty Friends of Clark Park get together for a Saturday afternoon cleanup, we can eliminate enough eyesores to feel that our work has made us better off. Of course, any of our group might feel still more advantaged to imitate our free-riding neighbors who spend Saturday watching football on television. But so long as there are enough of us to get the job done, the temptation to stay home can be overcome by friendly social persuasion and other incentives that will be discussed below, such as the pleasure of working together or a sense of public-spirited obligation. If, however, our numbers fall below the threshold needed for efficacy, these inducements will be soured by a sense of futility and exploitation.

Pleasurable Participation

Both Olson's logic and the Riker-Ordeshook calculus assume that members regard participation as a costly activity, either because it is inherently unpleasant or because engaging in it necessitates sacrificing greater pleasures. As one of my colleagues puts it, "They'd rather go to the beach." It is clear enough that most people feel this way sometimes, and some people always have better things to do than trying to influence political or organizational decisions. But to believe that everyone always feels burdened by political action seems unduly pessimistic and ignores the intrinsic benefits of participation described in Chapter 2. As one activist writes, "I believe that people have a (usually deeply sublimated) basic need for collective idealistic involvement, and that one of the most crucial factors for public interest organizing is tapping that need."[21] For others (especially leaders), the pleasures of participation depend less on identification with a cause and more on delight in the process itself—the enjoyment of the game, the excitement of struggle, the gratification of exercising skills rarely needed outside the political arena.

Though the fact that political activity can be a pleasure rather than a sacrifice undoubtedly explains much participation, one should not count on this possibility to be the chief incentive for either widespread or intensive involvement. Like most pleasures and sooner than many, the joy of participation runs into diminishing returns. A one-hour meeting can be fun, but four hours is torture. Even those happy few with a limitless taste for politics must sooner or later pay opportunity costs few can sustain, as when full-time activists condemn themselves to material poverty. Moreover, for the citizen truly devoted to participation, there remains the choice among competing claims on the time one can devote to civic affairs. You may have to say no to the United Way because you have already said yes to the Home and School Association, the Republican party, and the Spruce Hill Community Association. In making this sort of choice, even the person who loves politics must regard each action as costly in the sense that it takes time or other resources from alternative political involvements.

MORAL MOTIVES FOR PARTICIPATING

To some readers, Olson's pessimistic logic of participation seems premised on a depressing view of human nature as selfish and narrowly calculating. Olson himself vacillates on this question. At times, he admits his theory works best for political action oriented to economic goals, about which people are most likely to be rational and self-interested. At other points, however, he argues that the model applies even to altruists:

> The concept of the large or latent group offered here holds true whether behavior is selfish or unselfish, so long as it is strictly speaking 'rational.' Even if

the member of a large group were to neglect his own interest entirely, he still would not rationally contribute toward the provision of any collective or public good, since his own contribution would not be perceptible. . . . Selfless behavior that has no perceptible effect is sometimes not even considered praiseworthy. A man who tried to hold back a flood with a pail would probably be considered more of a crank than a saint, even by those he was trying to help.[22]

Altruism

Our calculus of participation points to a different interpretation of the effects of altruism. A person who values the welfare of others as well as of himself (has positive B_g as well as positive B_i) feels a greater motivational stake in the collective outcome. Olson argues that in large groups P is so small that the net quantity $P(B_i + B_g)$ must be insignificant. Nevertheless, so long as P is non-zero (even if it only represents, so to speak, a bucket against the flood), that quantity will be positive. Hence Olson's conclusion does not hold if the member "were to neglect his own interests entirely," but instead must assume that his personal costs of participation (C) outweigh his tiny contribution toward the common good. Therefore, altruism does increase the tendency to participate, but unless the individual feels his efforts have a perceptible impact, the logic of collective inaction will tend to dominate the behavior of even the citizen who cares about others. To overcome the problem of collective action, we need a morality less dependent than simple altruism on individual efficacy.

Duty

One partial solution is symbolized by the D term in the Riker-Ordeshook formula. Here the sense of duty, the belief that participation is an obligation of the good citizen, is not discounted by the individual's perceived lack of power. Instead, it functions as an additional selective incentive: the individual feels virtuous if she participates, guilty if she does not. The formula does imply, however, that the sense of duty is weighed against, and might be offset by, the cost the individual bears in participating. Common sense suggests this is so for most political behavior. Consider a Bostonian who on election day happens to be in the middle of a business trip to California. No matter how strongly she feels it is her duty to vote, she is unlikely to make a special trip back East just to get to the polls; the cost is simply too high.

For most people, moral incentives of this type are relatively weak; yet, paradoxically, they are extremely important in overcoming the collective-action barrier to participation, because they suffice to motivate less costly political acts that in the aggregate are vital to democracy. For example, survey evidence shows that the sense of civic duty is the best attitudinal predictor of who will vote.[23] Similarly, it is hard to find any better explanation of why large numbers of citizens send their modest checks to political candidates or organizations.

Conditional Participation

So far, we have treated moral motives as elements added on to a basically utilitarian decision process. Sometimes morality functions less pragmatically by imposing rules of conduct that people follow without calculating personal cost or practical effect. Under one such rule, which we may call the ethic of *conditional cooperation*, the individual remains unwilling to be the "sucker" who sacrifices when no one else puts out any effort, but if others do participate he genuinely wants to take part in the collective endeavor and would be ashamed to play the free rider. In terms of the Prisoner's Dilemma in Figure 3–1, a person who participates conditionally ranks the possible outcomes A ⟩ B ⟩ D ⟩ C, rather than the B ⟩ A ⟩ D ⟩ C preference ordering that we expect from a pure individualist.[24]

Besides this ethical norm, several other motives can produce the same pattern of conditional participation in what we would otherwise consider Prisoner's Dilemma situations: (1) The involvement of others can sharply cut the cost to the individual of participating. This is dramatically the case when people find safety in numbers for action that authorities would repress if few took part. (2) Like social occasions (which in fact they are), some opportunities to participate are great fun if enough others join in but are a depressing waste of time if they do not. (3) Actions that are expected to attract multitudes elicit "the desire to be there, to take part in history."[25] (4) After repeated interaction within a group that enforces a norm of conditional cooperation, people may learn that they profit most by reciprocating.[26]

Whatever their motive, people who follow a policy of conditional participation no longer need coercion or positive selective incentives to sustain their participation—as long as they expect others to participate. But once that expectation of cooperation breaks down, conditional participants prefer not to act, and the system of collective effort crumbles. Thus, under this decision rule, participation is volatile: Mass action may surge or collapse, as the delicate flower of mutual trust blossoms or withers.

Unconditional Participation

A second ethic of conduct offers a foundation for participation that is sturdier in principle, if seemingly utopian in practice. For people who follow a rule of *unconditional cooperation* in Prisoner's Dilemma situations, A ⟩ B *and* C ⟩ D. Such persons care most about the rightness of their own actions, regardless of what others do and regardless of individual or collective practical effect. It may seem that this rule can never describe the ordinary mass of humanity. Nevertheless, one of history's most influential leaders, Mao Zedong, believed it an ethic worth teaching. His parable "The Foolish Old Man Who Removed the Mountains" subtly mixes selflessness with the hope of practical results in an image that contrasts strikingly with Olson's crank who tried to bail out the flood. Retelling an ancient Chinese fable, Mao describes an old man whose home was overshadowed by two huge peaks:

> With great determination, he led his sons in digging up these mountains hoe in hand. Another grey-beard, known as the Wise Old Man, saw them and said derisively, "How silly of you to do this! It is quite impossible for you few to dig up these two huge mountains." The Foolish Old Man replied, "When I die, my sons will carry on; when they die, there will be my grandsons, and then their sons and grandsons, and so on to infinity. High as they are, the mountains cannot grow any higher and with every bit we dig, they will be that much lower. Why can't we clear them away?" Having refuted the Wise Old Man's wrong view, he went on digging every day, unshaken in his conviction. God was moved by this, and he sent down two angels, who carried the mountains away on their backs.[27]

It may seem that only a handful of saints could work so hard for a future they expect never to see. But the analogy Mao proceeded to draw was appropriate. The old man and his sons stood for the Chinese Communist Party, which began in 1920 as a secret gathering of twenty-one persons. According to Mao, they dug away at the twin mountains of feudalism and imperialism so persistently that they touched the heart of their God, the Chinese people, who joined them to revolutionize the most populous country on earth. Ironically, however, Mao's successors repudiated his policy of relying on moral incentives. This reversal is perhaps evidence that systems depending excessively on moral incentives cannot last—except perhaps for religious groups and other communities able to carefully select, thoroughly socialize, and, if necessary, expel their members.

Division of Labor and Mixture of Incentives

The selflessness of Mao's foolish old man is rare in politics, but uncommonness and unimportance are not the same. As in the parable, a relative handful who act as an inspirational or organizational nucleus can create the conditions necessary for the less remarkable activity of thousands or millions of others. Indeed, nearly all political action involves such division of labor. We should obviously expect those who contribute intensively to a common purpose to respond to stronger incentives than the less active rank and file. Often, their motives are qualitatively different as well.

Many revolutionaries and others working for social change are spurred by ideological commitment, zealously pursuing a utopian vision as they adhere to an ethic of unconditional participation.[28] Their organizing efforts can create the expectation of widespread action necessary to arouse followers who practice a rule of conditional participation. The relationship between organizers and masses in large demonstrations is an example.

More often, individualistic or selective incentives spur either or both groups. The nucleus, however selfless themselves, may set up an organization that sustains mass action through coercion or tangible inducements. Labor unions maintained by union shop agreements are a case in point. Conversely, moral incentives sometimes stir the mass of members rather than the leaders. Many lobbying groups consist of paid staff persons who solicit the altruistic donations of thousands of members. Similarly, politicians, often seeking primarily to advance their own careers, offer policies to attract the favor of millions of dutiful voters.

Because organizational nuclei consist of relatively few people, small-group pressures and satisfactions help explain their efforts, even when the structures they establish become huge. Indeed, one of the best explanations of how collective action crosses the line from small numbers, where Olson thought spontaneous participation quite possible, to large, where he considered it improbable, lies in recognizing that small-group processes affect the organizers. But if they are to succeed in mobilizing others, they must solve the problem of large-scale collective action, rejecting the mistaken assumption that everyone will be moved by the same mix of ambition, self-realization, friendship, and ideology that inspires their own intense commitment.

NOTES

1. Arnold S. Tannenbaum, "Unions," in James G. March, ed., *Handbook of Organizations* (Chicago: Rand McNally & Co., 1965), p. 740.

2. *Sierra Atlantic*, 6, no. 3 (1979), 8.

3. For a summary of such research, see Lester W. Milbrath and M. L. Goel, *Political Participation: How and Why Do People Get Involved in Politics?* 2nd ed. (Chicago: Rand McNally & Co., 1977), chaps. 3 and 4.

4. Mancur Olson, Jr., *The Logic of Collective Action: Public Goods and the Theory of Groups* (Cambridge: Harvard University Press, 1965). This classic has inspired a large literature. Citations, as well as original contributions, can be found in Norman Frohlich and Joe A. Oppenheimer, *Modern Political Economy*, Foundations of Modern Political Science Series (Englewood Cliffs, N.J.: Prentice-Hall, 1978), chaps. 2–5; and in Russell Hardin, *Collective Action* (Baltimore: Johns Hopkins University Press, 1982).

5. Olson uses the term "public goods," which has a strict technical definition seldom satisfied by real-world political objectives, so I follow Hardin in using the looser notion of "collective goods." Ibid., *Collective Action*, pp. 17–20.

6. Students at the University of Pennsylvania once created an organization with this name; other details are fictitious.

7. Thomas C. Schelling, *Micromotives and Macrobehavior* (New York: W. W. Norton & Co., 1978).

8. This was first demonstrated by Russell Hardin, "Collective Action as an Agreeable *n*-Prisoners' Dilemma," *Behavioral Science*, 16, no. 5 (1971), 472–81.

9. *The Logic of Collective Action*, p. 2.

10. "A Theory of the Calculus of Voting," *American Political Science Review*, 62 (1968), 25–42. I have augmented their formula by including a term for selective incentives and by differentiating benefits to other persons.

11. Olson is fuzzy about where to draw the line between "small" and "large." In *The Logic of Collective Action*, he cites evidence that committees of five perform best (p. 54); numbers of this magnitude are also congruent with the economic theory of oligopoly, from which he developed his logic. But in describing the effect of social pressure, Olson specifies only that the group should be small enough for face-to-face interaction. His general rule is that "the larger the group, the farther it

will fall short of providing an optimal amount of a collective good" (p. 35). Hardin, whose analysis valuably advances our understanding of the relation between size and latency, concludes that "the meaning of small is somewhat indeterminate and probably variable according to context." *Collective Action*, p. 48.

12. *The Logic of Collective Action*, p. 63, emphasis added.

13. On the women's movement see Jo Freeman, *The Politics of Women's Liberation* (New York: David McKay Co., 1975), chap. 4.

14. The line between coercion and positive inducement varies with the baseline established by the individual's expectations, which usually (though not always) correspond to the status quo. A precinct captain who works for the party in hope of getting a patronage job sees the job as a reward. Once she gets on the payroll, her continued politicking may depend on fear of being fired, a threat, or coercive incentive. The objective benefit that motivates action is the same in both cases, but the two situations differ psychologically and socially.

15. Note that "size" in Olson's theory refers to the number of decision-making units, which may be persons or organizations.

16. The same analogy was used by a real whistle-blower, Hugh B. Kaufman, after he exposed inadequate clean up of toxic chemical waste dumps by his employer, the U.S. Environmental Protection Agency. "I don't care whether I'm fired or not," he said. "I've helped raise the public consciousness. I've put my finger in the dike at a time when the civil servants, who I think are just trying to do a good job, were scared to death." *Philadelphia Inquirer*, February 15, 1983, p. 4A.

17. Hardin, *Collective Action*, pp. 55–61.

18. In a large system, even a close election is unlikely to be decided by one individual's vote, so some writers emphasize the prevalence of exaggerated perceptions of efficacy. See Robert Weissberg, "Political Efficacy and Political Illusion," *Journal of Politics*, 37 (1975), 469–87; and Terry M. Moe, *The Organization of Interests: Incentives and the Internal Dynamics of Political Interest Groups* (Chicago: University of Chicago Press, 1980).

19. Norman Frohlich, Joe A. Oppenheimer, and Oran R. Young, *Political Leadership and Collective Goods* (Princeton: Princeton University Press, 1971).

20. Schelling, *Micromotives*; Norman Frohlich et al., "Individual Contributions to Collective Goods: Alternative Models," *Journal of Conflict Resolution*, 19 (1975), 310–30; and Hardin, *Collective Action*, chaps. 3 and 5.

21. Neal T. Kilminster, "Problems of Collective Action: The Conflict Over Nuclear Energy" (unpublished paper, University of Pennsylvania, 1979).

22. *The Logic of Collective Action*, p. 64.

23. Brian Barry, *Sociologists, Economists, and Democracy* (London: Collier-Macmillan, 1970), pp. 15–19.

24. The concepts of conditional and unconditional participation are an extension of the analysis of work motivation in Communist systems developed by Amartya Sen, *On Economic Inequality* (New York: W. W. Norton & Co., 1973), pp. 94–100; and Carl Riskin, "Incentive Systems and Work Motivations: The Experience in China," *Working Papers for a New Society*, 1, no. 4 (1974), 27ff.

25. Hardin, *Collective Action*, p. 108.

26. Cf. Hardin's notion of "contract by convention," ibid.; and Robert Axelrod's "tit-for-tat" strategy, *The Evolution of Cooperation* (New York: Basic Books, 1984). In an effective society, it is hard to distinguish moral motivation from enforced conformity, because morality will be learned from social inculcation of norms that advance the enlightened self-interest of members.

27. *Selected Readings from the Works of Mao Tse-tung* (Peking: Foreign Languages Press, 1967), p. 261. Mao delivered this talk in 1945.

28. Various writers have noted that extreme but voluntary sacrifices seem to require utopian goals. In terms of the calculus of participation, if costs are great, selective incentives slight, and personal power small or uncertain, then an extremely large collective benefit is needed to make action psychically worthwhile.

CHAPTER 4

CONTEXT

Now that we have looked at what moves individuals to participate or, more often, not participate, we can address larger questions: Why do systems differ so much in extent and intensity of member participation? Why does activity within a given polity ebb and swell? What can be done to develop an active citizenry?

Two strategies exist for answering such questions. Most social scientists, especially those who depend on surveys, try to explain the behavior of systems by adding up the individual characteristics of their members. They first explain why people vary in political involvement by relating their actions to personal traits that pollsters can observe or ask about. Besides education, sex, race, age, income, and the like, these include beliefs and attitudes, some of which correspond to factors in our calculus of participation: efficacy (P), trust or cynicism about leaders' responsiveness (P), perceived importance of outcomes ($B_i + B_g$), and sense of citizen duty (D). Next they sum across individuals, hoping to account for why participation changes from time to time or place to place by finding differences in proportions of members who have characteristics conducive to political action. This research has its uses; unfortunately, they are severely limited. Adding up individual attributes to explain systems is to overlook the forest for the trees; or, more precisely, it is like explaining why forests grow lush or stunted by invoking only the quality of acorns and pine cones, neglecting soil, rainfall, sunshine, frost, wind, and fire.

The second strategy, which I prefer, works inward from systemic influences to individual choices and then outward again to systemic effects. Just as the botanist must know seeds, so also must the student of society understand individual motives and decisions. But most of the big forces transmitted through that personal calculus originate in the social context that shapes us all and offers the conditions within which we choose, whether or not we like the terms. In this chapter, we consider four aspects of that context: culture, organization, structure, and policies.

POLITICAL CULTURE

Let's begin with a tough test of my argument for the primacy of context. More than any other element in the calculus of participation, the sense of citizen duty seems like a purely personal trait. We all know that not everyone practices the habits that comprise good moral character in everyday life. Some, more than others, are honest employees, considerate friends, faithful spouses, loving parents. Similarly, some people are conscientious citizens while others cheat on taxes, litter streets, and neglect to vote.

We recognize these differences in civic virtue, and we pay tribute to the virtuous with admiration and praise. Indeed it is functional that we do so, because we thereby encourage behavior that benefits everyone. But this fact itself reveals that individual virtue is socially learned and reinforced. Not all societies accomplish this educational task equally well. Moreover, as with personal morality, the very definition of civic virtue varies among groups and over time. It is therefore mistaken to treat the sense of civic duty as primarily a characteristic of individuals. The widespread existence of such an attitude in a particular time and place is a social fact that exists when most members feel such an obligation, demand that others share it, and expect that others will in turn demand it of oneself, thus creating a socially reinforced structure of shared reciprocal expectations—in other words, a group norm.

Several other beliefs cohere with the norm of civic duty in a cultural syndrome that promotes participation. If you know that most members of your group feel obliged to be good citizens, then you can trust them to act when matters of concern arise. That trust, coupled with an ethic of contingent cooperation, produces collective action which, if effective, feeds back to convince you that by working with others you can indeed influence your polity; this in turn strengthens your loyalty to it. Thus widespread, mutually expected attitudes of civic duty, trust, efficacy, and allegiance together constitute a *participant culture* within which collective action occurs readily, even in the absence of tangible selective incentives. Conversely, a culture with the opposite characteristics—short-sighted self-centeredness, distrust of others, fatalism about oneself, and cynicism toward the system—seldom sustains the voluntary concerted action so familiar and essential in a healthy democracy.

Cultures vary dramatically in the degree to which they transmit attitudes conducive to widespread participation. Table 4–1 demonstrates this with results from surveys conducted in five nations during the early 1960s. Note how well civic attitudes correlate with collective action. Political cultures vary not only among nations but also within them. Observers of United States politics consider subcultures an important reason why Americans from different regions, states, classes, religions, and ethnic groups exhibit distinctive patterns of politics. Banfield and Wilson, for example, explain much of urban politics in terms of a clash between the "private-regarding" political ethos of poor immigrants and the "public-regarding" ethos of wealthier groups who take their values from the established Anglo-Saxon Protestant culture.[1]

If supportive social norms do so much to activate citizens, can anything be done to create and nourish a participant culture? Conflicting answers to this question are one of the great dividing lines between conservatives and radicals. Edward Banfield, whose research in several settings stresses the worth of a participant culture, nevertheless takes a pessimistic position:

> It may be impossible to bring about the changes that are needed. There is no evidence that the ethos of a people can be changed according to plan. It is one thing to engineer consent by the techniques of mass manipulation; to change a people's fundamental view of the world is quite a different thing, perhaps especially if the change is in the direction of a more complicated and demanding morality. . . . Nations do not remake themselves in fundamental ways by deliberate intention.[2]

Such fatalism has not always prevailed. H.D.F. Kitto describes the contrasting philosophy in ancient Greece:

TABLE 4–1 Political Cultures in Five Nations

	U.S.	U.K.	West Germany	Italy	Mexico
Efficacy: Percentage who say they can do something about an unjust national regulation	75	62	38	28	38
Duty: Percentage who say the ordinary person should be active in community affairs	51	39	22	10	26
Trust: Percentage who agree that most people can be trusted	55	49	19	7	30
Collective Action: Percentage who belong to an organization	57	47	44	30	24

Source: Gabriel Almond and Sidney Verba, *The Civic Culture: Political Attitudes and Democracy in Five Nations,* abridged edition (Boston: Little, Brown & Co., 1965), pp. 142, 127, 213, 249.

> The Greeks thought of the polis as an active, formative thing, training the minds and characters of the citizens; we think of it as a piece of machinery for the production of safety and convenience. The training in virtue, which the medieval state left to the Church, and the polis made its own concern, the modern state leaves to God knows what.[3]

But not all modern states shun the character-forming role. Communist regimes, especially during their more radical phases, have vigorously sought to create a "new" human being, believing, as Che Guevara said, that "society as a whole must become a huge school."[4] Opinions differ about how well Cuba, China, and other socialist states have succeeded in this task. But rejection of culture-molding state effort reflects not only pessimism about its feasibility but also scruples about means. After all, the Greek polis that most thoroughly succeeded in creating "citizens selflessly devoted to the common good" was not democratic Athens but regimented Sparta.[5] However appealing the communal vision that inspires cultural revolutionaries, the restrictions they impose on art, speech, thought, and individuality ultimately repel those raised in the liberal democratic tradition.

Is there no middle way? Cultures eventually respond, albeit with a lag, to material and political conditions. Rather than concentrate on indoctrination, polities may find that by reforming themselves they also produce lasting changes in their members. People whose safety, health, and livelihoods are secure learn that they are realistic, not foolish, to trust fellow citizens. Institutions that enable members to participate—and respond to those who do—foster a justifiable sense of efficacy. The more people shape decisions that affect their lives—not only in government but also everyday on the job—the more they will develop the habits and attitudes of the participant culture. So argue advocates of participatory democracy such as Carole Pateman, who believes that "a participatory system . . . is self-sustaining through the educative impact of the participatory process."[6]

ORGANIZATIONAL ENCOURAGEMENT

Pateman's statement amounts to a claim that participatory institutions promote participant cultures, as well as vice versa. Verba and Nie have gathered evidence that supports her faith and also illustrates one way in which participation is encouraged by our second contextual influence—organization. Their data show that, in the United States, people who are actively involved in unions and recreational groups also participate politically at higher rates. Partly this is because people often talk about politics when they get together, even if their immediate purpose is economic or social. But the data also suggest that nonpolitical organizations enable active members to practice citizenship skills that spill over to promote political involvement as well.[7]

Avowedly political organizations, such as parties and interest groups, no doubt also have a schooling effect. More important, they are a chief source of selective incentives, both material and social. The rewards they offer are especially crucial in motivating the unusual effort of activists and paid staff, who in turn lower costs of participation for other members, particularly by gathering and disseminating information that alerts them to political events and opportunities for action. Political organizations, like businesses, work harder when spurred by competition. Not surprisingly, areas with competitive parties tend to have higher rates of voting and campaign participation.[8] The powerful effect of organizations on participation is demonstrated by a comparative study of six nations: Austria, India, Japan, the Netherlands, Nigeria, and the United States. Despite the economic and cultural disparities among these countries, in every one of them organizational affiliation strongly affects how much citizens care about politics, how often they discuss politics with others, how often they vote, and how much they take part in campaign and civic activities.[9]

Given the strength of organizational influence, it is reasonable to expect individual participation to decrease whenever organizations weaken. A case in point is the much-discussed decline in United States voting turnout, which fell in every presidential election between 1960 and 1980, dropping from 63.1 to 52.6 percent before rising fractionally to 53.3 percent in 1984.[10] Between 1972 and 1976 alone, eighteen million people stopped voting![11]

To most observers, this long-term decline was a mystery, because four strong forces were working in the opposite direction. Potential voters became better educated (if education can be judged by years of schooling). The 1965 Voting Rights Act ended the terror and tricks that formerly barred blacks from the polls in many areas. Women, no longer content to defer to men in sexual or electoral politics, began to vote at the same rate as males.[12] And a series of reforms did away with many (but not all) of the registration barriers that had discouraged people from voting.[13] Two factors did work to lessen turnout: The changing age structure of the population swelled the numbers of young and elderly citizens—two categories whose members vote at lower rates—and the Twenty-sixth Amendment, by dropping the voting age to eighteen, enfranchised politically inexperienced young people, many of whom didn't exercise their new right. Nevertheless, statistical analysis shows that changing demographics and the youth vote together accounted for only about one-third of the turnout decline.[14]

Why, then, did so many people stop voting? An important reason is simply that most local party organizations were no longer so vigorous in getting people to register and vote. At least three influences undermined political parties during this period. The continuing spread of civil service and other good-government practices weakened the patronage-based incentive system on which traditional "machines" depended. The new dominance of television in campaigns diverted funds and effort that might have gone to supporting foot soldiers in the precincts. And the post-1968 reform of the Democratic party nominating process for a time excluded and alienated big-city organizations and their union allies.

Oddly enough, political scientists who write about turnout decline virtually ignore the organizational explanation.[15] Researchers seem unable to get outside the heads of survey respondents; but anyone who has watched or taken part in a traditional "vote-pulling" operation knows that responsive attitudes among voters are only one of the conditions necessary for a big turnout. Equally essential are organizational resources and effort: canvassers and telephoners who remind people of registration deadlines and election hours, cars and drivers who take them to the polls, babysitters who watch their children, and street-smart politicos who cajole, shame, or push citizens into performing their civic duty.

The appeal of attitudinal explanations stems from the ease of testing them with quantifiable evidence from surveys. What data support the party-atrophy theory of turnout decline? Systematic research that tests the hypothesis seems not to exist, but at least three important facts testify in its favor:

- The two attitudinal variables that researchers have succeeded in linking to turnout decline are party identification and feelings of external political efficacy (the belief that people like the respondent can influence government).[16] Party identification is as much a result as a cause of vigor in party organizations. As for external efficacy, the precinct-based party was, for many people, the chief means through which government could be made to respond to their needs.
- The sharpest single drop in turnout—from 60.9 to 55.2 percent—occurred between 1968 and 1972. This period coincided with the Democratic party reforms that weakened and embittered traditional party workers.[17]
- Voting fell off most among precisely that group of citizens who previously were the main constituents of patronage-based parties: the white working class. Between 1960 and 1976, the turnout rate among high-income whites slipped only a little—from 89.5 to 86.0 percent, but among low-income whites, the drop was sharp—from 71.3 to 57.3 percent.[18]

Regardless of the truth or falsity of this particular historical explanation, the general point should be clear: To understand participatory behavior, look not only at the characteristics, beliefs, and attitudes of individuals but also at the health of organizations that inform, assist, and motivate them. And when organizations weaken, understand that the fault often lies not only in decreased loyalty of their supporters but also in such causes as a changed legal climate, external competition, internal splits, and their own strategic mistakes.

STRUCTURE

Structure means features of a community, whether natural or artificial, that are normally beyond the control of groups or individuals and that change rarely, slowly, or not at all. We usually take structural influences as much for granted as the air we breathe, but by stepping back a bit from familiar situations, as in comparing one system with another, we can more easily appreciate the profound influence of structure on patterns of participation.

Physical Constraints

Nature imposes some elements of structure. Mountainous terrain, which keeps communities small and independent, nurtured the intensive participatory democracies of Switzerland and ancient Greece. Climate and seasons also play a role. As Kitto observes, direct democracy in a city the size of Athens would have been impossible without the mild Greek climate, which permitted regular outdoor assemblies of all male citizens.[19] In agricultural communities, it is foolish to expect farmers to participate much during the planting, growing, and harvesting seasons. This may explain the United States tradition of November elections, nestled between the harvest and the coming of harsh weather.

Physical arrangements not imposed by nature also have a marked effect. A residential pattern of peasants clustering together in villages surrounded by fields contributes to participatory decision making in Chinese farming communities. In contrast, the United States pattern of dispersed farm families housed on their own acreage neither requires nor facilitates intensive participation. Similarly, the central plazas common in European cities provide a focus for mass demonstrations, whereas sprawling American suburbs offer no such encouragement. (Parking lots are uninspiring sites for rallies, and mall managers discourage controversial activities.)

Communication patterns are another element of structure. The greater attention given national politics by American news media helps account for lower voting rates in state and local elections. New Jersey especially suffers from lack of local media. Until the 1970s, there was no television station in the state, and New York and Philadelphia still dominate their neighbor's airwaves. Thus a survey in 1979 found that only 21 percent of New Jerseyans could name their two United States Senators, whereas 75 percent in Massachusetts knew theirs.[20]

Jurisdiction

As the calculus of voting implies, people are more willing to take part in decision making when there is more at stake. A central structural property of any polity is its jurisdiction—the scope of outcomes it controls. American federalism, by sharing the powers of government among local, state, and national levels and among three constitutional branches, reduces the value to the citizen of participating in elections for any one office. A similar effect results when public powers are dispersed to separate quasi-governmental units, whether elective or appointive. For decades, reformers and professionals sought to remove specialized functions from the pernicious influence of "politics." They succeeded so well that the United States now has one governmental unit for every 2,703 persons,²¹ with a bewildering array of special-purpose districts and authorities for transportation, ports, water and sewers, fire protection, and schools. The loss of these powers leaves mayors impotent in dealing with issues of urgent concern to citizens, who thus are justified in caring little about municipal elections. And when voters choose special-purpose officials such as school board members, their relative invisibility and limited power typically produce low rates of participation.

Participation that is intense, extensive, and lasting becomes possible when collective decisions govern all important facets of life. Consider the long list of decisions that enabled an Israeli kibbutz to sustain interest in twice-weekly town meetings that often did not adjourn until after midnight:

> The annual budget, a new building program, the expansion of an agricultural branch, the election of officers and committees. . . . the stand to be taken on a political issue, the amount of activity to be devoted to a political campaign, the decision to admit an American anthropologist to the kibbutz to do research, the problem of the intellectual level of the children, the complaint of the women concerning kitchen facilities. . . . Should a student be sent to study in the city? Should a disturbed child be sent to a psychiatrist? . . . The problem of the women in the community, the participation of the younger people in community life, the meaning of a recent political event for the future of the kibbutz, the proper role of the Arabs in the national life of Israel—all are subjects for town meeting.²²

Rather than examining a tedious enumeration of all the other structural properties that affect participation, let us conclude this section by concentrating on two related influences that are both interesting and important.

Ease of Exit and the Possibility of Retaliation

Because getting together with others to influence large systems is costly and difficult, most people first try to solve problems through individual, rather than collective, action.²³ When conditions are bad, the simplest remedy for an individual is often to quit the system rather than to try to change it. This is the typical solution for consumers in a competitive economy. If the checkout lines at my neighborhood supermarket are too long, I can more easily walk an extra block to a better-run store than lobby for improvements with the managers of the closer one. Exit occurs in politics as well as in economics. During the Vietnam War, hawkish Americans displayed bumper stickers that advised dissenters, "America—Love It or Leave It." Thousands did just that, fleeing to Canada, Sweden, and other countries that seemed more peace-loving than their homeland. Despite such obvious examples, few people realized the general political relevance of exit until the economist Albert Hirschman published his widely read little book *Exit, Voice, and Loyalty*.²⁴

By "voice," Hirschman means precisely those actions we call "participation." After noting that economists focus on exit, and political scientists on voice, Hirschman observes that both overlook the important and nonobvious interactions that occur when people can choose between the two responses. In particular, Hirschman contends that if it is easy for people to leave, then they won't participate in efforts to change a poor situation. As he puts it, exit tends to drive out voice.

Hirschman's proposition identifies a key structural property affecting the amount of participation. Consider one of his most frequently cited examples, educational politics in American cities. In most metropolitan areas, parents unhappy with city public schools may transfer their children to parochial or private schools or may move to a nearby suburb. Consequently, parents able to leave have less incentive to become active in parent-teacher associations or in school-board politics.[25] As citizens sensitive to educational quality desert the system instead of working to improve it, a vicious cycle ensues. If, in contrast, there were only one school district in an area, those parents would be forced to stay and fight to maintain quality.

Does ease of exit always discourage voice? Must we restrict exit to promote participation? Matters are not so clear-cut. Ease of exit always reduces the individual's personal stake in acting to change system policies. However, ease of exit also affects another determinant of the decision to participate. One possible cost of participation is retaliation from authorities or others who dislike the participant's policies or tactics.[26] Severity of retaliation is limited by the possibility of exit. The easier it is for a member to leave when others make life unpleasant, the less punishment those others can inflict before the victim takes off.[27] As walls around prisons and East Berlin testify, systems that coerce members must always make departure difficult.

Ease of exit therefore works through two different channels both to discourage and to encourage participation. It is impossible to say in general which tendency is stronger, but Hirschman's hypothesis—that difficulty of exit fosters participation—is correct if retaliation is unlikely. Therefore, let us consider what strategies discourage reprisal.

First, participants can protect themselves by avoiding action that will provoke retaliation. Participatory acts vary from innocuous to bitterly controversial. Participation that hurts no one, such as community service, arouses no anger. We should expect, therefore, that when people find it hard to leave and guarantees against retaliation are weak, they will prefer nonconflictful participation. Evidence supporting this argument comes from the research of Verba and Nie. They compare participation rates in isolated or "bounded" villages, towns, and cities—from which exit is costly—with rates for suburbs and cities within metropolitan areas—where residents can more easily move from one jurisdiction to another. As Hirschman would expect, correcting for socioeconomic characteristics, total participation is higher in bounded communities of all sizes. But the greatest differences between isolated and nonisolated communities occur for activities that arouse little controversy: communal participation and particularized contacting. For the more conflictful voting and campaign activities, differences are small and inconsistent.[28]

The second, and more desirable, shield against retaliation is the enforcement of guarantees that protect the rights of participants. Our analysis implies that prohibitions against reprisal are most necessary when exit is difficult. Because exile from one's homeland is so painful, laws or norms comparable to the Bill of Rights are obviously needed before citizens can participate freely in national politics. For most people, the second most costly departure is to leave one's job unwillingly. Therefore, the full flowering of any work-related participation requires assurances against politically motivated firing and punishment. Paul Bernstein's survey of experiences with workplace democracy leads him to a similar conclusion:

> To persist, a participation system must be supported by the rights commonly associated with political democracy: freedom of speech and assembly, petition of grievances, secret balloting, due process and the right to file appeal in cases of discipline, immunity of rank and file representatives from dismissal or transfer while in office, and a written constitution alterable only by a majority or a two-thirds vote of the collective.[29]

When participatory rights have constitutional status, we can regard them as part of the structure of a polity. But rights begin—and, unhappily, sometimes end—when authorities depart from the practices of their predecessors—in other words, when they embark on a new policy. Moreover, policies that fall short of constitutional change can also powerfully affect amounts and patterns of participation. Let us look now at how they do it.

POLICIES

"At least in the short run," write Huntington and Nelson, "the values of the political elite and the policies of government are more decisive than anything else in shaping the participation patterns of a society."[30] Support for their argument is easy to find—for example, in the great contractions and surges in popular activity that occurred when Spain, Greece, and Brazil shifted from constitutional to authoritarian government and back again.

Governments (or other systems) can exert a continuum of effects on the costs members must bear if they wish to participate. Charles Tilly divides this continuum into three zones: At one extreme is *repression* (action that raises the cost of collective action); at the other is *facilitation* (action that lowers the cost of collective action). In between comes *toleration*, where the system neither represses nor facilitates.[31] His terms are useful, but our discussion is organized differently: First we examine legality and force, then facilitation and hindrance, and finally legitimation and support.

Legality and Force

The most obvious systemic power over participation is the simple ability to permit or forbid—to declare an activity legal or illegal or to ban some members from engaging in actions open to others. Employees do not run for workers' councils in factories where councils do not exist; until 1940, women did not vote in the province of Quebec, because only men were enfranchised;[32] and citizens of the Soviet Union do not engage in party politics except through the Communist party.

The control of the state over participation becomes most evident when it uses violence to enforce its commands. Governments usually apply force to suppress political activity—as in Chile during 1973, when the military executed thousands who had supported the deposed Allende government—but they can also employ it to protect participants, as when President Lyndon Johnson stationed federal marshals in southern polling places to ensure that blacks could vote.

Although laws are ultimately backed by force, victims of governmental repression are not always acting illegally, and official violence can chill the enthusiasm of would-be participants who do not contemplate illegal acts. For example, demonstrations against the Vietnam War markedly decreased in 1970, after Ohio national guardsmen at Kent State University shot twelve protesting students, killing four.

Facilitation and Hindrance

Many forms of participation cannot succeed unless authorities actively facilitate them. Can you imagine an election occurring just because the government tolerates voting? Who will bear the cost of printing ballots, renting polling places, hiring election officials, and counting votes? Merely to make an election possible is expensive, quite aside from the effort of inducing people to go to the polls. In the 1976 budget of the city of Philadelphia, the appropriation for the city commissioners, whose chief duty is to conduct elections, exceeded the budgets of the city council and the mayor's office combined.[33]

Governments can also encourage participation by manipulating selective incentives. Ancient Athens paid citizens to attend the Assembly. In modern times, governments typically use payments only to induce the participation of a relatively few persons, such as neighborhood organizers in community development programs, who in turn can stimulate the unpaid involvement of many more. When a government wants to directly induce activity by masses of citizens, negative selective incentives are cheaper than positive.[34] An obvious example is compulsory voting, enforced by levying a small fine against people who fail to turn out. The policy works well—in Australia, turnout rose from about 60 to 90 percent after it was introduced.[35]

Although violent repression furnishes bloody dramas for television news, subtler government policies can also hinder participation. For most people the calculus of collective action yields net incentives to participate that, at best, barely exceed zero; therefore, even slight governmental pressure on the cost side of the scale tips the balance toward passivity. For example, the chief explanation of the relatively low voting turnout rates in the United States compared with other Western democracies lies in the cumbersome registration procedures most American states inflict on citizens before permitting them to cast ballots.[36] Among the impediments states have imposed are lengthy residence requirements, closing dates for registration well before election day, literacy tests, and inconvenient places and times for registration.[37] By 1972, legislative and judicial action had greatly liberalized registration laws; nevertheless, Wolfinger and Rosenstone estimate that turnout in that year would have been 9 percent higher—12.2 million additional voters—if the least restrictive existing provisions had applied nationwide.[38] In 1977 the Carter administration introduced the Universal Voter Registration Act, a plan to promote election-day registration, which would have moved the United States closer to the system employed in most European countries. The bill was eventually withdrawn when opposition from Republicans, southern Democrats, and big-city Democrats made passage impossible.[39]

Besides their impact on participants' costs and selective incentives, government policies also affect other elements in the citizen's mental calculus. Perhaps most important, the extent to which members believe they can achieve their goals through collective action depends strongly on their perceptions of authorities' responsiveness. Revolution and venting of rage aside, it makes no sense to try to influence rulers who will neither listen nor be moved. This may be one reason why the high tides of leftist activism in the United States coincided with the progressive, interventionist administrations of the 1930s and 1960s. Similarly, the peak phases of activism on the right seem to occur during conservative administrations.[40]

Legitimation and Support

Besides its own policies that directly affect political participation, government plays a preeminent role in steering the policies of lesser associations as they encourage or suppress participation within their ranks.

We like to think that the modern state has a monopoly on the use of violence, but nongovernmental organizations also sometimes resort to force in order to intimidate members who want a larger voice in decisions. In a well-ordered society, the state regulates such violence—either by stepping in to prevent its recurrence or by legitimizing it through explicit authorization and tangible support. Two incidents involving the United Mine Workers show how the U.S. government, at different times, played both roles when first mine owners and then the union itself attempted to suppress collective action by miners.

In 1919, coal mine operators in southern West Virginia tried to destroy the U.M.W. by hiring private guards to evict union members from company-owned houses and to lock them out of the mines. The workers fought back, and by 1921 the struggle had become a small war. At the "Battle of Blair Mountain," aviators employed by the companies dropped bombs on miners who were marching on the coal fields of Logan County. The miners surrendered only after the federal government intervened on the owners' side with troops and its own squadron of bombers.[41]

Half a century later, Tony Boyle, an unworthy heir to leadership of the same U.M.W., hired contract killers to assassinate Jock Yablonski, who offered members a choice by daring to run against Boyle for the union presidency. This time the government acted to protect rank-and-file unionists. Boyle was prosecuted, convicted, and imprisoned for murder. The Department of Labor supervised a new election, in which the insurgent Miners for Democracy swept the top offices.[42]

In the movement for workplace democracy, violence is seldom an issue, but government financial and legal support often makes the difference between success and failure. In 1980, $2.3 million in loans from federal and county agencies enabled former employees at the McKeesport (Pa.) Steel Casting Company to buy the closed factory and return to their jobs as worker-owners.[43] In a larger and more publicized 1979 case, the Economic Development Administration killed a plan to revive the Campbell Steel Works in Youngstown, Ohio. A worker-community coalition needed $245 million in federal loan guarantees to purchase and modernize the plant, but the E.D.A. rejected their application.[44]

The few American legislative efforts to promote workplace democracy (most of which encourage employee stock ownership plans) look meager compared with the full-scale national commitments that have democratized industry elsewhere. The pioneer is Yugoslavia, which in 1950 enacted a law applying "management by collectives" to nearly all economic enterprises.[45] Yugoslavia is no longer unique. William Lafferty describes Norway as having accomplished "perhaps the broadest participatory spectrum ever achieved in a national polity." The strength of Norwegian government support for this transformation becomes apparent when one reads language like the following in an official document:

> It is a broad-based political goal—to which the Government assigns great importance—that democracy should be further developed and established *in all areas of society*. This implies that every individual should—to the greatest possible extent—have real influence on those decisions . . . which affect one's own living conditions.[46]

CONCLUSION

The ideas presented in Chapters 3 and 4 force us to reexamine assumptions that people often take for granted about political action.

Because personal costs and selective incentives commonly play a larger role than collective goals in the decision to participate, purely political beliefs, attitudes, and motives influence decisions to participate less than we usually think. Citizens' underlying concern about issues can remain steady; yet their involvement will fluctuate with changes in public policies and organizational stimulation, the two factors that most massively affect the costs, rewards, and chances for success of political action. The same logic should make us neither surprised nor upset (though perhaps a bit wary) when many participants act from essentially personal, apolitical motives—seeking companionship, career advancement, prestige, excitement.

None of this means that people care little about the ability to participate. History amply demonstrates that citizens will, on occasion, fight passionately for the right to govern themselves. Nor is it correct to say that people act only when they anticipate a personal payoff. Nevertheless, except for the most easily exercised rights, the majority in large systems spontaneously use participatory opportunities only sporadically—when an issue is of intense concern, prospects for effective action seem good, cooperation of others can be expected, and especially, when the conjunction of all these conditions makes civic action itself an occasion for joy and celebration.

But what if we hold to the participatory democrat's dream of widespread, sustained involvement in decision making? Then three hard lessons must be faced.

First, people will be least willing to participate regularly in large systems—precisely where most of us live and work. In Chapter 7, Olson's argument is augmented with others to show that only in small-scale settings can we expect participatory democracy to be both extensive and intensive.

Second, because the willingness of most people to participate is so sensitive to the price they pay to act, it is up to governments and organizations to minimize or defray the costs of participation. As Ralph Nader says, "Half of democracy is facility."[47] The common prejudice that people who "really care" about an issue can and should be willing to overcome all difficulties in "earning the privilege" of taking part leads to policies that exclude rational members with a real stake in decisions.

Third, we must recognize that participation, a central democratic value, conflicts with certain other cherished liberties. If we want the highest possible rates of participation, we must accept coercion—penalties that make people less free *not* to participate, whether in the form of legally imposed fines or the informal pressures of a small community. Moreover, people who are free to leave a polity without personal sacrifice are less inclined to exercise participatory rights. Fortunately, if you like at least *some* good things to go together, you can take comfort from the encouragement that civil liberties give to uninhibited participation.

Faced by so much difficulty, why not just leave politics to those who enjoy it? Even if you are willing to forgo the benefits of widespread participation reviewed in Chapter 2, a laissez-faire stance toward political action sacrifices another great democratic value—political equality. The next chapter is an analysis of the uneasy marriage of participation and equality and what can be done to ease the tension between them.

NOTES

1. Edward C. Banfield and James Q. Wilson, *City Politics* (New York: Vintage Books, 1966), pp. 234–40, 329–46; Wilson and Banfield, "Political Ethos Revisited," *American Political Science Review*, 65 (1971), 1048–62.
2. *The Moral Basis of a Backward Society* (New York: Free Press, 1958), pp. 157, 166.
3. *The Greeks* (London: Penguin Books, 1951), p. 75.
4. Ernesto Che Guevara, "Man and Socialism in Cuba," in *Man and Socialism in Cuba: The Great Debate*, ed. Bertram Silverman (New York: Atheneum, 1973), p. 343.
5. Kitto, *The Greeks*, p. 94.
6. *Participation and Democratic Theory* (Cambridge: Cambridge University Press, 1970), p. 42.
7. Sidney Verba and Norman H. Nie, *Participation in America: Political Democracy and Social Equality* (New York: Harper & Row, 1972), chap. 11, especially pp. 191–94.
8. Lester W. Milbrath and M. L. Goel, *Political Participation: How and Why Do People Get Involved in Politics?* 2nd ed. (Chicago: Rand McNally, 1977), pp. 132–34.
9. Sidney Verba, Norman H. Nie, and Jae-on Kim, *Participation and Political Equality: A Seven-Nation Comparison* (Cambridge: Cambridge University Press, 1978), chap. 7.
10. Carole Jean Uhlaner, "Turnout in the 1984 Presidential Election" (paper presented at the annual meeting of the American Political Science Association, 1985), p. 1.
11. According to an estimate by Thomas E. Cavanagh in "Changes in American Voter Turnout, 1964–1976," *Political Science Quarterly*, 96 (1981), 53–65. The dropouts were partially offset by new voters.
12. By 1984, the turnout difference between the sexes had entirely disappeared. Uhlaner, "Turnout in 1984," p. 5.
13. Raymond E. Wolfinger and Steven J. Rosenstone, *Who Votes?* (New Haven: Yale University Press, 1980), chap. 4. See also below, pages 47–48.
14. Cavanagh, "Changes in American Voter Turnout." The proportion would be even smaller if the base were adjusted for increases that could be expected because of the four favorable factors.
15. One exception is a journalist who writes very good political science—Thomas Byrne Edsall, *The New Politics of Inequality* (New York: W. W. Norton & Co., 1984), pp. 198–201. More typical studies include Richard A. Brody, "The Puzzle of Political Participation in America," in *The New American Political System*, ed. Anthony King (Washington: American Enterprise Institute, 1978), pp. 287–324; most articles in the special voting turnout issue of *American Politics Quarterly*, 9 (1981); and Paul R. Abramson and John H. Aldrich, "The Decline of Electoral Participation in America," *American Political Science Review*, 76 (1982), 502–21.
16. Abramson and Aldrich, "The Decline of Electoral Participation."
17. For an account of the exclusion of Chicago's regular organization delegates from the 1972 convention, see William Crotty, *Party Reform* (New York: Longman, 1983), chaps. 14–16.
18. Howard L. Reiter, "Why is Turnout Down?" *Public Opinion Quarterly*, 43 (1979), 297–311. The figures are based on surveys, which overstate voting, because more people say they remember voting than actually vote; nevertheless, these data give a good idea of trends and relationships. "High" and "low" incomes are the top and bottom quartiles, respectively.
19. *The Greeks*, p. 37.
20. Marc Fisher, "On Selling the State an Image," *Philadelphia Inquirer*, January 20, 1980, p. 3J.
21. Richard W. Boyd, "Decline of U.S. Voter Turnout: Structural Explanations," *American Politics Quarterly*, 9 (1981), 133–59.
22. Melford E. Spiro, *Kibbutz: Venture in Utopia*, augmented ed. (New York: Schocken Books, 1970), p. 92.
23. Samuel P. Huntington and Joan M. Nelson, *No Easy Choice: Political Participation in Developing Countries* (Cambridge: Harvard University Press, 1976), pp. 165–66.
24. *Exit, Voice, and Loyalty: Responses to Decline in Firms, Organizations, and States* (Cambridge: Harvard University Press, 1970).

25. Ease or difficulty of exit depends on individual circumstances as well as on structure. Non-Catholics, homeowners, and people with low income all find it harder than others to leave the public schools in their community.

26. A. H. Birch, "Economic Models in Political Science: The Case of 'Exit, Voice, and Loyalty,'" *British Journal of Political Science*, 5 (1975), pp. 69–82. Hirschman comments on retaliation in his *Essays in Trespassing: Economics to Politics and Beyond* (New York: Cambridge University Press, 1981), chap. 10.

27. In formal terms, the maximum punishment a rational individual will endure is that which inflicts a utility loss equal to the utility difference between staying in the present system and moving to the next best alternative (allowing for transaction costs of moving). This difference is precisely the same as the difficulty of exit, expressed in terms of utility.

28. *Participation in America*, chap. 13. Verba and Nie, who wrote before Hirschman's book appeared, account for this finding with several ad hoc explanations that are less satisfying than a prediction drawn from a more general theory.

29. "Necessary Elements for Effective Worker Participation in Decision Making," in *Workplace Democracy and Social Change*, eds. Frank Lindenfeld and Joyce Rothschild-Whitt (Boston: Porter Sargent, 1982) pp. 65–66.

30. *No Easy Choice*, p. 27.

31. *From Mobilization to Revolution* (Reading, Mass.: Addison-Wesley, 1978), pp. 100, 107.

32. William Mishler, *Political Participation in Canada* (Toronto: Macmillan of Canada, 1979), p. 26.

33. Adam Tait, ed., *1976 Bulletin Almanac* (Philadelphia: The Bulletin Company, 1976), p. 64.

34. Rewards are costly when they succeed; punishments, when they fail. Therefore, organizations generally use positive incentives when they need relatively few people to respond (e.g., organizers). When nearly everyone must comply, threats and moral suasion are cheaper. See David A. Baldwin, "The Power of Positive Sanctions," *World Politics*, 24 (1971), 19–38.

35. Alan Wertheimer, "In Defense of Compulsory Voting," in *Participation in Politics*, eds. J. Roland Pennock and John W. Chapman (New York: Lieber-Atherton, 1975), p. 279.

36. G. Bingham Powell, "American Voter Turnout in Comparative Perspective," *American Political Science Review*, forthcoming.

37. Stanley Kelley, Jr., Richard E. Ayres, and William G. Bowen, "Registration and Voting: Putting First Things First," *American Political Science Review*, 61 (1967), pp. 359–77.

38. *Who Votes?* p. 78. See their Chapter 4 for an excellent summary of registration laws and their impact.

39. "Election Reforms: Delay and Defeat," *Congressional Quarterly Almanac*, 33 (1977), 798–801.

40. This argument is a less formal version of a prediction by William A. Gamson, *Power and Discontent* (Homewood, Ill.: Dorsey Press, 1968), pp. 160–62.

41. Evelyn L. K. Harris and Frank J. Krebs, *From Humble Beginnings: West Virginia State Federation of Labor, 1903–1957* (Charleston: West Virginia Labor History Publishing Fund, 1960), pp. 152–54.

42. H. W. Benson, *Democratic Rights for Union Members: A Guide to Internal Union Democracy* (Brooklyn N.Y.: Association for Union Democracy, 1979), p. 237.

43. *Ocean County* (N.J.) *Times-Observer*, May 15, 1980, p. A4.

44. Stephen Sachs, "Political Obstacles to Workplace Democracy," *Workplace Democracy*, 10 (1983), 6–7. See also Gar Alperovitz and Jeff Faux, "The Youngstown Project," in *Workplace Democracy and Social Change*, eds. Lindenfeld and Rothschild-Whitt, pp. 353–69.

45. David Jenkins, *Job Power: Blue and White Collar Democracy* (Baltimore: Penguin Books, 1974), p. 94.

46. William M. Lafferty, "Political Participation in the Social-Democratic State" (paper presented at the annual meeting of the American Political Science Association, 1981), p. 22; emphasis added.

47. Talk at the National Conference on Citizen Participation, Silver Spring, Md., January 28, 1984.

CHAPTER 5

EQUALITY

Participation and political equality go together in the minds of most democrats. Participation in some form and amount is a necessary condition of democracy, and belief in the fundamental equality of humanity is the wellspring of democratic ideology. Indeed, many writers define democracy as a system that seeks to distribute power equally among all members.[1] It may therefore shock you to learn that in practice opportunities for more participation often produce *less* equality. The purpose of this chapter is to help you understand the conflict between these ideals by developing three important generalizations.

EXTENT VERSUS INTENSITY

Our first rule uses the distinction made in Chapter 1 between two ways the amount of participation can vary: extent and intensity. *Extent* refers to how many people participate. It depends on three quantities: size, or the number of persons in the affected population; eligibility, or the fraction of those affected whom the polity allows to take part in decisions; and turnout, or the proportion of eligibles who use the opportunities given them. *Intensity* indicates how much each member is permitted or required to do in the process of participating. Intensity has several dimensions: frequency (an initial election

53

plus a runoff demands more intensive participation than just a single election); duration (a three-hour meeting is more intensive than a one-hour meeting); financial cost ($1,000-a-plate political dinners are more intensive than $5-a-ticket picnics); and difficulty, whether physical, mental, or emotional (a person who speaks at a meeting participates more intensively than one who sits silently).

RULE 1: The more intensive the activity a system requires of members, the less extensive their actual participation.

This proposition follows immediately from the calculus of participation presented in Chapter 3. Intensive participation is more costly in time, money, or effort. More costly actions are less probable. Therefore, increased intensity reduces the likelihood that a typical member will turn out.

Despite this rule's obviousness to anyone used to thinking in economic terms, instances abound where advocates of more participation ignore Rule 1. Reformers have demanded that voters choose party candidates in primaries as well as select among them in general elections, and many states have substituted even more time-consuming rank-and-file caucuses for primaries. The effect on the extent of participation is overwhelming: The proportion of people who vote in presidential primaries is only about half as great as in the November election,[2] and the proportion who attend caucuses is a mere tenth of the turnout in primaries.[3] Similarly, participatory democrats often favor consensus decision making over majority rule and unrestricted speech over controlled debate, even though both practices lengthen meetings and drive away members.

In all such cases, people have reasons for supporting the more intensive process. Consensus decisions are intended to unify a group and protect minorities; full discussion is thought to produce wiser decisions; primaries are designed to break the rule of "bosses." Why shouldn't those who can tolerate, or even enjoy, such activities be able to engage in them? Is it not better for fewer people to participate meaningfully than for many to get involved only superficially? Perhaps so, especially if we focus on the developmental and intrinsic values of participation; however, serious doubts arise once we look at participation instrumentally, as a means through which individuals and groups struggle to influence policy. If those who act differ substantially from other citizens, then decisions will be biased in their favor, and the polity will neglect the interests of those who stay on the sidelines. Hence, the key question becomes, how much can we count on participants to resemble nonparticipants?

REPRESENTATIVENESS AND MOTIVATION

RULE 2: The less extensive the participation, the less the similarity between the policy preferences of participants and the preferences of the affected population.

At the extremes, the truth of this proposition is obvious: If all those affected are eligible and turnout is 100 percent, participants represent the population, because they *are* the population. One might be tempted to extrapolate, assuming that the fewer who participate, the more likely they are to differ from the entire group merely through the operation of chance. In fact, if participants are truly a random sample of the population, this will be true for small populations, but the proportion who participate from a large population has little effect on representativeness, so long as the absolute number of participants is reasonably big (about fifteen hundred or so).[4] Unfortunately, random processes rarely choose participants. Instead, they choose themselves, which is to say people who participate are motivated to act. Some motives—for example, the enjoyment of politics for its own sake—may be relatively independent of policy preferences. But most factors that spur citizens to act are linked with distinctive attitudes toward issues. To see why this is so, let us use the framework supplied by the calculus of participation to explore four factors that affect motivation: costs, selective incentives, special interests, and zeal.

Costs

American governments do strive to select citizens randomly for jury duty, but even this deliberate effort often fails to achieve representativeness, because the cost of service varies for different categories of the population. The higher opportunity cost that employed persons (or their employers) must pay to serve gives them a reason (or excuse) to be released from duty. Consequently, unless courts are strict in turning down requests to be excused, juries will tend to consist disproportionately of retirees and homemakers. What has this to do with decisions? Nothing, sometimes; but if you were on trial for robbing a senior citizen or raping a woman, a jury pool that is mostly elderly or female might give you reason to worry.

New England town meetings offer a more typical example, because town governments make no effort to structure who turns out. People who live in town are more likely to attend meetings than rural "backroaders," both because the townsfolk have less far to travel and because they get political information easily from the village gossip network. Does this affect the town's decisions? It will if the agenda includes proposals to pave country roads or to charge parents whose children ride the schoolbus.[5]

It is hard to generalize about how differential costs affect who participates and what policies they favor. But in evaluating methods and occasions for participation, you should always ask two questions: Who finds it easy and who finds it hard to engage in this action? How do these groups differ in their preferences concerning the issues at stake?

Selective Incentives

Those who participate to gain rewards or to avoid punishments differ from others in a peculiar way. They are more likely to have *no* policy preferences. More precisely, their individual payoffs usually outweigh whatever concern they feel for the collective outcome. Therefore, such people are willing to replace their own goals with the goals of the organization that feeds them. The patronage-based political party "machine" derives its vaunted adaptability from this power to discipline adherents.

Such a system is not always bad from a democratic point of view. If leaders of party organizations want above all to win votes in general elections (the arena of most extensive participation), they will adopt policy positions likely to win among the general electorate, regardless of what course they privately favor. In 1968, Mayor Richard J. Daley of Chicago—the prototypical machine boss—seemed an archvillain to opponents of the Vietnam War, because he supported the Johnson–Humphrey administration and his police beat demonstrators outside the Democratic National Convention. Yet, just two years later, the Daley organization threw its crucial backing to an antiwar senatorial candidate, Adlai Stevenson III.[6] Daley had read the mood of the electorate and realized that a pro-war candidate would lose. Did his party workers favor or oppose the war? It didn't matter. To keep their jobs, they needed to win elections, so they worked for the candidate whose policies pleased the majority of voters.

Making decisions by intensive participation helps organizations based on selective incentives, because of their members' relatively strong and dependable motivation. In New Haven, I once observed a sequence of events that illustrates the danger this advantage poses for those who would substitute intensive for extensive participation. In a hotly contested election that brought several hundred voters to the polls, a reform challenger displaced a "machine" adherent as Democratic leader of a ward. The victorious reformer, an idealist committed to participatory democracy, pledged that unlike his predecessor, he would never unilaterally decide whom to endorse for higher office. Instead, he would follow the majority will of monthly ward meetings open to all Democrats. At the first of these assemblies, about twenty-five people showed up. Only a few were supporters of the reformer. The voters who had elected him several weeks earlier were busy people who had work, children, and studies to attend to, so they followed the familiar logic of collective action. The majority at the meeting were party regulars whose city jobs depended on their political activity. They dominated the tense gathering, and the embarrassed reform leader found himself pledged to support a regular organization candidate for the state legislature. How democratic was the result of this experiment in participatory democracy? Which forum communicated the more legitimate voice of the people—the election where hundreds gave up a few minutes to vote, or the ward meeting, where two dozen sacrificed an evening?

Special Interests

As we saw in Chapter 3, people commonly conclude that participation is not worthwhile in collective-action situations; however, it often happens that not everyone has an equal individual stake in the group decision. People who stand to gain or lose a great deal more than others may find that action pays off, especially if the decision process requires or encourages intensive participation, which will drive down the number who act, thus increasing the relative influence of those who do get involved.

Everyone knows about the disproportionate influence of special-interest groups in national politics, but we less often recognize that the same sort of calculations enable less formal special interests to dominate in any setting open to intensive participation. Let me again draw on personal experience for a homely example. The city of Philadelphia once proposed to institute a resident-permit parking system for the crowded streets of my neighborhood. During a stormy community meeting, the most conspicuous organizer and vocal cheerleader for people opposing the plan was a millionaire landlord who did not live in the affected area. Why did so atypical a citizen care about this seemingly petty matter? His apartment buildings were inhabited largely by students whose cars were registered to out-of-town addresses, which meant that the city would not issue them permits.[7] If tenants found it hard to park near the landlord's buildings, fewer of them would want to live there. As demand fell, so would rents, occupancy rates, and profits.

Certainly it was legitimate for the landlord to try to protect his investment. In so doing, he promoted the interests of his tenants, who previously had been a latent group in local affairs. However, proponents of the plan had no organizer, so the parking authority officials received a one-sided impression of neighborhood opinion; opponents—mobilized by their landlord-organizer—seemed more numerous at the raucous, four-hour open meeting. Would a door-to-door poll have shown that the majority of residents supported the permit system? No one knows, for no poll was ever taken, and the plan was withdrawn.

Zeal

Not all participants are drawn to politics by financial rewards. Many care deeply about the principles or people affected by collective decisions. But issue-oriented activists also present a dilemma for democratic theory, because they tend to be unrepresentative in the positions they prefer as well as in the fervor of their feelings. Because they work so much harder than most, the policies and candidates they favor are more likely to prevail.

Even during the tranquil 1950s, when pragmatic professionals still ruled American political parties, a classic study showed that Democratic and Republican national convention delegates were far more ideological than ordinary party supporters. Republican delegates were much more to the right, and Democratic delegates more to the left than their respective rank-and-file followers, who differed from each other only moderately. Herbert McClosky and his coauthors speculated about why activists tend to be ideologues, and ideologues activists:

Through a process of circular reinforcement, those for whom politics is most important are likely to become the most zealous participants, succeeding to the posts that deal in the formation of opinion. Ideology serves the instrumental purpose, in addition, of justifying the heavy investment that party leaders make in political activity. While politics offers many rewards, it also makes great demands on the time, money, and energies of its practitioners—sacrifices which they can more easily justify if they believe they are serving worthwhile social goals.[8]

The differences that McClosky and his colleagues observed in the late 1950s became more pronounced in the ensuing decades.[9] The nominations of Barry Goldwater, George McGovern, and Ronald Reagan testify to the strength of zealous amateur politicians, and all candidates must steer in their direction, or else risk losing the money, effort, and opinion leadership they offer.

Summary

A political system that requires or encourages intensive participation raises the cost barrier to action so that typical members become increasingly uninvolved, though they are less often unconcerned and are seldom unaffected. Spurred to leap the higher hurdle are a smaller fraction of citizens who respond to unusual inducements—personal payoffs, a special stake in the outcome, or ideological commitment. But giving disproportionate power to such people is only part of the danger intensive participation poses to egalitarian democrats. Just as pervasive and fundamental is the bias of participatory democracy toward those who are already advantaged by societal inequalities.

SOCIAL CLASS

No aspect of participation has received more attention from researchers than its relation to social class, or, as they like to call it, socioeconomic status (SES) or socioeconomic resource level (SERL). Normally, SES is measured as a composite of three closely linked attributes: income, education, and occupational prestige, but some studies separate these components or concentrate on just one or two of them. Numerous investigations around the world lead to the same conclusion: "No matter how class is measured, the studies consistently show that *higher-class persons are more likely to participate in politics than lower-class persons.*"[10] This well-known relationship varies in strength for different types of participation—which brings us to our third key generalization.

RULE 3: The more intensive the form of participation, the greater the tendency of participants to overrepresent higher-status members of the population.

Although systematic research on this proposition is scarce, a great variety of settings yield evidence consistent with Rule 3. In their comparative survey of seven nations, Verba, Nie, and Kim found that "socio-economic resources play a more important role in relation to difficult acts." In every country they studied, SERL was less strongly associated with voting—the easiest political act—than with more intensive campaign and communal activities.[11] In small-group experiments, a Dutch social scientist, Mark Mulder, found that increasing the amount of time allowed for discussion resulted in a sharp rise in the influence of the most expert members.[12] Douglas Yates reports that leaders of block associations in New York City "were relatively successful members of their small communities."[13] In Yugoslav workers' councils and management boards, skilled and highly skilled workers constitute the largest single group—about 50 percent in 1966.[14] Local advisory boards that assist the United States government in managing public grazing lands are dominated by large ranchers; similarly, the more successful farmers are most active in local farm bureaus.[15]

Why do such findings occur with monotonous regularity? No doubt in part it's simply a matter of the cream rising to the top. The same qualities of intelligence, energy, and ambition that help people advance in school and on the job also push them to the forefront in political action. Rank-and-file members recognize merit by deferring to higher-status people. But elites also possess advantages that make them more willing and able to surmount the motivational obstacles to participation. Because they are better educated, they incur lower information costs in learning about decisions and how to influence them. Among the middle and upper classes, social norms more often inculcate the sense that one has a duty to engage in acts that make one a good citizen. And, most important, when they act politically the higher-status members of any group are usually more effective. An educated person who speaks before a group can anticipate a respectful hearing. Less articulate people share the fear of the Vermont villager who explained her silence at town meeting: "They'll say 'She's a fool!'"[16] Affluent, well-dressed businesspeople or professionals can readily gain access to high officials, who are likely to resemble and agree with them. Less-polished laborers or clerks will find themselves cooling their heels before minor functionaries and flak-catchers. In short, people of higher status more often find that participation pays off.[17] The process is easier and less threatening for them, and the decisions that result are typically more to their liking.

Note that all of these explanations, except possibly class norms, have to do with a person's relative status within a population of potential participants: In the land of the blind, the one-eyed man is king. For this reason, Rule 3 holds for any population, even if its status is low in the greater scheme of things. Thus, if eligibility is restricted to the poor, those who participate intensively will tend to be better educated, more skilled, and less poor than most people who qualify as "poor"; nevertheless, compared with the total population, these activists will of course be near the bottom of the status ladder.

RESPONSES TO INEQUALITY

Clearly, democrats face a quandary. Increased opportunities for more meaningful participation favor unrepresentative elements of the population. Political processes that are supposed to equalize power instead exacerbate economic and social inequalities. How can a polity respond to this dilemma? There are many ways to reduce the conflict between participation and equality, but none of them offers a perfect solution.

Cost-Reduction

Whatever the method of participation, managing it inefficiently raises members' costs of action and so, by our three rules, produces involvement that is less extensive, less representative, and more skewed toward high-status members. Therefore, *cutting the price citizens pay to participate should always be the first resort of those who desire egalitarian governance.*

The exact form that cost-reduction takes depends on the type of participation. Devices to encourage extensive voting include traveling registrars, postcard registration, election-day registration, numerous polling places, and more voting machines. Officials genuinely seeking broad consultation will schedule hearings for evening hours at halls near the people affected instead of demanding that citizens travel to government offices during the workday. Chairpersons of meetings will boost attendance if they distribute background information in advance, keep to a scheduled agenda, maintain germane discussion, and strive for expeditious decision making.

Nevertheless, once reasonably efficient practices are achieved, an irreducible minimum cost will persist, varying with the intensiveness of the decision-making method. Those who feel dissatisfied with the remaining inequality must turn to more drastic and controversial practices.

Compulsion

If too many people hurt themselves by passing up chances to influence decisions, then one solution is to "force them to be free." For example, the equalizing effect of compulsory voting is shown by the experience of the Netherlands, which stopped penalizing nonvoters in 1970. In the last election under compulsory voting, the difference in turnout rates between the most- and least-educated population was only 4 percent (97 percent versus 93 percent). In the first election after 1970, the gap spread to 15 percent (87 percent versus 72 percent).[18] Small fines suffice to compel voting, a low-cost act, but intensive forms of participation may require harsher penalties. William Hinton recounts how, as Chinese peasants grew weary of revolutionary meetings, gun-carrying militiamen prodded them with kicks and blows.[19] In other settings where members have much at stake, intensive participation can be compelled without violence. Unions withhold strike benefits from members who shirk their turns on the picket line. Cooperative workplaces can cut the wage shares of members who avoid the effort of self-governance. Nevertheless, in the United States, attempts to compel participation are likely to arouse resistance and resentment.

Constraint

Requiring low-status members to act boosts equality by raising the bottom; conversely, restricting the freedom of high-status members also equalizes by leveling down. The revolutionary government in China initially denied political rights to ex-landlords.[20] During militant stages of their movements, some United States civil rights and women's groups barred whites and males, respectively. One motive was the desire to prevent them from dominating meetings and leadership roles. Actions short of exclusion can also inhibit normally advantaged groups. In Malaya, less-educated Chinese citizens vote at higher rates than those with more schooling. Alvin Rabushka believes this reversal of the usual pattern occurs because "increased levels of education in urban Malaya lead to an awareness that one's vote is meaningless. . . . Malayan Chinese have been systematically discriminated against, disfranchised or otherwise reduced to a low level of political efficacy" by the poorer but more numerous Malays.[21] Less extreme are policies restricting the full use of resources that would otherwise give power to the wealthy—for example, United States laws setting limits on individual political contributions.

Stratification and Quotas

Not so openly coercive as compulsion and constraint are policies that stratify a population into categories that guarantee more humble groups a chance to take part. One way to do this is by setting up separate organizations for the downtrodden. In addition to disenfranchising the wealthy, the Chinese Communists established poor peasants' leagues and women's associations through which those formerly voiceless groups could speak.[22] Similarly, antipoverty programs in some American cities, including Los Angeles and Philadelphia, set up neighborhood poverty councils and imposed an income ceiling on eligibility for membership.[23]

Stratification is also a good device for ensuring that governing or advisory assemblies include all levels of a polity. At my university, the Council consists of delegates chosen separately by students, administrators, senior faculty, junior faculty, and clerical and blue collar workers. Less explicit criteria also can improve representativeness. In cities in the United States, segregated as they are by race and income, geographic districts produce more representative municipal councils than do at-large elections.

Quotas are an alternative to formally stratified constituencies. In 1972 the Democratic party imposed de facto race, sex, and age quotas on state delegations to its national convention. The party later backed away from some of these controversial rules, partly because when the population is complex, singling out just a few categories can result in underrepresentation of members not benefiting from quotas. Hence the party was attacked for neglecting ethnic groups, union workers, and elected party leaders.[24] Quotas are more tenable when the major divisions in a system are stable and simple. Thus production workers are supposed to comprise at least three-quarters of the membership of management boards of Yugoslav enterprises.[25]

Some perfectionist critics of participation overlook the equalizing effect of stratification. Researchers have, for instance, pointed out that workers' councils fall short of proponents' egalitarian ideals, because higher-status workers are overrepresented and more active. But compared with a top-down system, any worker-based council is a step toward equality. The same can be said of neighborhood councils, poverty boards, and so forth. Although the upper elements in each stratum will normally come to the fore, they and the interests they advocate would probably have remained invisible in either a hierarchy or an unstratified system of participation.

Randomization

When public opinion pollsters want an accurate picture of citizens' attitudes, they choose a random sample of the population. People who answer questions have no official standing, but the views they express have a great influence on politicians. Systematic survey research is a modern development, but the device of selecting citizens by lot has a long history, both for sharing the burdens of citizenship fairly (as in the military draft) and for distributing more equally the powers of government. Ancient Athenians used allotment machines to choose their council (five hundred persons who met daily) as well as many other officials.[26] Today in the United States, juries are one of the few participatory institutions selected by lot, and their role has declined as plea bargaining replaces trial by jury in all but a small fraction of cases. However, an influential political theorist, Robert Dahl, urges that we revive participation by lot as a partial solution for the dilemmas of participation in large-scale democracies (or "polyarchies," as he calls them):

> I propose that we seriously consider restoring that ancient democratic device and use it for selecting advisory councils to every elected official of the giant polyarchy—mayors of large cities, state governors, members of the U.S. House and Senate, and even the president.[27]

Could such councils work? In one notable instance, a group selected by lot serves effectively not as a mere advisor, but as a watchdog over executives. At the Scott Bader Commonwealth, an employee-owned British chemical manufacturer, a twelve-member "jury" annually reviews the performance of the firm's board of directors (who are mostly nonelected managers). If the jury is not satisfied, a process is set in motion that can lead to dismissal of directors.[28]

As Dahl notes, the laws of probability tell us that there is a good chance that small randomly selected panels will be quite dissimilar from the general population. For this reason, among others, he counsels against giving decision-making powers to groups selected by lot. The authority given the Scott Bader "jury" is a tolerable exception because its powers are limited, and it is but one element in a comprehensive democracy that includes elected councils and direct assemblies. But in larger, more complex systems, small panels chosen by lot—even though only advisory in function—could distort policy if, as the workings of chance imply, their membership is often seriously unrepresentative.[29] For this reason, some advocates of citizen participation urge still more use of large-scale sample surveys, not just as an informal adjunct to political campaigning but as an integral part of governmental policymaking.

Organization and Ideology

All the equalizing devices looked at so far are most feasibly implemented as policies of the system—rules of the game within which all members must play. There is, however, one important leveling strategy that depends mainly on the effort and beliefs of people who belong to the polity.

In a series of major studies, Sidney Verba and his colleagues developed evidence that organization and ideology are "the weapon of the weak": "(L)ower-status groups . . . need a group-based process of political mobilization if they are to catch up to the upper-status groups in terms of political activity. They need a self-conscious ideology as motivation and need organization as a resource."[30] In other words, disadvantaged persons are more likely to participate if their consciousness has been "raised" so that they relate their problems to their membership in an oppressed group—peasants, workers, blacks, women, Quebecois, Untouchables, homosexuals, or whatever. Such an identity is especially likely to grow and lead to action if fostered by an organization that competes for power in the name of the downtrodden. Around the world, Socialist and Communist parties are the leading examples, but labor unions, civil rights organizations, and nationalist movements play similar roles.

Organization and ideology are by no means inevitable mobilizing forces. Often they remain only a potential way to improve the welfare of suffering people. Schlozman and Verba found that jobless Americans in the 1970s did indeed participate politically at higher rates if they belonged to organizations; but only about a quarter of their sample of the unemployed were members of *any* group, much less one primarily devoted to helping people who lack work. As the authors dryly observe, "the present effects of this potential resource are quite limited."[31]

Their findings are consistent with the well-known "exceptionalism" of the United States: Class consciousness and class conflict are weaker here than in most other nations. This has been true in part because racial conflict intermittently takes center stage as the main cleavage in United States politics. Thus, it is not surprising to learn that the Verba thesis does hold true for

United States blacks. In the 1960s, blacks who were high in group consciousness far exceeded the activity rates of whites with comparable socioeconomic status.[32] Subsequently, as black versus white mayoralty contests increased in the United States, registration and turnout rates leaped among blacks generally.

THE DILEMMA PERSISTS

All these strategies for reconciling participation and equality entail some sacrifice of other values. Coercion and constraint restrict personal liberty. Stratification subtly reduces freedom by narrowing the range of settings within which individuals may act. Quotas clash with both merit and majority rule principles, as does participation by lot. Group-based organization and ideology ignite social conflict and spurn the universalism so dear to many believers in democracy.

Moreover, these devices offer only limited help in resolving the dilemma implied by our three rules. Most of them can succeed in equalizing member involvement only for less difficult acts of participation—of which voting is prototypical and most important. Thus, in their seven-nation study, Verba, Nie, and Kim show that, except in the United States, belonging to an organization counteracts the effect of social class in getting people to vote; but only in the Netherlands does it reduce the effects of class for more difficult political acts.[33] Similarly, in large democracies, it is hard to imagine coercing universal participation for anything other than simple acts such as voting. Such polities do sometimes constrain upper-status members by inhibiting costly types of involvement, but this strategy reduces the opportunity to participate intensively. Only stratification and random selection offer much hope of equalizing intensive participation (especially if the lucky winners are compelled to serve, compensated for their effort, or both—as with jurors). Although these two devices can produce an egalitarian result, like all systems of representation, they assume universal participation is impossible; indeed, they curtail the ability of most citizens to directly influence decisions entrusted to the small number of representatives.

In short, our equalizing strategies, singly or in combination, can lessen the conflict between participation and equality, and they may eliminate it altogether for easy acts; but they do not entirely solve the participatory democrat's dilemma. We must therefore take a fresh look at fundamental values.

Abandon Equality?

Some democrats who cherish participation as an end in itself are tempted to back away from their commitment to equality once they recognize the tradeoff between the two goals. Rousseau himself, as Dahl observes, seemed "surprisingly unconcerned" that the direct democracies he so admired in ancient Athens, the Roman republic, and his native Geneva were really open only to a privileged minority, who were freed for intense politicking by the labor of slaves, women, or other noncitizens.³⁴ Benjamin Barber, a modern disciple of Rousseau, condemns liberal instrumentalist democracy because it insists "on equality of participation without regard to quality of participation." He even expresses mixed feelings about the 1971 enfranchisement of women in Switzerland:

> Half of Switzerland's population is finally recognized as having rudimentary human rights, but as a result the expanded electorate participates far less. Village halls become too confined, village assemblies grow unwieldy, and twice as many voters are given the privilege of turning over to elected representatives what half as many once did for themselves. . . . And so, equality and justice seem to come only at the price of participation and community.³⁵

Most explicit of all is J. R. Lucas, who writes:

> Any system that calls for more than minimal participation will favor the active over the apathetic and the rich over the poor. . . . Participation is inegalitarian. It both requires and creates a certain degree of inequality. . . . Better that some should be able to participate than that none should.³⁶

Equality as a Conditional Value

Few values should always have absolute priority, without any regard for circumstances and competing considerations. Democratic theorists suggest that the value we place on equality should be made conditional on two important qualifications: strength of emotional concern and degree of conflict.

Even if we believe all members count equally, should we not give heavier weight in any particular decision to those who care more about what happens? Known as *the intensity problem*, this issue has long been a key argument against pure majority rule.³⁷ It has also served to rationalize observed inequalities of United States politics. Why shouldn't minorities rule if their greater activity shows they feel more strongly about outcomes than the passive majority?

As a defense of conventional interest-group politics, the intensity argument is decisively undermined by Olson's logic of collective action. Although there is no doubt some correspondence between political activity and strength of feeling (if only because our emotional attention tends not to stray too far from possible outlets for practical action), the participatory advantages of special interests, small groups, and higher-status persons give them political weight out of proportion to any plausible difference between the strength of their feelings and that of their less active fellow citizens. For example, who could contend that the unemployed have no stake in government economic policies? Yet, in the 1970s, among the 173 witnesses who testified to Congress about the Full Employment and Balanced Growth Act (Humphrey-Hawkins bill), only one was unemployed.³⁸ In small polities, there may be some justification for the advantage intensive participatory methods give to intense interests, but in large systems, the cards are already stacked against large latent groups.[39]

A second way to restrict the priority of equality is to make it important only when interests conflict substantially. Even in small groups, most people are quite willing to forgo participatory opportunities if they will not lose out by doing so. They are glad to "let George do it" if George can be counted on to do the same thing they would have done. This happy congruence is most likely if everyone shares pretty much the same interests, values, and preferences. Working from observations of this sort, Jane Mansbridge concludes that "equal power is unnecessary" if people have common interests and if other goals of power-sharing—equal respect and opportunities to exercise responsibility—are met by other means:

> [E]galitarians should order situations along a spectrum ranging from complete identity of interest to complete conflict and should be willing to pay more to get equal power as interests diverge. . . . In moments of conflict, when the goal is equal protection of interests, equalizing power will usually remain the ideal toward which a democratic polity must struggle.[40]

The Superior Legitimacy of Extensive Participation

Mansbridge's principle, combined with the argument of this chapter, suggests that when serious conflict is apparent or suspected, one price egalitarians should pay for equal power is to sacrifice their fondness for methods of intensive participation. These practices—including face-to-face meetings, lengthy discussion, and consensus decision making—may help produce better policies when conflict is low. They can also serve as exploratory or advisory aids to less intensive methods when conflict exists. But egalitarian democrats must assign ultimate legitimacy to those methods that encourage the most extensive participation. That means, to take just a few examples, that when intractable differences occur organizations should heed plenary assemblies rather than committees, ballots rather than long meetings, and elected representatives rather than self-selected activists.

Except for such examples and frequent abstract references to more and less intensive methods of participation, the channels through which ordinary members influence their polities have not been examined. Let us turn to that task now, beginning with the decision-making ideal that demands the most of members—direct democracy.

NOTES

1. For examples, see sources cited by Jane J. Mansbridge, *Beyond Adversary Democracy* (New York: Basic Books, 1980), p. 334.

2. Nelson W. Polsby and Aaron Wildavsky, *Presidential Elections*, 6th ed. (New York: Charles Scribner's Sons, 1984), p. 105 (citing studies by Austin Ranney).

3. Judging from 1976 Democratic data reported in Austin Ranney, "Participation in Precinct Caucuses," in *Presidential Politics: Readings on Nominations and Elections*, 2nd ed., ed. James I. Lengle and Byron E. Shafer (New York: St. Martin's Press, 1983), pp. 173–75.

4. The line between "small" and "large" here depends on how much variety exists among members and on how strict a standard one sets for "representativeness." Readers familiar with statistics will recognize that when participants are a random sample, turnout is equivalent to the sampling fraction, which has little effect on the standard error once the sample exceeds a few thousand. For more about this, see note 29 below.

5. Mansbridge, *Beyond Adversary Democracy*, chap. 9.

6. Milton L. Rakove, *Don't Make No Waves, Don't Back No Losers: An Insider's Analysis of the Daley Machine* (Bloomington: Indiana University Press, 1975), pp. 101–5.

7. Students could change their registrations, but then they would be exposed to the exorbitant rates insurance companies inflict on city-dwellers.

8. Herbert McClosky, Paul J. Hoffman, and Rosemary O'Hara, "Issue Conflict and Consensus Among Party Leaders and Followers," *American Political Science Review*, 54 (1960), 406–27; quoted passage from p. 421.

9. Norman H. Nie, Sidney Verba, and John R. Petrocik, *The Changing American Voter* (Cambridge: Harvard University Press, 1976), pp. 200–205; Barbara G. Farah, M. Kent Jennings, and Warren E. Miller, "Convention Delegates in the Post-Reform Era," in *Presidential Politics*, ed. Lengle and Shafer, pp. 264–74.

10. Lester W. Milbrath and M. L. Goel, *Political Participation: How and Why Do People Get Involved in Politics?* 2nd ed. (Chicago: Rand McNally College Publishing Co., 1977), p. 92. Their Chapter 4 provides an inventory of research supporting this statement, with many citations.

11. Sidney Verba, Norman H. Nie, and Jae-on Kim, *Participation and Political Equality: A Seven-Nation Comparison* (New York: Cambridge University Press, 1978), pp. 120, 75.

12. "Power Equalization Through Participation?" *Administrative Science Quarterly*, 16 (1971), 31–38.

13. *Neighborhood Democracy: The Politics and Impacts of Decentralization* (Lexington, Mass.: Lexington Books, D. C. Heath and Co., 1973), p. 70.

14. Gerry Hunnius, "Workers' Self-Management in Yugoslavia," in *Workers' Control: A Reader on Labor and Social Change*, ed. Gerry Hunnius, G. David Garson, and John Case (New York: Vintage Books, 1973), p. 299.

15. Grant McConnell, *Private Power and American Democracy* (New York: Alfred A. Knopf, 1967), pp. 209, 234.

16. Mansbridge, *Beyond Adversary Democracy*, p. 23.

17. See Sidney Verba and Norman Nie, *Participation in America: Political Democracy and Social Equality* (New York: Harper & Row, 1972), p. 337. Verba and Nie argue that the American political system rewards activity, not SES per se, but their interpretation conflicts with the data in their own Figure 20–1, which show an interaction effect: High SES and high activity in combination increase "concurrence" (agreement on priorities between participants and officials), but *low* SES and high activity combine to *depress* concurrence.

18. Data of Galen Irwin reproduced in Verba, Nie, and Kim, *Participation and Political Equality*, p. 7.

19. *Fanshen: A Documentary of Revolution in a Chinese Village* (New York: Monthly Review Press, 1966), chap. 23. The Communist party opposed such acts of "commandism."

20. James R. Townsend, *Political Participation in Communist China* (Berkeley: University of California Press, 1969), pp. 67, 118.

21. "A Note on Overseas Chinese Political Participation in Urban Malaya," *American Political Science Review*, 64 (1970), 177–78.

22. Hinton, *Fanshen*, passim.

23. J. David Greenstone and Paul E. Peterson, *Race and Authority in Urban Politics: Community Participation and the War on Poverty* (Chicago: University of Chicago Press, 1973), p. 174.

24. William Crotty, *Party Reform* (New York: Longman, 1983), chap. 12.

25. Hunnius, "Workers' Self-Management in Yugoslavia," p. 278.

26. Aristotle, *The Constitution of Athens and Related Texts*, trans. Kurt von Fritz and Ernst Kapp (New York: Hafner Press, 1974), pp. 116–47.

27. *After the Revolution? Authority in a Good Society* (New Haven: Yale University Press, 1970), p. 149. Benjamin Barber makes a similar proposal in *Strong Democracy: Participatory Politics for a New Age* (Berkeley: University of California Press, 1984), pp. 290–93.

28. Daniel Zwerdling, *Democracy at Work: A Guide to Workplace Ownership, Participation and Self-Management Experiments in the United States and Europe* (Washington, D.C.: Association for Self-Management, 1978), pp. 147–49.

29. If you are willing to work through a few statistical concepts and symbols, it is easy to show why committee-size random panels are often unrepresentative even when drawn from a small population. The risk that a random sample will differ from the population is measured by the sampling error, $\sigma_{\bar{x}}$. A formula for this measure is

$$\sigma_{\bar{x}} = \sigma \sqrt{\frac{1-f}{N}}$$

where σ is the standard deviation of the full population (a measure of how much its members differ from one another); and f is the sampling fraction, or number of people in the sample (N) divided by the number in the population. If you plug in a range of values for N and f, you will discover that a manageable panel of, say, ten members produces a large sampling error for almost any size population, whether one hundred or one million. On the other hand, a sample the size of a typical public opinion poll (an N of about 1,500) yields a low sampling error no matter how large the population. Note also that, for a given size panel and population, the sampling error will be less if members of the population are similar to each other (σ is low). Hence a relatively homogeneous polity (the Scott Bader Commonwealth, perhaps, or many American suburbs) can use small random panels with less risk of getting a distorted view of member preferences. For more about $\sigma_{\bar{x}}$, see Hubert M. Blalock, *Social Statistics* (New York: McGraw-Hill, 1960), or in any other good text.

30. Verba, Nie, and Kim, *Participation and Political Equality*, pp. 14–15.

31. Kay Lehman Schlozman and Sidney Verba, *Injury to Insult: Unemployment, Class, and Political Responses* (Cambridge: Harvard University Press, 1979), p. 263.

32. Verba and Nie, *Participation in America*, chap. 10.

33. *Participation and Political Equality*, chap. 7.

34. *After the Revolution?* p. 84.

35. *The Death of Communal Liberty: A History of Freedom in a Swiss Mountain Canton* (Princeton: Princeton University Press, 1974), pp. 5, 273. Barber's lament points to the fact that the reverse of Rule 1 also holds: A more extensive population of eligible participants *requires* less intensive participation (or a lower turnout rate). In Chapter 7, we take a closer look at problems that size creates for participatory democracy.

36. *Democracy and Participation* (Baltimore: Penguin, 1976), p. 230.

37. The classic analysis is by Robert A. Dahl, *A Preface to Democratic Theory* (Chicago: University of Chicago Press, 1956), chaps. 4 and 5.

38. Schlozman and Verba, *Injury to Insult*, p. 339.

39. Mancur Olson presents perhaps the most damning indictment yet of special-interest influence in his sequel to *The Logic of Collective Action*. He blames them for the misfortunes listed in his title, *The Rise and Decline of Nations: Economic Growth, Stagflation, and Social Rigidities* (New Haven: Yale University Press, 1982). Olson specifically rebuts the pluralist thesis (or hope) that bargaining among groups produces something like a social optimum. See his pages 36–37, and compare with Charles E. Lindblom, *The Intelligence of Democracy: Decision Making Through Mutual Adjustment* (New York: Free Press, 1965), especially chap. 18.

40. *Beyond Adversary Democracy*, pp. 240, 248.

CHAPTER 6

DEMOCRACY

Until about two centuries ago, the meaning of *democracy* remained, as in its Greek roots, "rule by the people"—a system where authority over any public decision rests directly with the collectivity of members. Self-government of this sort was usually thought possible only in small polities. The word acquired a new and less restricted meaning largely because of the success of the United States Constitution, which reconciled the democratic value of popular sovereignty with the capacity to govern a large territory. Although the Founding Fathers had preferred to call the system they devised a "republic," by the middle of the nineteenth century, democracy was thoroughly identified with representative government, in which citizens participate authoritatively only by electing leaders, who then have the power to make laws and other binding policies.[1]

Consequently, today we use one word—democracy—for two related but distinct systems of participation. It is as if we had only "precipitation" to refer to both rain and snow. Just as we might then talk about "liquid precipitation" and "frozen precipitation," so also we refer to "direct democracy" and "representative" (or "indirect") democracy when we want to distinguish between the ancient and modern forms. This clumsiness in our language is confusing, because only a partial overlap exists between the values, processes, and problems of direct and representative democracy.

The obscuring of the old meaning would not matter so much if direct democracy were only ancient history, but it remains very much alive today, both in practice and as an ideal. As flourishing political practice, direct democracy remains the principal means of local self-government for millions of people around the world, in places as diverse as Chinese villages, Swiss *Landsgemeinden*, Israeli kibbutzim, and New England towns. Moreover, within representative democracies, leaders gather to decide issues in committees and assemblies that pose for them the same possibilities and problems that direct democracy offers ordinary citizens in local government. And in countless nongovernmental settings—unions, workplaces, clubs, faculty meetings—people make decisions directly and democratically.

As a challenging political ideal, direct democracy possesses a persistent appeal that is evident in the nostalgia felt for the town meeting, in the fascination of scholars with Athens' Golden Age, and in the recurrent attraction of youth to utopian communities. To some theorists, this allure is a dangerous delusion that arouses "impossible demands for a democracy which is too pure and too perfect to exist,"[2] but it inspires others to propose imaginative reforms that they hope will intensify participation in modern societies.

In this chapter, we take a quite practical look at issues most of us face when we participate in groups that try to make decisions directly and democratically while embedded in larger systems that necessarily must be governed in other ways. Our first order of business will be to explore the distinctive ideals that justify vesting decision-making power directly in a group's membership, because the practice of direct democracy cannot be understood unless one appreciates the values that inspire it.

IDEALS OF DIRECT DEMOCRACY

Of the three general benefits of participation that we considered in Chapter 2, believers in direct democracy give relatively short shrift to instrumental utility. Instead, they stress its developmental and intrinsic virtues. Closely related to these two values are four distinctive ideals that advocates of direct democracy believe it can and should achieve: action, discussion, consensus, and community.

Action

In the calculus of participation that provides a framework for much of our analysis (see Chapter 3), a cost is attached to the effort of participating, as if the costless or preferred state is to be politically passive. Proponents of direct democracy abhor this idea, for they share the Greek ideal of the active life, not so much because they think action pleasurable (though it may be that), but rather because only through action can individuals achieve what they hold to be the true goal of life: attainment of excellence. Instrumental success or failure matters less than daring to express your own personhood by attempting to work your will on the society in which you live. As the philosopher Hannah Arendt put it, "Courage, which we now feel to be an indispensable quality of the hero, is in fact already present in a willingness to act and speak at all, to insert one's self into the world and begin a story of one's own."[3] Like the Athenian leader Pericles, people who share this approach to life hold in contempt those who shrink from political effort: "We do not say that a man who takes no interest in politics is a man who minds his own business; we say that he has no business here at all."[4]

Discussion

According to theorists of direct democracy, political action should take the form of talk—not the bombast of self-serving rhetoric but something more like true conversation, in which all participants both speak and listen to one another. Through discussion, each person can come to understand how other members see, think, and feel. Ideally, according to Benjamin Barber, "Talk engenders empathy, nourishes affection, and engages imagination"; listening to a fellow citizen should involve the frame of mind: "I will put myself in his place, I will try to understand, I will strain to hear what makes us alike."[5]

Consensus

Whenever underlying interests are not fundamentally irreconcilable, the outcome of discussion should be a public decision acceptable to all. Consensus can result from two effects of talk: one intellectual, the other emotional. Through imaginative brainstorming, participants may invent new options that integrate the interests of all, even though their separate interests remain distinct. Through empathetic understanding, participants may arrive at altruistic identification of their own highest good with the well-being of other members or of the group as a whole. They learn to "will the general will."

Nearly everyone prefers a unified group, but advocates of direct democracy are more likely than others to strive for, or even insist on, consensus rather than resort to the quick expedient of majority rule. Barber expresses this attitude forcefully:

> Majoritarianism is a tribute to the failure of democracy: to our inability to create a politics of mutualism that can overcome private interests. It is thus finally the democracy of desperation, an attempt to salvage decision-making from the anarchy of adversary politics. . . . Wherever possible, the strong democrat will try to defer decisions on which there is not yet agreement rather than to win a majority victory that leaves behind a legacy of dissatisfaction.[6]

Community

Public action, mutual discussion, and consensual decisions are intensely social pursuits. Hence, direct democracy has always been closely associated with community—a setting where people know each other as individuals, treat one another as friends, and share norms that give meaning to their lives. It may seem that such a community must exist before its members can govern themselves directly, but advocates of direct democracy believe causality runs strongly the other way. Again, Barber is the best spokesperson for this school of thought: "Far from positing community a priori, strong democratic theory understands the creation of community as one of the chief tasks of political activity in the participatory mode."[7] To people who share his belief, the appeal of direct democracy lies not only in its empowerment of ordinary members but also in its creation among them of bonds of unity and friendship, the hope it offers of overcoming loneliness and alienation.

ISSUES IN THE PRACTICE OF DIRECT DEMOCRACY

The values of action, discussion, consensus, and community appeal to nearly everyone. In practice, however, direct democracy almost always involves certain basic problems. Idealists who fail to anticipate, recognize, and deal with these issues risk having their hopes dashed, for any one of them can render a polity ineffective. At the extreme, these dangers can turn democratic dreams into nightmares.

Of all the barriers to direct democracy, size is most fundamental. Chapter 7 explains why large size and direct democracy seem incompatible and explores how they might be reconciled. In the meantime, let us focus on three other crucial issues: conflict, leadership, and interdependence.

Conflict

Discussion, consensus, and community are characteristics of what Jane Mansbridge calls *unitary democracy*. These practices reflect the assumption that all members have fundamentally compatible interests. People who hold this belief view the making of group decisions as a cooperative effort to solve common problems. Through discussion, a solution should emerge; when it does, no vote is needed, because everyone should recognize and accept its correctness. Indeed, a formal vote "signals . . . the passing of a belief that decisions have a correct solution" and therefore "is the crucial mark of the legitimacy of conflict."[8] To admit that divisions exist among members might undermine solidarity, whereas the bonds of community are strengthened every time a group achieves consensus.

Contrasting with unitary democracy is the model Mansbridge labels *adversary democracy*. This approach to government assumes that unresolvable conflicts are inevitable—usually because members' interests or tastes fundamentally differ on at least some issues but also because even people who agree on goals often disagree about how to achieve them. Adversary democracies make decisions by voting, a process that enables the group to act and recognizes that legitimate differences exist within it. To give everyone a fair chance to prevail and to protect those who do not, adversary democracies rely on such formal devices as civil liberties, rules of procedure, and secret ballots.

The emotional solidarity and common purpose of unitary democracy are often attractive, perhaps especially to people whose everyday lives are dominated by the impersonal competitiveness of a market economy. Although Mansbridge may be right in believing that "we in America are starved for unitary democracy,"[9] in the United States we encounter unitary ideals and practices wherever face-to-face democratic decision making is feasible—in local governments, labor unions, social organizations, committees, and work groups. Because unitary democracy is both enticing and common, we must understand the dangers that arise from rigid insistence on its assumptions and procedures.

First, excessive emphasis on unity can lead to denying or suppressing differences. When internal conflicts are ignored or defined away, possibilities for structuring participation in a more egalitarian way will be neglected, and members with natural advantages will unduly dominate collective decisions.[10] In extreme cases, the mere expression of disagreement becomes traitorous.[11] Advocates of direct democracy do not envision this sort of a priori, eternal unanimity when they stress the values of consensus and community. Instead, they believe consensus will emerge after initial differences are fully and frankly expressed. Nevertheless, pressure to achieve agreement sometimes produces false consensus, beneath which members censor their secret doubts.

When members are willing to clash, consensual decision processes often break down. Protracted discussion may drive away the exhausted majority of members, leaving an unrepresentative rump minority to rule. If two factions have equal staying power, the group may be unable to act at all, which can be disastrous for everyone. Or, if the smaller faction prefers the status quo, failure to act is tantamount to minority rule. Especially when religious or ideological doctrine is at stake, the unitary tendency to see opponents as evil or wrong leads to expulsion or exit of dissidents. When extremely frustrated, people who do not believe in counting heads sometimes resort to breaking them. Thus, during the Chinese Cultural Revolution, student factions unable to resolve differences by endless discussion turned to kidnapping, torture, and pitched battles.[12]

As the occurrence of schisms suggests, unitary democracies can avoid internal conflict at the cost of exacerbating conflict at their boundaries. Most proponents of direct democracy celebrate diversity and believe participation enables people to overcome differences of race, class, religion, or sex. For example, Mary Parker Follett, a pioneer theorist of participatory democracy, urged that neighborhoods be the basic unit of government primarily because she thought them more diverse than other possible constituencies. "In a neighborhood group you have the stimulus and the bracing effect of many different experiences and ideals. And in this infinite variety which touches you on every side, you have a life which enriches and enlarges and fecundates; this is the true soil of human development. . . ."[13] But dissimilar people unquestionably have more trouble reaching consensus, so the more heterogeneous the group, the more it needs to resort to adversary procedures. Therefore, direct democrats who especially cherish consensus and community are tempted to encourage a politics of insular, homogeneous groups that are all too ready for fanatical struggle with outsiders. In the United States, this issue has arisen in controversies over community control and neighborhood self-government.[14]

How can we avoid the pitfalls of unitary democracy while honoring as much as possible the attractive unitary ideals? Mansbridge believes that if we learn to distinguish between adversary and unitary situations, we can switch back and forth between decision-making methods tailored to fit the perceived conflict or compatibility among underlying interests. My observation and experience suggest that many groups would have difficulty adjusting procedures in the way she advises. I recommend instead a single set of premises and practices that integrates elements of both unitary and adversary democracy.

First, *always expect and accept conflict among members.* Disagreement must always be legitimate, whether it takes the form of bringing to the agenda an uncomfortable issue or standing as a minority of one against an otherwise unanimous conclusion. Unity should be founded on explicit recognition of diversity, on agreement to disagree. Too strong a unitary ideal aggravates whatever conflict occurs by raising the stakes from the immediate issue to the very coherence of the community. One of the worst effects of the rule of consensus is the pressure it puts on individuals to suppress their true feelings. Democrats should adhere to the tradition of Tocqueville and J. S. Mill, as described by Jack Lively: "Far from welcoming democracy as a means of inaugurating an age of perfect concord, they saw it primarily as a possible context in which men could retain their self-identity and individuality, their self-respect and self-assertiveness. . . ."[15]

Second, *always strive for consensus, but avoid insisting on it.* Unity should be an aspiration, not a requirement. Discuss an issue until the last possible moment as you strain for a synthesis founded on empathy and insight. When that search appears to have succeeded, it is still usually worthwhile to ask for a formal vote, both to ensure that no silent objectors have been neglected and to acknowledge that dissent would be entirely legitimate. All too often, the "sense of the meeting" untested by a vote really reflects only the wishes of a domineering chair or the reticence of doubters.

Third, *not every issue requires equal persistence in trying to achieve consensus.* In deciding whether to continue discussion or to resort to a vote, you need to make a series of judgments: Are existing disagreements due to fundamentally conflicting interests, or do they stem from disputes over factual matters that might be resolved by investigation and reasoning? Is the issue important enough to justify investing additional decision-making time? How numerous are the dissidents, and how strongly do they feel about their position? Has every viewpoint had a fair chance to be heard? Would a prolonged meeting cause departures that would reduce the representativeness of those who finally decide?

Fourth, *when conflicts persist, consider the use of other adversary decision procedures besides majority rule.* There are middle ways between the paralysis of unanimity and the divisiveness of majority dictatorship. Sometimes it is possible to remove inflammatory issues from the collective agenda, leaving them instead to individual or subgroup discretion, just as modern nations refrain from legislating religious belief and sexual morality. When this is not possible, try replacing majority rule with the rule of proportional outcomes—"distributing goods on the basis of the numerical strength of the competing factions."[16] Examples include taking turns, deciding by lotteries, sharing valued offices, and dividing up appropriations according to a formula. Such devices are especially desirable when majority rule might produce a permanent minority, one that, having little hope ever to win, will be tempted to disrupt or desert the group.

Leadership

The crucial role of leadership is usually so obvious that observers traditionally define political systems by the number, powers, and origins of their rulers: monarchy, aristocracy, oligarchy, party dictatorship. The special role of an elite is also recognized in representative democracy, which social scientists define as an arrangement in which leaders acquire power by competing for citizens' votes.[17]

Alone among political orders, direct democracy—rule by the people—appears to proclaim the possibility of governance without leaders.[18] Unfortunately, members of direct democracies neglect the need for leadership at their own peril. Just as repressed emotional needs produce neuroses, so also denial of political necessities manifests itself in governmental disorders. Democrats who lack conscious understanding of the proper role of leadership often display unstable, harmful attitudes toward leaders. Three patterns seem especially common: rejection, exploitation, and adulation.

Rejection: Some adherents of direct democracy are so strongly egalitarian that they reject any differences in power or status. An extreme version of this attitude produces what Jo Freeman calls the norm of "structurelessness." She describes how it affected feminist groups during the early years of the women's movement:

> The idea that there was some relationship between authority and responsibility, between organization and equal participation, and between leadership and self-government was not within their realm of experience. . . .

Some radical feminists became so hostile toward any woman who gained wider fame that they drove certain leaders out of the movement.[19]

More often, leaders stay with the group but change their behavior to make their influence less obvious. Among some groups, individuals capable of eloquent oratory make a habit of hesitant, inarticulate speech. In many democracies, any desire or willingness to lead must be hidden lest one be thought "power-hungry." Melford Spiro's account of the kibbutz applies equally to university faculties:

> It seems apparent that part of the refusal to accept an official position has become a pose. . . . The kibbutz would be suspicious of a chaver [member] who agreed to run for office as soon as he was approached by the nominating committee. The first answer is always, "I don't want it"; this is the answer one is expected to give.[20]

Skepticism toward people in authority is generally a healthy protection against abuse of power. The danger for direct democracies is not so much their suspicion of leaders as the temptation to deny that leaders exist or are needed. When leaders are rejected, they must hide; when they cannot operate openly, they must manipulate; when they are not formally chosen, they cannot be formally deposed. Freeman develops these themes in an essay that offers valuable lessons for many organizations besides the women's groups for whom she originally wrote:

> Structurelessness becomes a way of masking power, and within the women's movement it is usually most strongly advocated by those who are the most powerful (whether they are conscious of their power or not). . . . When informal elites are combined with a myth of structurelessness, there can be no attempt to put limits on the use of power. . . . If the movement continues to deliberately not select who shall exercise power, it does not thereby abolish power. All it does is abdicate the right to demand that those who do exercise power and influence be responsible for it.[21]

Exploitation: The second democratic pitfall derives not from egalitarianism but from the voluntarist ethic that underlies the procedural norms of discussion and consensus. In many democratic groups, the logic of collective action produces a phenomenon that Mancur Olson calls "the exploitation of the great by the small."[22] Leaders (whether formal or informal) normally feel a greater commitment to group goals. That is often why they become leaders in the first place; in any case, they soon come to feel personally responsible for purposes they have done more than others to shape. The combination of greater concern and greater influence induces leaders to make unusually great efforts toward collective purposes. Conversely, the rank and file are all too often tempted to play free rider.

Obviously, such irresponsibility weakens the overall effectiveness of the group, but more insidious, members' exploitation of leaders undermines the quality of leaders and their commitment to democratic values. Feigned unwillingness to serve becomes real, as potential leaders contemplate disproportionate burdens rewarded only by egalitarian jealousy. Those who do serve become contemptuous of the membership, who appear lazy and unworthy of their ultimate decision-making power. In a familiar process, corruption begins with leaders' desire to compensate themselves for extraordinary sacrifices that would otherwise go unrewarded. William Hinton describes how this process unfolded in a Chinese village among peasants who had led the revolutionary land reform:

> Since they spearheaded every drive, led in beating the "struggle objects" [former landlords], poured out their sweat . . . and above all, risked their lives through the long cold nights as they stood guard against counter-attack, they felt entitled to special privileges. Many of them thought it unfair to receive no return for service to the people beyond the *fanshen* [land distribution] in which all shared. . . . As heroes of the hour, these began in small ways to help themselves. When some article among the hundreds confiscated from the gentry caught their fancy, they took it when nobody was looking. If some comely woman aroused their passion, they seduced her if she was willing. If she were a "struggle object," they took her whether she was willing or not.[23]

Adulation: After hearing that direct democracies reject and exploit leaders, you may think it strange that they are also inclined to excessively venerate and defer to them. But swings from one extreme to another are common in the lives of individuals and groups. Sometimes, there is a direct historical sequence, as when a polity that has floundered through the hazards of anarchy turns in desperation to strong central authority. Cults of personality in direct democracies also have deeper origins in their distinctive values of consensus and community.

The unitary assumption can justify extremely unequal divisions of authority. Vesting great power in a leader cannot hurt members if they all want the same goals, because then members themselves would make the same decisions if they were in the leader's place.[24] In large polities, this argument based on unity has a long, infamous history as a rationalization for various forms of absolute rule. But even in small polities, where the assumption of a common interest is more often valid,[25] the dominance of an exalted leader is sometimes the very basis of group unity. In her study of nineteenth-century American utopian communities, Rosabeth Moss Kanter found that they often "combined participatory democracy with centralized control." They decided routine matters in participatory fashion, but issues affecting the definition, structure, or character of the community were the special prerogative of a charismatic leader whom the others regarded with awe. By enshrining the leader's will above their own, members avoid conflicts over crucial issues that might otherwise threaten their sense of community. Moreover, in a peculiar way, deference reinforces egalitarianism. In Kanter's words, "members of a group gain equality through their relation to the leader"; they attain brotherhood and sisterhood by common subordination to a single parental figure.[26] In recent times, the hazards of excessive desire for community and commitment have been revealed in the bizarre behavior of some religious and political cults.

Democratic Leadership: In posting warning flags by pitfalls along the democratic path, I do not mean to suggest that there exists any basic incompatibility between direct democracy and effective leadership. Purely negative lessons risk leaving you like the staff of Helpline, a crisis-intervention center that Mansbridge studied: "Everyone in this participatory democracy had trouble imagining what truly democratic leadership would look like."²⁷ The brief sketch that follows may give you some idea of what to look for and of what you can do to help your own democratic groups succeed.

In a democracy leadership cannot depend upon a single individual. In part, this is because leadership is inherently relational. The dangers of rejection, exploitation, and adulation all stem as much from expectations and behavior of followers as from the practices of leaders. Effective democracies also rely on more than just one leader. By distributing or rotating responsibilities, democracies develop resilience, lighten leaders' burdens, and approach equality. In sharing authority, however, democracies must avoid utopian denial of the division of labor. Dogmatic insistence on equality above all other values destroys not only efficiency but also the personal satisfaction that results when tastes and talents are matched with tasks.

Democracy requires the balanced judgment of common sense in other ways as well. Excessive enthusiasm for any one component of the democratic value system—community or voluntarism or equality—starts a group sliding into the traps of adoring, exploiting, or rejecting leaders. Similarly, leaders themselves must avoid the temptation to adopt various simplistic, extreme patterns of behavior. Of these, the most common results from the fallacy that, because democrats oppose dictatorial authority, democratic leaders should be passive and nondirective. A better guide to practice comes from Lewin, Lippitt, and White, whose classic experiments distinguished democratic leadership not only from the authoritarian style but also from the ineffectual pattern they called "laissez-faire," in which the leader participates minimally, with "no attempt to appraise or regulate the course of events."²⁸

If democratic leaders are neither dictatorial nor passive, what form does their activity take? With respect to decision making, democratic leaders are not merely active but interactive. Through close ties and frequent consultation with members, they should be able to propose actions that are closely attuned to members' aspirations. But the test of a leader's success rests in the members' judgment. If a leader cannot persuade members to approve his initiatives, he must be willing to rise above prideful stubbornness by seeking new proposals that correspond better to members' desires.

The search for solutions that synthesize the wishes of all, or almost all, members requires that the leader be constantly inventive, though new ideas can be found not only in solitary reflection but also by enlisting other members in brainstorming. However, purely intellectual solutions seldom suffice to bridge differences or inspire collective effort, so the effective leader must be value oriented, fostering and invoking the extrarational commitments that unify members through a shared sense of distinctive identity and purpose.²⁹

For democratic communities, the most fundamental value is the sanctity of democracy itself, so the leader must be constantly protective of the process. She must know that the right to speak belongs to the timid as well as the clamorous. She must recognize that the majority within an assembly often differs from the majority of the entire community, and somehow find ways to make the two compatible. She must act as the responsible agent of legitimate decisions, while always shielding dissenters who might someday persuade the group to adopt quite different policies.

While respecting members' political rights, the democratic leader must be demanding in reminding people of their collective responsibilities. These include both the obligation to participate in governance and the need to honor policies upon which the community has previously agreed. Leaders who allow free riders to exploit fellow citizens do not serve their communities well. A fair sharing of burdens is the best guarantee that all will be willing to shoulder them.

In all of the qualities described so far, democratic leaders are oriented inward, focusing on the values, wishes, and actions of their own policies. But in perhaps the most difficult task of all, the leader links the group to its environment, interpreting for members the requirements of the world outside. Because external demands often respond so little to the internal popular will, interdependence is a third major difficulty in the practice of direct democracy.

Interdependence

In this age of mechanized transportation and electronic communication, it is no secret that interdependence makes old boundaries obsolete. Superhighways and commuter rail lines force cities and suburbs to join in regional transit authorities. The drift and flow of pollution require states to yield powers to federal agencies. Ballistic missiles and instantaneous capital transfers make nations themselves inadequate protectors of their citizens' safety and prosperity.

Obviously, interdependence poses problems for any political system, but it threatens the essential character of direct democracies. It is no accident that the direct-democratic tradition draws its inspiration from Greece, Switzerland, and New England—all areas where rugged mountains once divided the population into small, isolated, nearly self-sufficient communities.[30]

Why do direct democracies flourish best in the rocky soil of self-sufficiency? Two explanations seem especially compelling. First, if a community is self-sufficient, then by definition it meets within itself all the needs of its citizens. This means that their collective decisions can potentially determine everything that matters to each member. Consequently, the incentive to participate is great enough to meet even the requirements of direct democracy, which of all forms of government demands the most from citizens. Conversely, as the life of a community becomes increasingly shaped by external forces, its internal decisions seem less and less consequential, so citizens no longer consider intense participation worth their while.[31]

Second, because direct democracies demand so much, they benefit if their citizens believe in the superior legitimacy of their own decision-making methods. When the democratic community becomes interdependent with other polities, it may play an active role in shaping the decisions of the larger system of which it is now a part, but it must do so through processes that are hard to reconcile with its customary internal practices. Members will have trouble adjusting to the new order, and for some the price of acceptance may be increasing cynicism about the old norms of equality, discussion, consensus, and community. How this happens will become clearer as we examine five ways in which direct democracies link themselves to other systems with which they are interdependent: hegemony, subordination, mutual adjustment, bargaining, and expansion.

Hegemony occurs when a democracy maintains its own autonomy by forcing others to give up theirs. Through superior power, the group preserves its internal simplicity in the face of a complex world. A familiar example is ancient Athens, whose citizens not only dominated a large population of slaves but also established hegemony over the other city-states of the Delian League. Modern cases are also easy to find. Some democratic workplaces grow by hiring new employees who are not allowed to share the participatory rights of the original worker-owners. Similarly, in university departments and schools, a relative handful of faculty members democratically decide curricular requirements that shape the programs of thousands of students.

As these illustrations show, hegemonic "democracies for the few"[32] can survive a long time despite inconsistency between their internal and external practices. To do so, they need a legitimating doctrine to justify the sharp separation between their own citizens and the others whom they dominate. The mixture of fact and myth in such doctrines varies, as does the basis for the claim of superiority—race, education, age, virtue, experience, religion, and sex have all been used in one setting or another. But once belief in the doctrine begins to weaken among either rulers or the ruled, the democratic norms of the hegemonic group create strong moral pressure for change.[33]

From the perspective of the less powerful, another group's hegemony implies their own *subordination*. Because they are small, direct democracies must usually bear the brunt of adjustment to interdependence while larger systems call the shots. Thus, towns are subject to state law, and units within a firm must work within an overall corporate plan. Subordination is not always tyrannical or even undemocratic. For example, unfettered employee "democracy" in a government agency would be decidedly antidemocratic if it permitted public servants to ignore the will of the people as a whole. Constraints must be imposed on any unit that exists within a larger, interdependent system; otherwise, that unit unilaterally dominates others. Subordination within a hierarchy is one way to communicate and enforce such constraints. Within organizations, however, accusations of "manipulation" and "pseudoparticipation" often arise when leaders attempt to encourage participation without first explaining the scope of discretion that the smaller unit will enjoy.

Although hierarchy is sometimes an unavoidable way of coming to grips with interdependence, people generally dislike subordination. Even if commands embody sensible decisions, the mere fact that others have decided makes people feel unfree. Groups, like individuals, prefer to adjust to one another as they think best, retaining the feeling of autonomy despite the fact of interdependence. Of the many ways separate decision makers can practice *mutual adjustment*, the most familiar is the market. If, for example, a firm run by worker-owners finds that consumer demand for a product has fallen, no government agency or corporate headquarters need tell them to shift production into a more profitable line—they decide that for themselves. The outcome may be the same—an adjustment to the environment—but the social process and the feelings it engenders are totally different.

Just as a democracy that establishes hegemony over other groups must sharply distinguish its internal and external norms, so must any democracy that hopes to survive within a market system. Strain is inevitable when people must practice empathetic cooperation toward fellow members but calculating competitiveness toward outsiders. Moreover, internal solidarity is undermined by the economic gaps that open up when members must be paid what external competitors are willing to offer. Nevertheless, democratic norms on the whole have more in common with market principles than with hierarchy. Both democracies and markets are based on formal equality, reason, and consent; whereas hierarchies depend on rank, authority, and obedience.

Marketlike adjustment occurs when external units are numerous. When relevant groups are few in number and balanced in strength, then *bargaining* becomes possible, as each unit seeks to negotiate the terms of its interdependence with others. As with hierarchy and markets, strain arises because attitudes and behavior required for successful bargaining partially clash with those that best promote internal harmony. Bargaining always involves a mixture of shared and conflicting interests, but the adversarial element is more salient than within a direct democracy, especially one with strong unitary norms. Threats are common in bargaining, and there is always danger that talk will give way to struggle involving mutual punishment. Democracy itself can be endangered if specialists in external conflict turn their adversarial skills to use inside the group. Less sinister but equally threatening to power sharing is the pressure that bargaining always creates toward centralization. Labor unions, for example, must delegate much discretion to negotiating committees or business agents, even when the rank and file retain the right to reject proposed contracts. No matter how resolutely egalitarian the polity itself may be, the world outside usually finds it easier to deal with a single authoritative spokesperson.[34]

If hierarchy, mutual adjustment, and bargaining create tension for direct democracies, would it not be sensible simply to expand the democratic community? If a worker-owned firm must hire new employees, can it not give them equal membership rights? If two union locals negotiate with the same employer, should they not merge? If several neighborhood groups work together on common problems, would they not be more effective as a single association? In all realms where participation occurs, expansion is commonplace, whether through merger or natural growth. Nevertheless, expansion poses the most severe threat of all to direct democracy, because as the number of participants increases the character of democracy undergoes radical change. Let us therefore turn to the crucial effect of size on participation.

NOTES

1. For a detailed account of this shift in usage, see Robert A. Dahl and Edward R. Tufte, *Size and Democracy* (Stanford: Stanford University Press, 1973), pp. 4–12.

2. Giovanni Sartori, *Democratic Theory* (Westport, Conn.: Greenwood Press, 1962), p. 54.

3. *The Human Condition,* Anchor Books edition (Garden City, N.Y.: Doubleday & Company, 1959), p. 166.

4. Thucydides, *History of the Peloponnesian War,* trans. Rex Warner (New York: Penguin Books, 1954), p. 147.

5. *Strong Democracy: Participatory Politics for a New Age* (Berkeley: University of California Press, 1984), pp. 202, 175.

6. Ibid., pp. 198, 107.

7. Ibid., p. 133.

8. *Beyond Adversary Democracy* (New York: Basic Books, 1980), p. 13.

9. Ibid., p. 301.

10. For a good example, see Goldie Shabad, "Strikes in Yugoslavia: Implications for Industrial Democracy," *British Journal of Political Science,* 10 (1980), 293–316.

11. Unitary assumptions have justified harsh treatment of minority factions in American labor unions and other nongovernmental associations; Grant McConnell, *Private Power and American Democracy* (New York: Alfred A. Knopf, 1967), chap. 5.

12. For two accounts that are all the more chilling because they are written by a sympathetic reporter, see William Hinton, *Hundred Day War: The Cultural Revolution at Tsinghua University* (New York: Monthly Review Press, 1972); and *Shenfan: The Continuing Revolution in a Chinese Village* (New York: Random House, 1983).

13. *The New State: Group Organization the Solution of Popular Government* (Gloucester, Mass.: Peter Smith, 1965; originally 1918), pp. 196–97. Since she wrote, increased ease of commuting has made neighborhoods far more homogeneous.

14. For an eloquent condemnation of overemphasis on community in city planning, see Richard Sennett, *The Fall of Public Man* (New York: Alfred A. Knopf, 1977), chap. 13.

15. *Democracy* (New York: St. Martin's Press, 1975), p. 138. Lively contrasts their attitude with the unitary position of Rousseau and Marx, who believed consensus possible once societies eliminate social and economic differences that cause political conflict. Note that Benjamin Barber explicitly dissociates his "strong democracy" from the unitary assumption, which he finds "relatively benign" in small face-to-face communities but "vicious" in larger settings. He advocates "institutions that facilitate the search for common ends without sabotaging the individuality of the searchers, and that can acknowledge pluralism and conflict as starting points of the political process without abdicating the quest for a world of common ends. . . ." *Strong Democracy,* pp. 148–50, 155.

16. Mansbridge, *Beyond Adversary Democracy,* pp. 266–67.

17. Joseph A. Schumpeter, *Capitalism, Socialism, and Democracy,* 3rd ed. (New York: Harper & Row, 1950), chap. XXII.

18. I do not count anarchy as a political order here, but some versions of participatory democracy verge on anarchism.

19. Jo Freeman, *The Politics of Women's Liberation: A Case Study of an Emerging Social Movement and Its Relation to the Policy Process* (White Plains, N.Y.: Longman, Copyright © 1975 by Jo Freeman), pp. 105–6, 121. In a quite different context, Digby Baltzell traces the long-standing contempt and disrespect for leaders in Pennsylvania politics to the egalitarian, power-rejecting tradition of Quakerism. See his *Puritan Boston and Quaker Philadelphia: Two Protestant Ethics and the Spirit of Class Authority and Leadership* (Boston: Beacon Press, 1979), especially chap. 18.

20. *Kibbutz: Venture in Utopia*, augmented edition (New York: Schocken Books, 1970), p. 97. See also Mansbridge, *Beyond Adversary Democracy*, chap. 16.

21. Jo Freeman, "The Tyranny of Structurelessness," in *Women in Politics*, ed. Jane S. Jaquette (New York: John Wiley & Sons, 1974), pp. 203, 207, 212. Michael Walzer makes a similar argument: "Formally shapeless discussion provides an absolutely open field for the manipulative craft of a few people. The crucial feature of orderly procedures is that they identify such people as responsible agents: the chairman himself, the mover of this or that motion, and so on." *Political Action: A Practical Guide to Movement Politics* (Chicago: Quadrangle, 1971), p. 71. For a balanced view of when structureless forms are valuable or disadvantageous, see Jane Mansbridge, "Feminism and the Forms of Freedom," in *Organization and Bureaucracy*, ed. Frank Fischer and Carmen Sirianni (Philadelphia: Temple University Press, 1984), pp. 472–81.

22. *The Logic of Collective Action: Public Goods and the Theory of Groups* (Cambridge: Harvard University Press, 1965), pp. 22–36.

23. *Fanshen: A Documentary of Revolution in a Chinese Village* (New York: Monthly Review Press, 1966), pp. 225–26. Copyright © 1966 by William Hinton. Reprinted by permission of Monthly Review Foundation.

24. Mansbridge, *Beyond Adversary Democracy*, chap. 17.

25. Ibid., chap. 20.

26. *Commitment and Community: Communes and Utopias in Sociological Perspective* (Cambridge: Harvard University Press, 1972), pp. 118, 131–32.

27. *Beyond Adversary Democracy*, p. 193.

28. Sidney Verba, *Small Groups and Political Behavior: A Study of Leadership* (Princeton N.J.: Princeton University Press, 1961), chap. IX. Verba provides an excellent summary of the Lewin, Lippitt, and White experiments.

29. Philip Selznick, *Leadership in Administration: A Sociological Interpretation* (New York: Harper & Row, 1957); and Thomas J. Peters and Robert H. Waterman, Jr., *In Search of Excellence: Lessons from America's Best Run Companies* (New York: Harper & Row, 1982).

30. For a sensitive essay on the relation between geography and political character, see Benjamin R. Barber, *The Death of Communal Liberty: A History of Freedom in a Swiss Mountain Canton* (Princeton: Princeton University Press, 1974), chap. IV.

31. The erosion of participatory communities by growing interdependence is a pervasive theme in the literature. For examples, see Barber, *Death of a Communal Liberty*, chap. IV; H.D.F. Kitto, *The Greeks* (New York: Penguin Books, 1951), chap. 9; and Hinton, *Shenfan*.

32. The phrase is borrowed from Michael Parenti, *Democracy for the Few*, 2nd ed. (New York: St. Martin's Press, 1977).

33. Compare the explanation of American reformism in Samuel P. Huntington, *American Politics: The Promise of Disharmony* (Cambridge: Harvard University Press, 1981).

34. Note that Dahl and Lindblom define *bargaining* as "a form of reciprocal control among leaders." Robert A. Dahl and Charles E. Lindblom, *Politics, Economics and Welfare: Planning and Politico-Economic Systems Resolved into Basic Social Processes* (New York: Harper & Row, 1953), p. 324, emphasis added.

CHAPTER 7

SIZE

The number of people in a group profoundly affects all aspects of the members' life together. Nowhere is this more evident than in the way decisions are made. Norms of direct democracy that work beautifully for ten create an entirely different atmosphere for a hundred and become virtually infeasible for a thousand. As their numbers grow, most polities resort to electing representatives; but because the appeal of direct participation remains so strong, attempts are often made to reconcile it with large size. This chapter presents and evaluates four such efforts: decentralization, referendums, community assemblies, and indirect elections. But first let us get a clearer idea of how size restricts our ability to practice pure direct democracy.

THE LOGIC OF NUMBERS

In an ideal direct democracy, every member participates actively in discussions aimed at reaching consensus. How large can a community get before this goal becomes impossible? There is no magic number that limits direct face-to-face democracy, but Bertrand de Jouvenel has suggested a useful formula that shows the relentless tradeoff between numbers and the cost and quality of participation.[1] Suppose, de Jouvenel says, that a decision-making group is willing to devote t minutes to meeting together; suppose also that for adequate discussion each member must be able to speak for at least *m* minutes. Then *n*, the maximum number of participants, is given by:

$$n = t/m$$

For example, if a group is willing to meet for three hours and each member wants to speak at least ten minutes (a frustratingly brief time in a meeting of that length), then the membership cannot exceed eighteen. We can play around with these numbers, but something always has to give. Increase *t*, and we run into all the opportunity costs of time. Decrease *m*, and individual contributions soon become so brief that the meeting will be a mockery of reasoned discussion and meaningful consensus.

Committees, Assemblies, and Crowds

The conclusion is imprecise but inescapable: A discussion that gives ample opportunity for every member to participate actively is possible only in meetings that range from two or three to, at most, two or three dozen people. Thus full realization of direct-democratic ideals requires a group so small that the most apt label is that proposed by Robert Dahl: *committee democracy*.[2] Innumerable committees, work groups, and clubs fall within this range, but no government of any consequence has ever included so few citizens.

Instead, the number of eligible participants in classic direct democracies typically runs into the hundreds. Groups of this size, which may be called *assembly democracies*, partially achieve direct democratic ideals, but they make substantial compromises in doing so. A strong sense of community can develop because all members are able to gather together in a meeting small enough so that each person is recognizable as an individual. All points of view can be expressed in discussions that often result in a genuine sense of the meeting, but only if most members are willing to remain silent, allowing unofficial spokespersons to represent their ideas. Thus the goal of equal development of all through active participation must be compromised; but if the assembly meets often enough, each individual can sooner or later make a contribution, especially if the assembly delegates tasks to smaller groups and makes a determined effort to share assignments among all members.

Assemblies sometimes grow much larger than a few hundred people. At the height of the "Shanghai Commune" phase of the Cultural Revolution in China's largest city, over one million assembled to hear an address by municipal leader Zhang Chunqiao.[3] But the quality of such gatherings declines rapidly as numbers increase. They become *crowds* rather than true assemblies, and among social theorists, the reputation of crowds has long been deservedly poor. Robert Michels's indictment is typical and accurate:

> The crowd . . . is always subject to suggestion, being readily influenced by the eloquence of great popular orators; moreover, direct government by the peo-

ple, admitting of no serious discussions or thoughtful deliberations, greatly facilitates *coups de main* of all kinds by men who are exceptionally bold, energetic, and adroit. It is easier to dominate a large crowd than a small audience. The adhesion of the crowd is tumultuous, summary, and unconditional. Once the suggestions have taken effect, the crowd does not readily tolerate contradiction from a small minority, and still less from isolated individuals. A great multitude assembled within a small area is unquestionably more accessible to panic alarms, to unreflective enthusiasm, and the like, than is a small meeting, whose members can quietly discuss matters among themselves.[4]

The size at which an assembly ends and crowd processes take over is, like the upper limit for a committee, imprecise and variable. But, as Dahl points out, "it is significant that in the modern world, six hundred seems to be about the limit for legislative bodies."[5] We may take this number as a rough ceiling beyond which reasoned deliberation becomes impracticable, while the lower bound on assemblies merges with the upper limit for committees.

How Size Limits Can Vary

Under what conditions is it safe to let a democratic group grow toward the upper limit of size for its type? We frequently rely on committees and assemblies to make decisions in workplaces, voluntary associations, and governmental subunits. Things can go seriously wrong if people expect all the virtues of committee democracy in a group too large to succeed in that mode, or if they create an assembly so numerous that it can only accomplish a parody of democracy. The size ranges noted above are too broad to rule out such errors, but de Jouvenel's formula tells us that groups can be larger if members are willing to spend more time meeting together or each member needs less time in which to speak.

Figuring out whether people will be generous or grudging in the time they are willing to devote to collective decision making should be a familiar exercise. Return to Chapters 3 and 4, and take into account the various factors, individual and contextual, that affect the motivation to participate. To cite a few examples, we could infer that a direct democratic community can afford to be somewhat larger if it has power over decisions that are vitally important to members; if they lead simple lives that offer few distractions to compete for their leisure time; or if meetings offer an enjoyable occasion for friendship and socializing. All these criteria are met in agricultural communities that farm collectively or cooperatively. It is no accident that such places provide many of the best examples of assembly democracy in action.

The amount of time members will need to take part effectively depends most obviously on the efficiency with which deliberations are conducted. Truly "structureless" groups *must* remain small. Conversely, groups that are ably chaired and whose members are experienced in democratic process can afford to grow more than others.

Perhaps the most important influence reducing feasible size is diversity. When only a few differences of opinion exist, fewer spokespersons can adequately express the views of a larger number of others. Diversity of a more fundamental sort also matters. People who share the same culture, education, and past experience communicate more quickly because they can rely on shared meanings and implicit understandings. Members of homogeneous groups are also less likely to feel they all need to take part in order to protect their interests. Therefore, the proportion who actually participate may shrink without arousing much concern. This means that homogenous communities can more easily retain the forms of direct democracy despite considerable growth of population. Conversely, diverse and contentious polities must more quickly resort to representative democracy as their numbers increase. By similar reasoning, a group of large but stable size will find direct democracy less satisfactory when it experiences an increase in conflict among members.

Even if we assume conditions favorable for generous size limits, most political and economic entities in modern societies are too big for committee or assembly democracy. Usually this fact leads to the conclusion that members can participate authoritatively only by intermittently electing leaders and representatives; however, people continue to seek ways to reconcile the direct-democratic tradition with the reality of large-scale organization. In the remainder of this chapter, we look at four such attempts.

DECENTRALIZATION

If few people can participate meaningfully in huge systems, then why not return as much power as possible to small units of organization? In United States politics, the attraction of grass-roots democracy cuts across the ideological spectrum. Whether in the guise of community control or new federalism, neighborhood action or local self-reliance, Democrats and Republicans, radicals and conservatives all invoke the rhetoric of decentralization so constantly that, in Grant McConnell's words, "the ideal plainly touches something very close to the heart of the dominant ideology."[6]

Olson's logic of collective action and de Jouvenel's formula both tell us that people will be more willing and more able to participate effectively in small units. Nevertheless, precisely because grass-roots imagery is so alluring, this section is devoted to pointing out fallacies of decentralization, as a result of which powers can be devolved to smaller units without really achieving participatory values. The purpose here is *not* to argue against decentralization per se but rather to seek the sort of balance advocated by E. F. Schumacher, the English prophet of small-scale technology and organization:

> For constructive work, the principal task is always the restoration of some kind of balance. Today, we suffer from an almost universal idolatry of giantism. It is therefore necessary to insist on the virtues of smallness—where this applies. If there were a prevailing idolatry of smallness, irrespective of subject or purpose, one would have to try and exercise influence in the opposite direction.[7]

In the United States, giantism is a pervasive fact, but our political ideology idolizes smallness and decentralization. Therefore, we need to pay attention to conditions that interfere with the ability of decentralization to promote democratic goals.

Large Units

Grass-roots rhetoric is often used to protect or enhance the power of decision units that are themselves far too big for self-government through participatory committees or assemblies. For example, turning decisions over to states or corporations often does little to promote participatory democracy, although there may be much to recommend such decentralization in terms of other values, such as efficiency. Always remember that, compared with most political and economic organizations with which we are familiar, the scale required for direct participation is very small indeed.

Excessive Interdependence

It is one thing to delegate nominal authority to small units. It is quite another to ensure that those units have sufficient control over outcomes important enough to motivate people to participate. Otherwise, members will learn that the real decisions are made or negotiated at higher levels, and participation will atrophy. Decision-making units must encompass reasonably self-contained patterns of commerce, transportation, work, or social interaction. As Karl Hess puts it, "If local liberty has no material base, then it ultimately has no base at all."[8] For this reason, many advocates of participatory democracy are enthusiastic about "appropriate technology"—low-energy, human-scale devices that might enable small communities to exist more independently without excessively sacrificing material or intellectual standards. Examples include the personal computer, the bicycle, and a multitude of alternative, or "soft," energy sources, including solar house-heating, windmills, and small dams. In contrast, "hard" energy sources—nuclear power, petroleum, huge electrical grids—virtually dictate political interdependence and large-scale centralized organization.[9]

Centralized Communications

No matter how realistic the material basis for decentralization, members will not participate if they are uninformed about opportunities to affect decisions. Few people will get involved in local self-government if all their political information comes from network television and national newsmagazines. It is no accident that Switzerland, the democracy with the most vigorous tradition of direct participation, also has—in proportion to population—the greatest number of newspapers, none of which has true mass circulation.[10] Decentralized politics depends upon decentralized attention. If people are to participate in a small unit, they must have and use a source of information devoted to that unit, even if it is as humble as a mimeographed newsletter.

Disregard for Inequalities

Technology is not the only force behind the modern trend toward large-scale politics. As Tocqueville foresaw, the "irresistible passion" for equality also pushes democratic nations toward centralized authority.[11] Conversely, all efforts to decentralize power create tendencies toward inequality among citizens. If participatory democrats keep this problem in mind, they can sometimes decentralize in such a way as to protect essential equalities. In other instances, a widening of political or economic differences may be the unavoidable price of increased participatory opportunities.

The first link between small units and inequality is the most dangerous. Because of the logic so clearly laid out in Madison's tenth *Federalist* paper, small units are more likely than large to split along simple, enduring factional lines, which may provide the basis for tyranny of one faction (whether majority or minority) over the other. A larger, more diverse system will be relatively independent of such local struggles and therefore better able to protect the rights of losers in its subunits. The federal government has played this role with respect to southern localities where blacks were denied voting rights before 1965. In principle, the danger of political tyranny in small units is easily solved. Decentralize all the powers you wish, but reserve to a larger entity the function of guaranteeing the integrity of the democratic process itself.

A second connection between decentralization and inequality is primarily economic. Whenever local units are given full control of their own resources, differences in endowments, skill, effort, and luck inevitably result in uneven success and failure. In the United States, local control over school finances produces tremendous differences in educational spending between rich and poor districts. Socialist societies, in which economic equality is a fundamental value, face the same dilemma when they decentralize their economies in order to encourage worker or peasant participation in decision making. The differences in prosperity among Yugoslav enterprises or Chinese farming villages can be just as great as among their counterparts in capitalist systems.[12] In response, central governments can tax the rich and give to the poor; but excessive taxation will destroy the incentive to participate in collective enterprises, just as it is assumed to destroy the initiative of capitalists.

A third tie between decentralization and inequality results from the different constituencies who participate in small and large systems. Large-scale decision making necessarily confines most citizens to voting, which, because it is a less costly act, fosters widespread and therefore relatively egalitarian involvement. Participatory democrats prefer small units because they permit more "meaningful" participation than voting, but we know from Chapter 5 that such intensive participation will be less representative. I see no easy way out of this tradeoff between centralized bureaucracies responding (albeit clumsily) to the wishes of broad electorates and smaller, grass-roots councils responding disproportionately to local activists and elites.[13]

DIRECT LEGISLATION

Given that it is so hard to adjust a large-scale world to the needs of committee and assembly democracy, one solution is to adapt direct democracy to meet the requirements of scale. Let the people decide, adherents of this view say, but as the basic mode of action, replace time-consuming discussion with direct legislation, in which an unlimited number of citizens can participate through the quick act of voting. We already recognize the advantages of voting to elect leaders, and the same device can enable the people to take back from remote representatives the right to determine policies directly. Indeed, according to one vision of the future, every home could become a polling place, with citizens learning about issues through personal computers, then electronically communicating their wishes to a central computer!

Terminology

In order to describe and appraise the actual and potential use of direct legislation, a note on vocabulary is essential to prevent confusion. The common term for direct legislation is *referendum,* a word which has both narrow and broad meanings. In the United States, the stricter use of *referendum* means "a popular vote on a bill that a legislature has already passed"; in effect, citizens are given a chance to veto the decisions of their representatives. Some polities also permit the *initiative,* in which ordinary citizens, through petitions, originate a measure as well as vote on it. Unfortunately, *referendum* is used broadly to include *both* forms of direct legislation (the narrower referendum and the initiative). In addition, you will also encounter the older European term *plebiscite,* which can mean any referendum (in the broad sense) but usually connotes a vote on fundamental issues such as national identity, political boundaries, type of regime, or the acceptability of a leader. Finally, those troubled (as many are) by the criteria for making Latin plurals will be reassured to know that *referendums* is not only easier to remember than *referenda,* it is also etymologically more respectable.[14]

History and Use

Although ideas such as the electronic referendum may be visionary or even frivolous, the basic notion of direct legislation has a long and honorable history. In Switzerland (which also has an ancient tradition of direct assembly democracy in local communities), the referendum dates back into the Middle Ages. Modern Switzerland has used the referendum on the national level as often as all other nations put together—more than three hundred times since

1848. Switzerland permits a referendum on any federal law or decree if 50,000 citizens sign a petition within ninety days after the act was published. The Swiss require referendums on some international treaties and on all amendments to their constitution, which can also be amended by popular initiative.[15] In addition, the Swiss make frequent use of referendums in their cantons and local communities. As a result, "There is hardly a Sunday in Switzerland without an election or a referendum somewhere at the federal, cantonal, or local level."[16]

Although Switzerland alone makes direct legislation so basic a part of normal decision making, referendums have played a crucial, if less frequent, role in other nations. Italy was created "by a series of referendums in which overwhelming majorities turned out to vote for the unification of their country."[17] The United Kingdom, Ireland, Denmark, and Norway used referendums to decide on membership in the European Economic Community. Charles de Gaulle relied on plebiscites to transform the French political system—establishing the Fifth Republic in 1958, the independence of Algeria in 1961 and 1962, and the direct election of the president in 1962.[18]

Unlike most other democracies, the United States has never held a nationwide referendum. However, most Americans have frequent opportunities to vote on policy questions, because all fifty states provide for state or local referendums (in the narrow sense), and twenty-three states permit initiatives.[19] Although Oregon has been the most frequent user of the initiative,[20] California is best-known for the device. In 1978, the famous Proposition 13 (a severe restriction of property taxes in that state) touched off a nationwide drive against taxes and government spending that culminated in the election of President Ronald Reagan and the impressive success of his legislative program in 1981.

Besides tax cutters, many other advocacy groups increasingly resorted to the initiative during the 1970s and 1980s. In 1982, statewide initiatives included eight nuclear freeze resolutions, five "bottle bills" to require deposits on beverage containers, and seven efforts to reform utility regulation. Some states debated more unusual issues. Voters in Idaho, for example, decided to permit denturists as well as dentists to sell dentures (a measure intended to save money for senior citizens).[21] Between 1970 and 1982, the number of statewide initiatives increased from ten to fifty-five, prompting the author of a best-seller to discern a "megatrend" from representative democracy to "participatory democracy."[22]

Does Direct Legislation Return Power to the People?

Unsurprisingly, for a device intended to give power back to the people, direct legislation is extremely popular. National polls in the United States show that 77 percent of the public endorse the idea, a figure that reaches 85 percent among Californians, who also believe by a three-to-one margin that voting on propositions is a more effective way to influence government than voting on candidates.[23] The referendum certainly seems like an egalitarian, populist institution, but does it really give the people more power than voting in elections?

Evidence shows that elected officials are chosen by a broader electorate than that which typically votes on propositions. Referendums (especially if they occur frequently) increase the intensity of participation a polity asks of citizens. By the analysis in Chapter 5, we should expect the extent of participation to decline unless voting is compulsory. During the 1970s, turnout in Swiss national referendums averaged 42 percent, whereas 52 percent voted in the 1975 Swiss federal election.[24] A comparable 14 to 17 percent "dropoff" in voting on questions as opposed to candidates occurs in American states.[25] In some local referendums, dropoff rates exceed 80 percent.[26]

According to Rule 3 in Chapter 5, we should also expect that referendum voters are higher in educational and economic status. Research in the United States consistently shows that the poor and less educated are much more underrepresented among people who vote on propositions than among those who vote on candidates.[27] Class bias in participation may help account for the conservatism of many referendum results, a tendency otherwise puzzling to observers who remember that radicals and progressives originally championed direct legislation. After noticing the trend, some American conservative leaders began to advocate a national initiative and urged their followers to exploit opportunities for state and local initiatives.[28]

From a global perspective, the possible class bias of direct legislation is less important than its impact on basic configurations of power. Does direct legislation strengthen rulers, special interest groups, or the broader public? The crucial factor in answering this question is how and by whom propositions are initiated: There are three basic cases: (1) government-initiated plebiscites; (2) citizen initiatives; and (3) mandatory referendums.

Government-Initiated Plebiscites. Some governments pose questions to the people in order to dodge a tough decision. Such was the case when Great Britain held its first nationwide referendum, at the initiative of a Labour government that feared "tearing itself asunder" over whether or not the country should remain in the European Economic Community.[29] Passing the buck to the people in this fashion can hardly be said to reduce popular power. Historically, however, leaders able to pick the occasion for referendums have more often used them to establish an identity between themselves and the people at the expense of other competitors for power. Charles de Gaulle inimitably expressed the spirit of this strategy when he spoke to the French people before a 1961 referendum: "I need, yes I need, to know how things stand in your minds and hearts. And therefore I turn to you, over the heads of the intermediaries . . . the question is one between each man and woman amongst you, and myself."

Despite his grandeur, de Gaulle retained enough respect for the people to resign eight years later when voters rebuffed his plan to establish regional councils and restructure the French Senate.[30] But the plebiscite generally has a bad name because autocrats from Napoleon to Hitler exploited the device to put a seal of popular approval on their own power.

Citizen Initiatives. Referendums initiated by citizen petitions are less vulnerable than plebiscites to executive manipulation, but power in this case passes not so much to "the people" as to the interest groups that organize petition drives and finance advertising campaigns. Some of these groups are ideological or issue oriented, such as the environmentalists who sponsored many recent United States initiatives. The advantage that committed citizens gain from the initiative refutes one common objection to referendums: that they supposedly fail to allow for the intensity of different voters' policy preferences.

However, the high cost of referendum campaigns in large polities also gives a great advantage to a second type of group: economic special interests. In 1980, for example, the ten largest contributors to initiative campaigns in American states were three electric utilities fighting antinuclear power proposals, three tobacco companies resisting antismoking questions, and four oil firms.[31] The fact that these companies were put on the defensive might seem to show that the initiative gives foes of economic vested interests at least a chance to win. David Magleby, however, reaches a more pessimistic conclusion as a result of his analysis of California propositions between 1954 and 1982. "Proponents cannot spend an initiative into law," he finds, but opponents "can virtually guarantee the defeat of an initiative if they significantly outspend the proponents."[32] Evidence from other states leads to a similar, but less absolute, conclusion. Outside California, opponents with a big financial edge succeeded in 79 percent of campaigns between 1976 and 1981, as compared with the 100 percent rate Magleby found in California.[33]

Mandatory Referendums. Mandatory referendums (as on constitutional amendments in Australia, Switzerland, and all American states except Delaware) seem most likely to enhance the power of ordinary voters, who get the final say without depending on a prior decision by politicians or interest groups to put a question to them. In Australia, voters have flaunted their independence of parliamentary leaders by defeating 28 of 36 proposed amendments.[34] In Switzerland, 100 of 138 obligatory referendums have passed, but Aubert and others convincingly argue that voters gain influence because leaders must anticipate their reactions: "Parliament is dealing with bills which it knows will be subject to a popular vote, and it prepares them with appropriate prudence, seeking the good will of voters through compromises and by offering guarantees."[35]

Does Direct Legislation Achieve Direct-Democratic Values?

Much of the enthusiasm for referendums arises from the desire to intensify direct popular participation. As one activist exclaimed, "The referendum is participatory democracy to the *n*th degree!" Others, as Butler and Ranney observe, would disagree:

> Some advocates of participatory democracy are not enthusiastic about direct legislation as the right path to human development. They do not agree that voting in initiative and referendum elections is the kind of participation that best elicits the human potential. After all, they argue, voting demands only the most minimal commitment and effort by the citizen. . . . Voting is conducted in secret and therefore irresponsibly. Voters need not engage in any confrontation between their preferences and opposing preferences. All in all, then, voting is a most passive, undemanding, uninspiring, and unimproving kind of civic participation, vastly inferior to taking an active part in the discussion of issues in town meetings, local caucuses, and other types of face-to-face assemblies.[36]

Does the attempt to reconcile direct democracy with large numbers through voting mistakenly produce an altogether different sort of participatory politics? To answer this question, let us appraise direct legislation with respect to the values we have associated with direct democracy: action, discussion, consensus, and community.

Action. Although voting on propositions is certainly a more perfunctory activity than the meetings and assemblies that participatory democrats idealize, a more appropriate comparison for evaluating referendums should be between citizens voting for candidates only and citizens voting on candidates *and* on policy questions. By this standard, referendums clearly intensify the activity of voters who take part in them, especially of those who put great effort into organizing petition drives and campaigning for or against questions.[37] However, evidence indicates that direct legislation in the United States seldom increases the extent of participation. Only in rare cases do more people turn out to vote just because a question is on the ballot; and states with initiatives do not experience higher turnout than states without them.[38]

Discussion. Controversial referendums surely stimulate political discussion, but the nature of the dialogue they produce differs from that pictured in the direct democratic ideal. Instead of a conversation among friends aimed at a synthesis acceptable to all, the yes/no posing of the typical proposition forces a debate from which only one side can emerge victorious. Recognizing this defect, Finland, in 1931, and Sweden, in 1957, experimented with referendums that gave voters three choices, but in neither case did the moderate option win.[39] Benjamin Barber proposes another multichoice format, in which voters would be asked not only to vote yes or no but also to indicate the strength and certainty of their opinions. To pass, a referendum would have to win on two occasions, separated by six months during which everyone could consider the detailed information about people's feelings obtained from the first vote. Barber reports that this device was used for centuries in the Republic of Raetia, now part of Switzerland.[40] His plan might work well if everyone respected its spirit, but there is danger that some voters will overstate the strength of their preferences in order to gain an advantage over others.

Consensus and Community. Such proposals aside, ordinary referendums create a clearly adversarial situation, to which they offer a majoritarian solution. The referendum is therefore a device hard to reconcile with the goals of consensus and community. Indeed, one traditional objection to the referendum is that legislatures are better able to produce solutions that take into account many points of view. As Butler and Ranney note, legislative "discussions approach the small-group ideal far more closely than the discussions preceding referendums."[41] Legislatures are in fact assemblies that do much of their work through committees, so we should not be surprised that they exhibit many of the virtues assembly and committee democracies are supposed to develop. Would it not be better therefore to leave large-scale policymaking to representatives? Do referendums gain direct citizen participation at the price of sacrificing direct-democratic values?

Not always. Sometimes an overwhelming referendum tally proves the existence of a near-consensus that one side had previously disputed. For example, the 90.7 percent approval that French voters gave in 1962 to the treaty establishing Algeria's independence defused a conflict that threatened to explode into civil war.[42] Some plebiscites establish or affirm the very existence of a political community, as when 99.9 percent of Norwegians voted to separate from Sweden in 1905.

Perhaps the best reason to consider the referendum more sympathetically is given by the experience of Switzerland. Among the political leaders of that linguistically and religiously divided nation, the consensual decision-making principle of "amicable agreement" is ubiquitous.[43] Yet Switzerland is also the foremost user of that majoritarian device, the referendum. This seems incongruous, but the existence of the referendum may explain why the Swiss so widely and successfully practice amicable agreement. With the threat of a referendum hanging over their plans "like the sword of Damocles,"[44] parliamentary leaders are forced to accommodate proposals to the wishes of minority factions who might organize referendums if they were excessively displeased. Although the leadership might reasonably expect to win such contests, they have no guarantee of victory, and in any case the campaigns would be expensive.

In general, the possibility of resorting to decisive referendums may enhance the viability of a political system whose consensual habits would otherwise produce too much delay and stalemate. Indeed, the ability to shift from unitary to adversarial methods that Mansbridge deems necessary can be accomplished by having two distinct decision systems: a consensual process for normal issues and a strongly decisive alternative to use in adversarial situations when deadlock would be intolerable. The majoritarian referendum is one such device; others include authoritarian leaders, impersonal formulas, and divine guidance. Consensual democratic systems *need* their opposites; and among those opposites, the referendum at least has the virtue of deriving from *some* elements of direct-democratic ideology.

REFERENDUMS BASED ON LOCAL ASSEMBLIES

Mindful of the deficiencies of the referendum with respect to the values of discussion, consensus, and community, some participatory democrats have revived a plan first put forth by Thomas Jefferson, who sought a way to reconcile the virtues of direct democracy with the need to govern a large republic. Jefferson proposed dividing the counties of his day into smaller wards:

> The mayor of every ward, on a question like the present [revision of the Virginia constitution], would call his ward together, take the simple yea or nay of its members, convey these to the county court, who would hand on those of all its wards to be the proper general authority; and the voice of the whole people would be thus fairly, fully, and peaceably expressed, discussed, and decided by the common reason of the society.[45]

Terrence Cook and Benjamin Barber offer detailed proposals for Jeffersonian assemblies that would provide a forum for face-to-face discussion of larger issues, after which those attending would cast votes to be added up statewide or nationwide.[46] The assemblies would meet as often as monthly (Cook) or weekly (Barber), and if they were to accomplish their intended purpose, most meetings would surely last for several hours. Thus their proponents are calling for political participation far more intensive than anything our system now demands of citizens. We could therefore expect a severe decline in the extent of participation (compared with elections or conventional referendums) and a most troubling problem of unrepresentativeness.

A preview of how community assemblies would work is offered by the nearest approximation to them in contemporary politics: the party nominating caucuses in Iowa and other states. Although some observers see the caucuses as grass-roots democracy in action, others severely criticize them for low turnout rates, lack of secrecy in balloting, and the advantage they give well-organized interests. That their results can differ from methods that encourage more extensive participation has been vividly and frequently demonstrated. For example, in 1984 Senator Gary Hart defeated Walter Mondale by a 46 percent to 43 percent vote of the 600,000 citizens who turned out for the nonbinding Wisconsin Democratic presidential primary; but Mondale captured 60 percent of Wisconsin delegates compared with Hart's 30 percent, because delegates were selected four days later by caucuses in which only 30,000 people participated.[47] Like caucuses, referendums based on local assemblies would surely have a severe bias in favor of better-educated citizens and organized groups. This would not matter too much if their function were purely informational and advisory (as Barber proposes that they be during an initial phase), but if their votes had binding authority, the results would be dismaying to anyone who values political equality.

INDIRECT ELECTIONS

Another device intended to combine the participatory virtues of small groups with the ability to encompass large memberships is systematic indirect representation. One such plan was put forward in 1918 by Mary Parker Follett.[48] She proposed a "new state" based on neighborhood groups in which every citizen could participate. The neighborhoods would send representatives to district groups that would in turn send delegates to city councils, and so on through state and national legislatures. At each stage, the numbers meeting together would be kept small enough to permit true discussion. Mathematically, systems like Follett's are easily conceivable. Just five levels of representation (in addition to the basic neighborhood units) would suffice to include the entire voting-age population of the United States; yet at each level the number of people eligible to meet together would average only forty-five.

Like plans for local-assemblies democracy, Follett's proposal would require intensive participation from every citizen. Follett in fact wrote in those very terms:

> We have seen in considering direct government that the activity of every man is not enough if we mean merely his activity at the polling booths. With the inclusion of all men and women (practically accomplished) in the suffrage . . . , the *extensive* work of the democratic impulse has ended. Now the *intensive* work of democracy must begin.[49]

For this reason, plans like hers seem best suited to workplaces and other settings to which people devote a great share of their time. Thus the influential management theorist Rensis Likert urges a new approach to corporate structure closely akin in spirit to Follett's vision. Instead of treating hierarchy as a chain of boss–subordinate pairs, Likert recommends that organizations operate as structures of small participatory groups joined vertically by "linking-pin" individuals who belong to two or more groups.[50] Many modern firms have heeded Likert's advice. (It is worth noting that Mary Parker Follett was a management consultant as well as a political theorist, and her writings on management are now read more widely than are her political works.)

Political parties and voluntary associations often base their constitutions on similar principles. Nevertheless, with notable exceptions (such as the parliamentary selection of prime ministers), modern democratic governments avoid indirect elections. Forbidding the people to vote for top officials seems unacceptably elitist in a democratic age. When citizens' influence must be transmitted through several intervening layers, their impact is likely to be delayed and attenuated. Moreover, systems of indirect representation in parties and other organizations frequently turn out to transmit more influence from the top down than from the bottom up. Thus, even when many levels of representatives exist, as in the United States, citizens usually elect most of them directly. The constituencies into which voters are grouped vary in size, but nearly all are "large" compared with the requirements of participatory democracy. From this fact arise the distinctive character, problems, and strengths of electoral participation—the subject to which we now turn.

NOTES

1. "The Chairman's Problem," *American Political Science Review*, 55 (1961), 368–72.

2. Dahl divides democracies into four types: committee democracy, primary democracy (which I call assembly democracy), referendum democracy, and representative democracy. See his *After the Revolution?* (New Haven: Yale University Press, 1970), pp. 67–77.

3. Victor Nee, "Revolution and Bureaucracy: Shanghai in the Cultural Revolution," in *China's Uninterrupted Revolution: From 1840 to the Present*, ed. Victor Nee and James Peck (New York: Random House, Pantheon Books, 1975), p. 360. Nee describes how the Cultural Revolution drew inspiration from precedents for direct democracy in the Communist tradition, especially the Paris Commune of 1871. Zhang, a rising leader in 1967, was later imprisoned as one of the disgraced Gang of Four.

4. *Political Parties: A Sociological Study of the Oligarchical Tendencies of Modern Democracy*, trans. Eden and Cedar Paul (New York: Free Press, 1962), p. 64.

5. *After the Revolution?* p. 70.

6. *Private Power and American Democracy* (New York: Alfred A. Knopf, 1967), p. 96.

7. *Small Is Beautiful: Economics As If People Mattered* (New York: Harper & Row, 1975), p. 66.

8. *Community Technology* (New York: Harper & Row, 1979), p. 29.

9. Amory Lovins, *Soft Energy Paths: Toward a Durable Peace* (New York: Harper & Row, Colophon Books, 1979). For a general review of appropriate technology initiatives, see George McRobie, *Small Is Possible* (New York: Harper & Row, 1981).

10. Jurg Steiner, *Amicable Agreement Versus Majority Rule: Conflict Resolution in Switzerland*, rev. ed., trans. Asger Braendgaard and Barbara Braendgaard (Chapel Hill: University of North Carolina Press, 1974), p. 117.

11. Alexis de Tocqueville, *Democracy in America*, ed. Phillips Bradley, vol. II (New York: Random House, Vintage Books, 1945), p. 103.

12. This is not to say there is no difference in income distribution between worker-managed and capitalist economies. Inequalities *among* firms may be comparable, but *within* their own firms, workers generally distribute income more equally. For more about this subject, see Chapter 11.

13. On this and other biases of decentralized small units, see McConnell, *Private Power and American Democracy*, chap. 4.

14. According to David Butler and Austin Ranney, who edited the invaluable collection *Referendums: A Comparative Study of Practice and Theory* (Washington, D.C.: American Enterprise Institute for Public Policy Research, 1978), pp. 4–5.

15. Jean-Francois Aubert, "Switzerland," in Butler and Ranney, eds., *Referendums*, pp. 39–66.

16. Steiner, *Amicable Agreement Versus Majority Rule*, p. 77.

17. Philip Goodhart, "Referendums and Separatism I," in *The Referendum Device*, ed. Austin Ranney (Washington, D.C.: American Enterprise Institute for Public Policy Research, 1981), p. 139.

18. Vincent Wright, "France," in Butler and Ranney, eds., *Referendums*, pp. 139–67. In their appendices A and B, Butler and Ranney list all national referendums up until 1978.

19. For a summary of requirements, see David D. Schmidt, *Initiative Procedures: A Fifty-State Survey*, INR Special Report (Washington, D.C.: Initiative News Service, Inc., 1983).

20. Ranney, "The United States of America," in Butler and Ranney, eds., *Referendums*, p. 76.

21. Schmidt, *Ballot Initiatives: History, Research and Analysis of Recent Initiative & Referendum Campaigns*, INR Special Report (Washington, D.C.: Initiative News Service, Inc., 1983).

22. John Naisbitt, *Megatrends: Ten New Directions Transforming Our Lives* (New York: Warner Books, 1984), chap. 7.

23. David B. Magleby, *Direct Legislation: Voting on Ballot Propositions in the United States* (Baltimore: Johns Hopkins University Press, 1984), pp. 9–10.

24. Aubert, "Switzerland," p. 45.

25. Magleby, *Direct Legislation*, pp. 83–87.

26. Schmidt, *Ballot Initiatives*, pp. 26–34.

27. Magleby, *Direct Legislation*, chap. 6.

28. For example, Richard A. Viguerie, *The Establishment vs. The People: Is a New Populist Revolt on the Way?* (Chicago: Regnery Gateway, 1983), pp. 195, 257–62. For different explanations of conservatism in Swiss referendums, see Barber, *The Death of Communal Liberty*, pp. 258–74. Efforts to assess the liberalism or conservatism of referendum outcomes in the United States find mixed results. See Ranney, "The United States," pp. 82–85; and Schmidt, *Ballot Initiatives*, pp. 52–54.

29. David Butler, "The United Kingdom," in Butler and Ranney, eds., *Referendums*, p. 214.

30. Wright, "France"; quotation from p. 147.

31. Schmidt, *Ballot Initiatives*, pp. 17–18.

32. *Direct Legislation*, pp. 147–48.

33. Computed from data in Schmidt, *Ballot Initiatives*, pp. 14–23.

34. Don Aitkin, "Australia," in Butler and Ranney, *Referendums*, pp. 124–28.

35. Aubert, "Switzerland," p. 45.

36. *Referendums*, p. 33.

37. In California, however, these functions have been increasingly professionalized by a multi-million-dollar "initiative industry" of firms that collect signatures and conduct mass mailings. See Larry L. Berg and CB Holman, "The Initiative Process and Its Declining Agenda Setting Value" (paper presented at the annual meeting of the American Political Science Association, 1985); and Magleby, *Direct Legislation*, chap. 4.

38. Magleby, *Direct Legislation*, pp. 95–98.

39. Sten Sparre Nilson, "Scandinavia," in Butler and Ranney, eds., *Referendums*, pp. 191–92.

40. *Strong Democracy*, pp. 286–89.

41. *Referendums*, p. 36.

42. Wright, "France," p. 144.

43. Steiner, *Amicable Agreement Versus Majority Rule*, p. 23 and passim.

44. Ibid., p. 93.

45. Letter to Samuel Kercheval, July 12, 1816, in Adrienne Koch and William Peden, eds., *The Life and Selected Writings of Thomas Jefferson* (New York: Random House, 1944), p. 676. See also pp. 660–76.

46. Terrence E. Cook, "Community Assemblies Democracy: A Latent Theme in Democratic Theory" (paper delivered at the annual meeting of the American Political Science Association, 1978); Barber, *Strong Democracy*, pp. 267–73.

47. *New York Times*, April 8, 1984, p. 36; Marvin Stone, "These Wearying Caucuses," *U.S. News and World Report*, April 23, 1984, p. 82.

48. *The New State: Group Organization the Solution of Popular Government* (Gloucester, Mass.: Peter Smith, 1965), especially chap. 27.

49. Ibid., p. 256; emphasis in the original.

50. *New Patterns of Management* (New York: McGraw-Hill, 1961).

CHAPTER 8

ELECTIONS

For a long time, conventional political scientists virtually equated "participation" with voting in elections. As other chapters show, we are now aware of many more opportunities for action by ordinary members of political systems. Unfortunately, while sensitizing us to these possibilities, some enthusiasts of intensive participation have grown disdainful of elections. In an especially pungent put-down, Benjamin Barber claims that

> our primary electoral act, voting, is rather like using a public toilet: we wait in line with a crowd in order to close ourselves up in a small compartment where we can relieve ourselves in solitude and in privacy of our burden, pull a lever, and then, yielding to the next in line, go silently home.[1]

The act of voting is indeed quick, simple, and secret. These qualities may appear deficient compared with those of more demanding, informative, and communitarian acts, but they are also strengths that make voting paramount among all forms of democratic participation. Because ballots can be cast quickly and simultaneously, electoral democracies are potentially unlimited in size. Because voting is easy, more people take part in elections than in any other political action. Because votes are standardized and quantifiable, suffrage is the only power resource divided equally among all eligible citizens. Because voting constitutes a clearcut choice, elections both legitimate conflict and peacefully resolve it.

Journalists and academics lavish attention on elections. Perhaps their preoccupation is a way of paying tribute to the virtues just listed, but often it seems instead that the media see in elections only an entertaining spectator sport and political scientists, only an unending source of data for number crunching. Rather than vainly attempt to distill the huge literature they have created, this chapter will try to drive home just a few lessons that we all often forget. Briefly put, they are that rules matter, elections matter, and participation matters.

RULES MATTER

Many citizens take electoral rules for granted, allowing them to fade into the political background, where it is easy to overlook their powerful impact. Yet they affect everything that happens in elections, including the choices offered, the decisions voters make, the extent of participation, and who wins.

To demonstrate these and other points, it will help to use an imaginary example. Suppose that three candidates are running for office—Mr. Clean, Ms. True, and Mr. Macho. They are competing for the support of voters who, analysts say, can be grouped into three camps: Greens, Blues, and Khakis. Here is how the groups compare in size and in their rankings of the candidates:

Group	Size	Preference Ordering		
Greens	35	Clean	True	Macho
Blues	25	True	Clean	Macho
Khakis	40	Macho	True	Clean

Plurality Versus Majority Rule

The easiest point to demonstrate about electoral rules is that they can decide who wins. To most people, *democracy* means "majority rule," which they suppose simply requires that the candidate who receives more votes than any other should win. In fact, this criterion—which does govern most United States elections—is not majority rule but *plurality rule*. *Majority rule* means that the winner must have at least one vote more than half the total number cast. When there are only two candidates, the plurality and majority rules give the same result, but when there are three or more candidates, they often choose different winners.

Under plurality rule, if all groups vote for their first choice, Mr. Macho will win our fanciful election with 40 percent of the vote. Who would win under majority rule? No one! You can see immediately why we so often use the plurality criterion: *Majority rule does not guarantee a winner.* To ensure a majority, we must narrow the field to just two candidates. Often this is done by holding a second, *runoff* election; under the most common procedure, if no candidate receives fifty percent of the votes, the two top finishers in the first election advance to the runoff. In our example, the qualifiers would be Mr. Clean and Mr. Macho. How would they fare in the runoff? Clearly, Blues would join Greens in supporting Clean, so he would beat Macho, 65 to 35 percent. Thus with two different election rules—both seemingly "democratic"—we get contrary results.

So far we have assumed that voters cast ballots strictly in accord with their true preferences. But election rules also affect what people do in the voting booth. Suppose that before the election, opinion polls reveal the distribution of first-choice preferences. Plurality rule will tempt Blues to desert Ms. True because she cannot win and because by voting for their second choice, Mr. Clean, they can prevent a Macho victory. Theorists call this *insincere*, or *strategic*, voting—"insincere" because people are not voting for their true first choice; "strategic" because they are adjusting their plans in reaction to what they expect others will do. Such responses to the "wasted-vote" dilemma definitely occur among real voters. In the 1980 United States presidential election, third-party candidate John Anderson's support was as high as 29 percent in early polls, but on Election Day only 7 percent of voters actually marked ballots for him.[2] Some of Anderson's fall-off may have reflected changes in true preferences, but most of it probably resulted from strategic behavior based on voters' belief that he had no chance to win. In contrast, under the majority runoff system, the Blues would probably not abandon Ms. True in the first round because they would anticipate a second chance to defeat Mr. Macho in the runoff.[3]

Thus voters will behave differently under the two election rules. What about candidates? In both plurality and majority elections, Ms. True will realize—once polls give her the bad news— that she has no chance to win. To avoid the cost and frustration of a losing effort, she may decide to drop out of the race. This logic is probably the major reason why two-party systems are so persistent in countries where plurality elections predominate.

The chance that Ms. True will abandon the field is greater under plurality rule than in a majority runoff system. With a runoff, her supporters are more likely to vote sincerely in the first round, so if she wants to "send a message," she will not be embarrassed by a misleadingly low vote. Moreover, a good showing in the first round may enable her to win concessions from other candidates, if they believe her endorsement in the runoff will sway Blue voters.[4] From this example, you can see that majority runoff rules encourage the entry and persistence of more candidates or parties than do plurality systems, but by the second stage voters necessarily gather into two large coalitions. This has been the experience of France under the Fifth Republic, where a majority runoff system has grouped the numerous political parties into two camps—one socialist and communist, the other centrist and conservative.

Proportional Representation

Under either plurality or majority elections, large groups of voters will feel left out. If Macho wins, only the Khakis will be happy. If Clean prevails, the Greens will rejoice, but the Khakis will be miserable, and the Blues, only grudgingly satisfied. People often think majority and plurality rule unfair because the governments they produce represent only the winners rather than all the people. To avoid this supposedly undesirable result, many countries have adopted electoral systems based on proportional representation (PR).

Details of PR systems vary tremendously, but the essential idea is simple: Parties should be represented in government in proportion to the number of votes they win in elections.[5] To do this requires that voters choose an assembly rather than a single leader (such as a president) and (usually) that electoral constituencies be represented by more than one person. In the purest form of PR (approximated in Israel and in the Netherlands), the entire nation constitutes a single electoral district, and parties win legislative seats in close proportion to the number of votes they receive nationwide.

How would proportional representation affect our imaginary election? The objects of choice would probably become the Clean, True, and Macho parties rather than individual candidates. Minority parties will not be shut out of the legislature, so citizens have no obvious incentive to vote insincerely. Because no party expects a strategic dropoff in support and because their leaders are assured of seats in parliament, all parties will stay in the election.

So far, PR sounds pretty appealing. But another look at our example shows that it suffers from one major drawback. Under PR, the Macho party should win 40 percent of the seats, the Clean party 35 percent, and the True party 25 percent. But most legislatures operate by majority rule, so who will govern? If—as frequently happens under PR—no party wins an electoral majority, then parties must bargain with one another to form a coalition—an oftimes protracted process that can result in weak governments. Many PR systems—including Italy and the French Fourth Republic—have experienced chronic instability and frequent paralysis.[6]

Electoral Rules and the Extent of Participation

The impact of rules on the choices offered voters in turn affects their willingness to turn out to vote. In our example, if Ms. True carries on her crusade, Blues can cast futile votes for a sure loser or turn to a lesser-of-evils candidate. If True drops out, Blues have only the second option. In either event, their enthusiasm for voting will be diminished. In contrast, under PR, the True party will be in the race, and every vote it receives will give it a chance for more legislative seats. Voter enthusiasm under PR is also encouraged because parties tend to offer undiluted ideological or group appeals, whereas parties in plurality and majority systems tend to adopt similar positions (a phenomenon discussed at length later in this chapter). Under which system would you be more likely to vote? PR, of course—and evidence shows that most people think the same way. Median turnout in nine countries using PR is 87 percent compared with only 71 percent in seven presidential systems (which necessarily use plurality or majority rule).[7]

So far, we have seen that rules make a difference in sincerity of voting, decisiveness of elections, and extent of voter turnout. Unfortunately, none of the rules we have considered ranks best by all three criteria. Is there some other electoral system that would perform better? To seek an answer to this question, let us return to the first question we posed about electoral rules: How do they affect who wins? But now we also ask, who *should* win?

The Condorcet Criterion

Under plurality and majority-runoff rules, our example yields two different results. Which is preferable? Mr. Macho has the largest group of intense supporters, but everyone else dislikes him. Mr. Clean beats Macho in a one-on-one contest, so is it not more democratic that Clean win? But if we accept this test for the choice between Clean and Macho, should we not also accept it between *any* pair of candidates? In other words, should we not elect the candidate who can beat *all* the others one-on-one? If you agree, you are endorsing the criterion for democratic choice first established by the Marquis de Condorcet, a great French theorist of democracy who, ironically, died a prisoner of the French Revolution.[8]

To establish the Condorcet winner, we must run a round-robin series of elections between the three pairs of candidates. When you have done the calculations, you will discover a surprising result. Neither the plurality victor (Mr. Macho) nor the runoff-majority champion (Mr. Clean) can withstand the Condorcet test. Instead the Condorcet winner is the third candidate, Ms. True. She defeats Macho by a margin of sixty to forty and sweeps Clean sixty-five to thirty-five. What is True's secret? Although her core supporters, the Blues, are the smallest group, she is the second choice of everyone else. Thus her victory leaves no one terribly unhappy, whereas both Macho and Clean are worst choices for many voters.

The Condorcet Paradox

If the Condorcet criterion produces outcomes that make most voters reasonably satisfied, why do we almost never see elections that use the Condorcet procedure of pairwise choices? There are two reasons. First, the round robin can get extremely cumbersome because the number of pairs increases more rapidly than the number of candidates. In the 1981 New Jersey gubernatorial primary, Democratic voters had to choose among thirteen candidates, which means that there were seventy-eight possible pairs. (A somewhat less awkward way of getting the same information would be to ask each voter to rank-order all the candidates.)

The second problem is less obvious but more fundamental. To visualize it, let's diagram the results of our imaginary election. An arrow between two candidates indicates that the candidate at the tail of the arrow defeated in a pairwise election the candidate at the point.

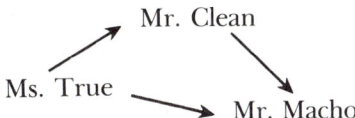

Note the clear ranking (or transitive ordering) among the candidates: True beats both Clean and Macho; Clean beats Macho; Macho beats no one. Now suppose the Greens reverse their preference between True and Macho so that they rank Macho second and True third. If you work out the Condorcet election again, you will find a new and perplexing result. Just as before, True defeats Clean, and Clean defeats Macho; but this time Macho wins over True. Here's the new diagram:

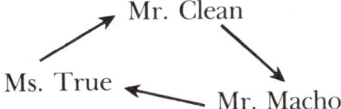

This electoral possibility is called a *cycle* or *Condorcet paradox*. You can imagine the confusion and endless disputes such an outcome would cause among voters. Thus the ultimate drawback to the Condorcet procedure is that *Condorcet winners do not always exist,* and when they do not (i.e., when there is a cycle), the procedure not only makes the presence of a cycle painfully obvious but also fails to produce any clear-cut winner. Thus the Condorcet procedure, like PR, sometimes fails the test of decisiveness.

Does the fact that plurality and majority-runoff rules are decisive mean they eliminate the possibility of cycles? No—they only hide cycles by making what seem to be definite choices between candidates. In fact, as Kenneth Arrow first proved, no democratic decision rule can preclude intransitive social choice.[9] If the underlying preference pattern is cyclic, the social choice will be unstable and manipulable, so whoever controls nominations controls the result. Thus, in our modified example, *any* winner can lose the next election if paired against the right opponent, even though voters' preferences remain constant.

This possibility of disequilibrium and arbitrary electoral choice greatly troubles some theorists. They forget that *the ultimate test of elections is not how logically they aggregate individual preferences but rather how persuasively they produce a social choice that all citizens will peacefully accept.*[10] We therefore need above all an election procedure that is decisive and avoids revealing the existence of cycles. At the same time, we would prefer a procedure that chooses the Condorcet winner when one exists. Are there any methods that show promise of accomplishing both goals? Of the many that have been suggested, two are especially interesting—one old and one new.

The Borda Method and Manipulation of Results

The Borda method is named for its inventor, Jean-Charles de Borda, who was a friend of Condorcet.[11] You may have used Borda's method in clubs or on committees, and baseball writers employ it to choose most-valuable players. Each voter ranks the n candidates in order of preference. The candidates then receive points according to how high they stand in the voter's ranking—usually $n - 1$ points for the highest ranking candidate, $n - 2$ for the second, and so on, down to zero for the least preferred. These scores are added up, and the candidate with the most points wins. To see how the Borda method works, try it out for our original configuration of preferences of Greens, Blues, and Khakis. You should get these results:

		Mr. Clean	Ms. True	Mr. Macho
Points from:	Greens	70	35	0
	Blues	25	50	0
	Khakis	0	40	80
Total Points		95	125	80

In this case, there is a Condorcet winner—Ms. True—and the Borda method does elect her. In fact, research shows that the Borda method performs quite well in selecting Condorcet winners a high percentage of the time (when they exist).[12] Yet when there is no Condorcet choice, the Borda method nevertheless produces a winner. (Try it for our cyclic example.) Is the Borda procedure then the perfect compromise? Not quite. Like the Condorcet procedure, the Borda method lacks simplicity—expressing preferences and calculating results gets complicated when there are many candidates or voters. This is one reason you may have encountered the Borda rule in small groups but almost surely not in large-scale elections, where it would be hard to administer.

The Borda method also suffers from a second, more fundamental weakness: It allows people to manipulate results too easily. In our original example, suppose the Greens realize that their favorite, Mr. Clean, is fated to lose a three-way Borda contest. They could introduce a fourth candidate, Mr. Clone, whose positions and appeal are almost identical to Mr. Clean's. If all voters insert Clone just below Clean in their preference orders, we obtain a new matrix of points:

	Clean	Clone	True	Macho
Greens	105	70	35	0
Blues	50	25	75	0
Khakis	40	0	80	120
Totals	195	95	190	120

Ms. True is still the Condorcet choice. (Run the pairwise elections if you doubt this.) But the entry of Clone tips the Borda count in favor of Clean. The Borda method is also vulnerable to another form of manipulation—the false reporting of preferences so that the strongest challenger to one's favorite loses points. Thus, in the example just given, the Blues might protect True by ranking Macho second, even though they really like him less than Clean. This would cost Clean fifty points, putting True back in the lead.

When the possibility of this strategy was brought to Borda's attention, he loftily replied, "My scheme is only intended for honest men."[13] Unfortunately, as James Madison wrote in *The Federalist Papers,* number 51, "If men were angels, no government would be necessary." Because the possibilities for manipulating Borda elections are too obvious, the method has few advocates in the rough-and-tumble world of real politics.

Approval Plurality Elections

In the late 1970s a number of people independently invented a new way of voting—the *approval ballot*.[14] This method allows each voter to vote for (or approve) as many candidates as he wishes. Unlike the Borda method, the approval ballot counts each vote equally—making no distinction between first and second or third choices. In two-person races, voters would presumably approve only one candidate, because to vote for both is tantamount to not voting at all. But in multicandidate races, the approval ballot enables voters to escape from the strategic dilemma of whether to desert their first-choice candidate. In our example, the Blues would no longer feel torn between loyalty for Ms. True and worry about wasting their votes. Instead, they could vote for her *and* for their second choice, Mr. Clean.

In principle, the approval ballot might be combined with numerous decision rules, including plurality, majority-runoff, and proportional representation; but most analysts concentrate on the approval plurality combination. Many believe it compares favorably with other electoral systems according to all six of the criteria we have used:

> —*Decisiveness:* Like the Borda and single-vote plurality methods, approval plurality guarantees a winner—something that PR and the Condorcet procedure cannot promise.

—*Simplicity:* Unlike the Condorcet and Borda methods, the approval plurality system should be easy to administer, even with numerous candidates or voters. As a one-stage method, it also avoids the extra effort of runoff elections.

—*Sincerity:* Under approval plurality, a rational voter never has an incentive to abandon her first-choice candidate. This is a great advantage over the single-vote plurality system, which so often places the voter in a strategic dilemma.

—*Selecting Condorcet Winners:* Even when Condorcet choices exist, approval plurality does not guarantee their victory. Nevertheless, theoretical analyses and simulations indicate that they have as good or better a chance of winning under approval plurality than under single-vote plurality or majority runoff.[15] You can get an idea of why this is so from our example, in which True is the Condorcet choice. First, the approval ballot's encouragement of sincere voting means that she will hold the support of all twenty-five Blues. Second, many Greens and Khakis may approve her also if they strongly prefer her to their third-ranking candidates. If enough of them do. she will emerge with more votes than either Clean or Macho.

—*Manipulability:* In contrast to the Borda method, single-vote plurality, and majority runoff, entry of candidates appears unlikely to affect who wins under approval plurality unless a new candidate can beat the previous winner one-on-one. This is perhaps the strongest argument for approval plurality as an electoral reform in the United States, where crowded fields of candidates have become common in primaries and nonpartisan elections. In addition, the encouragement approval plurality gives to sincere voting for first-choice candidates protects it more than some other systems against the second type of manipulation, strategic voting.[16]

—*Participation:* Because approval plurality enables voters to avoid dilemmas about "wasting" votes and deciding between equally valued candidates, it might promote greater turnout than single-vote plurality and majority-runoff systems, though it would probably not boost turnout as much as PR does.

Although approval plurality does not score perfectly on every criterion, taken together our six tests give it higher marks than any other electoral system we have considered.[17] These judgments are, however, based mostly on theory rather than experience. Until some jurisdiction is bold enough to try out the new method, we cannot be sure how voters, candidates, and parties will react to it. Thus we have a long way to go before we know whether approval plurality will fulfill or deserve to fulfill the prediction of one advocate, who sees it as "the election reform of the twentieth century."[18]

Despite the intriguing qualities of the approval ballot, the purpose of this section has been less to introduce that reform than to sensitize you to how rules, preferences, and strategies combine to affect the results of participation in any electoral situation. That understanding may help you avoid becoming a victim of poor rules or clever manipulation. In addition, concepts you have met here will be useful as we establish the second major lesson of this chapter: Elections make a difference even when it seems they do not.

ELECTIONS MATTER

If you have ever done any political canvassing, you have surely met people who say, "Why should I vote? Elections don't make any difference anyway." (Or perhaps you have used this excuse to justify your own inactivity.) Some people who say this really mean, "*My vote* won't make any difference," a claim that is usually true in large-scale elections (as we saw in Chapter 3).[19] But many others simply do not believe that it matters *who wins* the election. Paradoxically, they may be right—but only *because* elections have a powerful effect. To put it another way, when democracy works well, elections *seem* not to matter. Let us explore three reasons for this.

Anticipating Passionate Majorities

Elections appear meaningful to most voters only when candidates offer them a clear choice between conflicting policies. Politicians know, however, that there are some policies they cannot advocate without committing political suicide. Specifically, they will not knowingly take a stand contrary to the desires of a *passionate majority* of voters. Frohlich and Oppenheimer explain the logic behind this conclusion:

> The defining characteristic of a passionate majority issue is that people on the majority side . . . won't trade their vote . . . on this (most important issue) for victory on the other issues. It follows that any politician who takes a minority stand on a passionate majority issue would lose to an opponent who took the majority stand on that issue. Thus, on any passionate majority issue, no win–oriented politician should be expected to espouse the minority position. Therefore, issues which a majority feel most strongly about would never enter into the electoral arena because political contenders would never find it worthwhile taking opposing positions on those issues. . . . *Passionate majority issues are protected by the democratic process, per se, without the necessity of constant contention in the electoral arena.*[20]

How do politicians know which positions are protected by a passionate majority? They don't know for sure, but their careers depend on skill in anticipating the reactions of voters. As long as politicians anticipate successfully, passionate majorities remain sleeping giants. Only when a politician makes a mistake or puts principle ahead of political survival does it become obvious that elections enable passionate majorities to rule.[21]

A vivid illustration of this principle occurred in a 1958 Arkansas congressional election. Through the 1950s almost all southern politicians supported the passionate (white) majority insistence on racial segregation. For this reason, among others, voters often showed little interest in congressional elections, and incumbents sometimes ran unopposed. As the 1958 election approached, Brooks Hays, a popular Little Rock congressman, was in this enviable position.

However, when President Eisenhower used troops to enforce a court order desegregating public schools in Little Rock, Hays courageously tried to mediate the crisis, making evident to all that his personal attitudes about race were moderate. Amid an extraordinary surge of public interest, the segregationist majority turned against Hays, and he was defeated by a write-in opponent.[22]

The Hays story shows that democratic rule is not always morally virtuous. (Note, however, that segregationist politics thrived in the South only so long as most blacks were kept from the polls. After the 1965 Voting Rights Act ended electoral discrimination, a new majority emerged, and racial moderation became almost essential for political success in the region.) But whether or not we like the results, the fact that elections force officials to anticipate and submit to passionate majorities greatly limits their ability to do as they might like. Were it not for this invisible effect of elections, many public policies might depart much further from popular desires.

Performance Accountability

Quite understandably, voters are most predictably passionate in demanding that governments protect their lives and livelihoods. Because promises can never substitute for a proven record of preserving peace and prosperity, national elections usually hinge on the economic and foreign-policy performance of the people in power.[23] As a result, electoral campaigns typically seem to consist mainly of incumbents claiming credit for every favorable development, their opponents blaming them for every misfortune, and both sides abusing statistics as they squabble about whether we really "never had it so good." Although writers of civics texts and editorials complain about inattention to "the issues," such petty, boring electioneering pays tribute to one crucial fact—*elections create a powerful incentive for rulers to please the ruled*—in their performance in office, if not in their debates.

As with anticipated reactions generally, evidence about how this influence works depends on the occurrence of "mistakes"— performance that fails to meet popular demands because the incumbent either could not control events or chose a course that he or she judged best for the country despite its unpopularity. Between 1948 and 1984, four incumbent presidents eligible for reelection did not return to office. Truman in 1952 and Johnson in 1968 refused to run again after they became mired in unpopular wars (Korea and Vietnam) that earned them extremely low poll ratings. Ford in 1976 and Carter in 1980 lost bids for reelection after terms in which the economy did badly. Adjusted for inflation, median family income fell almost 2 percent during the Nixon-Ford term and about 3 percent during the Carter administration. (Median male income dropped 7 percent and 8 percent, respectively.)[24] In contrast, four other incumbents (Eisenhower, Johnson, Nixon, and Reagan) ran for reelection and won. All had succeeded in raising real median incomes.

How elections affect official performance becomes easier to see because voters have short memories. Instead of evaluating an incumbent's performance during an entire term, they seem to give extra weight to recent events. "What have you done for us *lately*?" is their motto. Politicians understand this, so most of them try to make the economy boom just before elections. Between 1959 and 1976, six of the seven largest industrial democracies (including the United States) experienced election-year GNP growth rates that were nearly double the rates of nonelection years.[25] Conversely, administrations that want to cool down the economy generally do so immediately after elections. As a result, economic fluctuations tend to follow the electoral calendar. The pattern is so well known that it has a name—the *political business cycle.*

Again, the occurrence of a "mistake" proves the rule. Under President Jimmy Carter, the economy followed the opposite pattern. Unemployment fell and income rose during his first two years in office, but in 1979 and 1980, the economy went into a tailspin. This reversal of form may have resulted from events beyond any president's control (the Iranian oil embargo and OPEC oil price increases); but Carter's popularity suffered nonetheless, and he lost the White House to Ronald Reagan. During President Reagan's first term, the political business cycle reappeared. In 1981 and 1982, median real income fell, and unemployment rose to the highest levels since the Depression; but 1983 and 1984 were years of buoyant growth, and Reagan won reelection in a landslide.

Convergence on Position Issues

Peace and prosperity allow little room for disagreement—nearly everyone favors them. Politicians used to call such questions "motherhood" issues, but as the abortion controversy has made motherhood controversial, we must resort to the technical term *valence issue*, which means a "condition that is positively or negatively valued by the electorate."[26] Not all issues are so one-sided. On many policies, called *position issues*, voters' preferred outcomes differ across a range of alternatives. For such questions, surely we can expect elections to stimulate conflict and meaningful choice, can't we?

On the contrary. Plurality and majority-rule electoral systems create pressures on candidates to take similar stands on any position issue that is foremost in the minds of most voters. Figure 8–1 shows why. The horizontal axis represents possible positions on the issue. You can think of them as ranging from extremely liberal on the left to extremely conservative on the right. More concretely, this scale might stand for the extent to which government policies should favor low-income people (on the left) or the affluent (on the right). The vertical axis counts voters; thus the graph represents the relative numbers of voters who consider each possible policy position ideal. Analyses of this sort are called *spatial models.* They became influential in political science chiefly as a result of the work of Anthony Downs.[27]

FIGURE 8–1 Party Convergence

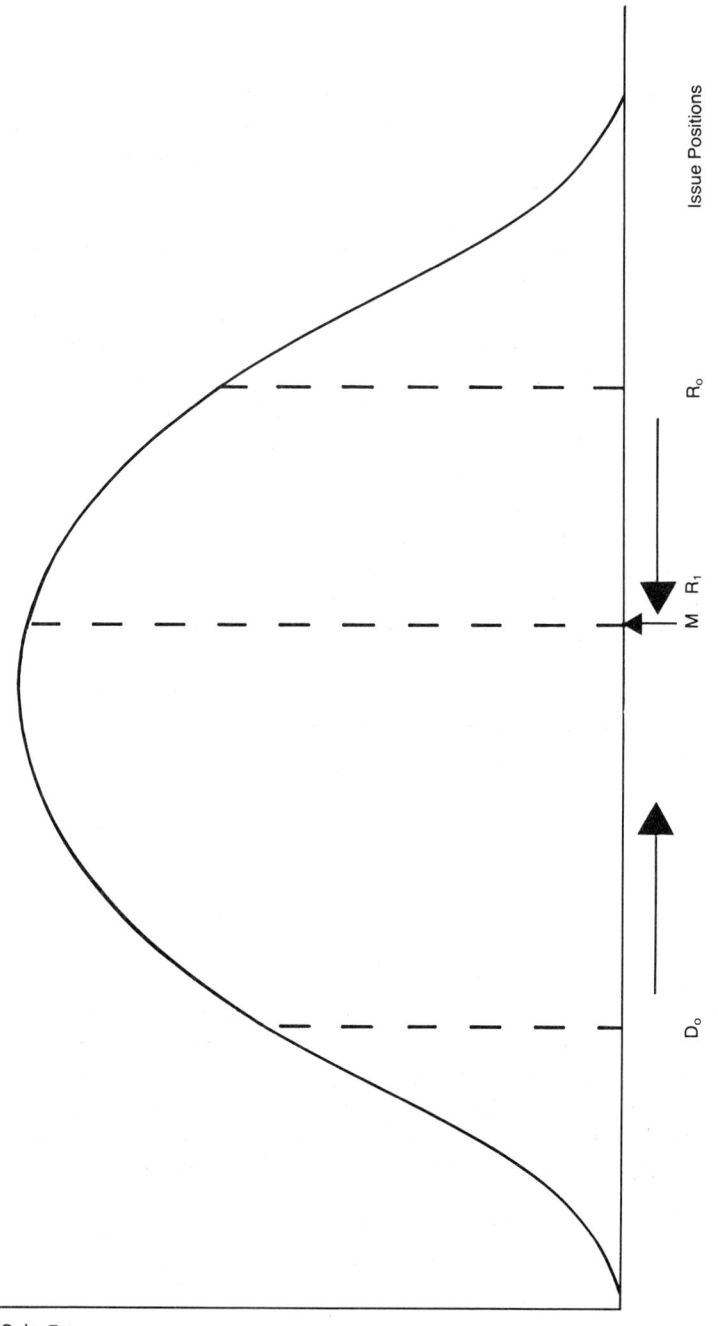

Suppose that the contending candidates (or parties) offer voters a distinct choice by advocating policies D_0 and R_0. Assume also that each citizen votes for the party whose policy is closer to her ideal point. If candidate D (a Democrat) stays at D_0, candidate R (a Republican) can win a big majority by attracting votes from centrist voters with a move to R_1. True, R's new position will be less satisfactory to voters on the extreme right, but they are less numerous than the moderates and they have nowhere else to go. (They can abstain in disgust or vote for a third-party candidate. Under plurality or majority rule, the third party has no chance for success, so the two responses are equivalent except that voting for a protest candidate sends a clearer message.) This is approximately what happened in 1972, when George McGovern's sharply liberal policies helped cause a debacle for the Democrats. Similarly, reversing the parties' strategies, Barry Goldwater's determination to offer "a choice, not an echo" enabled Lyndon Johnson to capture the center and a landslide victory in 1964.

To avoid such disasters, Downs argues, practical politicians will normally converge toward the center. More precisely, if there are only two candidates, their best strategy is to espouse the position favored by the *median voter*—that lucky person located at M, with equal numbers of fellow citizens to the left and to the right.[28] This tendency toward *convergence* on position issues maddens ideologues at both extremes, who decry it as "me-tooism," or "a choice between Tweedledum and Tweedledee." Many political scientists have also thought that convergence renders electoral choice meaningless.[29] But in fact, it can be shown that *the median voter's position is the Condorcet choice.*[30] Therefore, parties that do not offer this centrist choice actually subvert majority rule! To get an intuitive sense of this claim, suppose the parties adopt positions D_0 and R_0. Then no matter which wins, large numbers of voters will be dissatisfied because the policies they like best are a long way from either party's position. In contrast, position M minimizes the aggregate distance between the chosen policy and voters' ideal points. It thus yields the greatest happiness (or least unhappiness) for the electorate as a whole.

Implications for Participation

Let's step back a moment to take stock. We've seen that, in two-candidate elections under plurality rule, skilled politicians whose main goal is to win will:

—take similar stands on issues about which a majority might become passionate;
—if already in office, try hard to convince voters they have delivered the goods on valence issues; and
—converge toward the median on any position issue that is a dominant concern to most voters.

What then is left for citizens to vote about? No wonder their choices seem so often to hinge on traditional party loyalties, the attractiveness of candidates' personalities, or the emotional appeal of thirty-second television ads. And no wonder also that so many voters think elections matter so little that they do not bother to participate. But we now know, paradoxically, that elections appear to matter least when they actually are working best—pressuring politicians to perform satisfactorily and inducing them to adopt policy positions that conform to majority desires. As Downs observes, "rational behavior by political parties tends to discourage rational behavior by voters."[31] In an effective democracy, it is not the futility but the power of electoral participation that weakens the incentive to participate.

PARTICIPATION MATTERS

Downs's paradox may leave you feeling less cynical about elections but no less apathetic about voting in them. If competition induces candidates to offer similar policies, do citizens have any reason to participate other than their sense of obligation to preserve a democratic process that seems to work almost too well? The answer is yes, because the forces toward consensus and convergence are far from all-powerful. Offsetting them are three processes that give great advantages to groups who participate more extensively or intensively. First, activists within parties exert influences that pull platforms apart. Second, which policies will satisfy a majority depends on the preferences of those citizens who actually vote, and they may differ noticeably from the population as a whole. Third, passionate minorities can exploit the electoral process to control their favorite issues.

Activism and Intraparty Democracy

If you know the history of modern presidential elections, you have probably noticed that the Downsian model of convergent platforms no longer fits reality as well as it once did. From 1940 through 1960, elections conformed rather closely to the pattern. But from 1964 to 1984, obvious ideological gaps opened between the contenders on at least four occasions—1964, 1972, 1980, and 1984. Why did the parties not converge?

The Downs model assumes that parties and candidates treat policies only as a means to their real goal, which is to win office. This premise had more validity when professional politicians controlled party organizations that consisted largely of obedient patronage employees. By the mid-twentieth century, however, civil service and other reforms depleted the resources that had enabled traditional party machines to reward loyal workers. Simultaneously, the rapidly increasing ranks of well-educated citizens created within parties a rival force of amateur politicians, volunteers whose contributions of money and effort depend not on material payoffs but on enthusiastic commitment to candidates' policies.[32]

These activists extended the ideals of democracy and participation from general elections to internal party processes, especially the nomination of candidates. Choices formerly reached by bargaining among a handful of leaders (who, of course, always met in smoke-filled rooms) came to be determined instead in the open sunshine (and rain and snow) of interminable campaigns centered on primaries and caucuses open to all party members.

Party members, however, constitute only a part of the general electorate; those who bother to vote in primaries or attend caucuses are a still-smaller group; and activists who work intensively on behalf of candidates are even fewer. In accordance with Chapter 5's Rule 2, these successively smaller groups tend to be successively less representative of the population as a whole. Nevertheless, politicians who want to be nominated must adopt policy positions that please the activists. The policies best able to galvanize amateurs vary from election to election, but in general, Democratic activists are ideological liberals, and Republicans ideological conservatives.

The resulting situation is depicted in Figure 8–2. The internal politics of the two parties are dominated by the populations represented by the smaller curves on the left and right. To win nomination, we might suppose, candidates will have to position themselves near the medians within their parties, M_d and M_r. But to win the general election, the most advantageous position is at M, the median for the entire electorate.[33]

Thus every candidate must seek to win in two different electoral phases by responding to two distinct electorates. The issue positions that succeed among activists during the nomination phase tend to produce candidates who are far apart ideologically. During the general election, these divergent positions become a liability, as the nominees must respond to the centripetal pull of the larger electorate. But the candidates' ability to converge toward the general median is severely limited—sometimes by the sincere convictions that first made them attractive to party ideologues; often by the embarrassment of appearing inconsistent; and always by the fear of losing activists' indispensable financial and organizational support.

What do party militants gain in return? When Senators Goldwater and McGovern suffered overwhelming losses, it appeared that ideologues' victories within their parties merely guaranteed them defeat in November. Some activists in each party learned from these debacles that they should back centrist politicians such as Richard Nixon and Jimmy Carter, who compensated for ideological imperfection by offering more realistic prospects of winning.

In 1980, however, issue-oriented conservatives of the Republican right—for decades the largest and most persistent category of activists in the United States—achieved a satisfying triumph when they came to power behind Ronald Reagan, who had succeeded Barry Goldwater as leader of the ideological wing of the Republican party.[34] Would not the median-voter model predict the defeat of a candidate such as Reagan? Yes, but not if either (or both) of two conditions obtain: (1) A valence issue such as economic prosperity (or lack thereof) is more salient in voters' minds than the position issue of general ideological stance. As we have seen, the economy worked very much in Reagan's favor both in 1980 and in 1984. (2) The opposing party also fails to

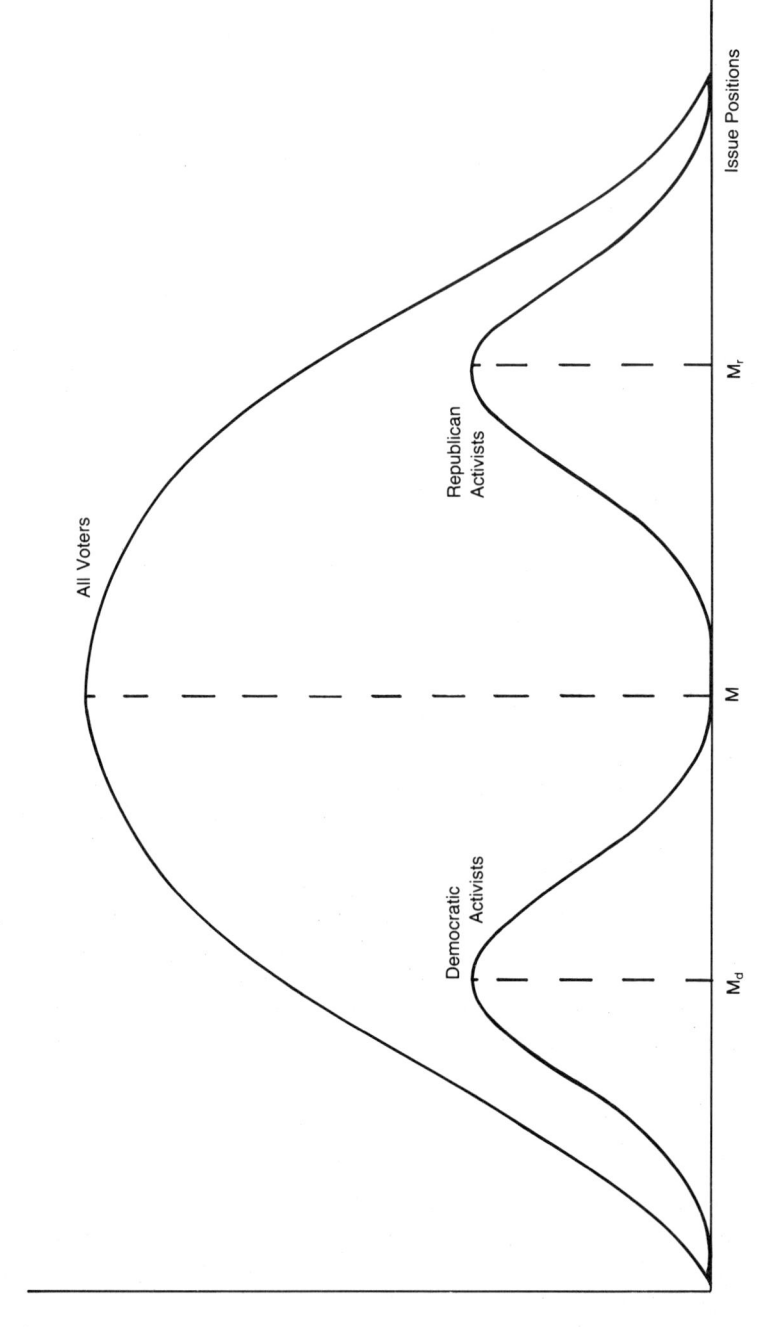

FIGURE 8-2 How Activitists Pull Parties Apart

take a position near the median. Walter Mondale in 1984 and (to a lesser extent) President Carter in 1980 were both pulled to the left by pressures from the most active constituencies of the Democratic party. In this way, the militants of both parties exist in high-risk symbiosis with each other. Each group has a better chance to win if the other succeeds in pulling its party away from the center; but each then makes an all-or-nothing gamble, for when Republican conservatives capture the White House, Democrats of the left lose much more than they would under the rule of Republican moderates, and vice versa.

The Reagan victories show that people who participate intensively in political campaigns can win disproportionate influence. But notice that a price is paid for the participatory nomination process. If neither party occupies the position favored by the median voters of the general electorate, then the ideal majoritarian outcome—the Condorcet choice—cannot prevail. Intraparty democracy triumphs at the expense of interparty democracy.

Majority Rule Depends on Who Votes

Despite the disproportionate influence of activists, which party and which policies will win still depends on who votes in the general election. Citizens who come to the polls therefore have an advantage over those who do not. For reasons explained in Chapter 5, better-educated people, who also tend to be more prosperous, vote at higher rates than the less educated and less affluent. Although weaker for voting than other forms of political action, such class bias exists at the polls except when offset by legal compulsion, group consciousness, or party mobilization. These equalizing forces have always been feebler in the United States than in other industrialized democracies, and in recent decades they have declined even further. Between 1964 and 1980, voters became a substantially more prosperous group than the population as a whole, as is shown in Figure 8–3, which charts the course of class bias in voting turnout.

Note that the Republican candidate won in each of the five years when class bias in turnout was greatest; conversely, in the three years when class bias was least, the Democrats won. Thus members of each economic stratum are rewarded for voting at high rates (compared with the other stratum) by the victory of the party more likely to pursue economic policies in their favor. Among the outcomes that vary according to which side holds power are unemployment, inflation, size of the public sector, level of personal income taxes, and extent of economic inequality.[35] In other words, although each party may attempt to please a majority of voters, *who constitutes the majority depends on who turns out to vote.* The opposing forces exerted on the two parties by their core activists, contributors, and loyalists mean that each is better suited to appeal to a different popular majority. The Democrats have an advantage when less prosperous people vote more nearly in proportion to their numbers. The Republicans win when voting turnout is strongly skewed toward the affluent.

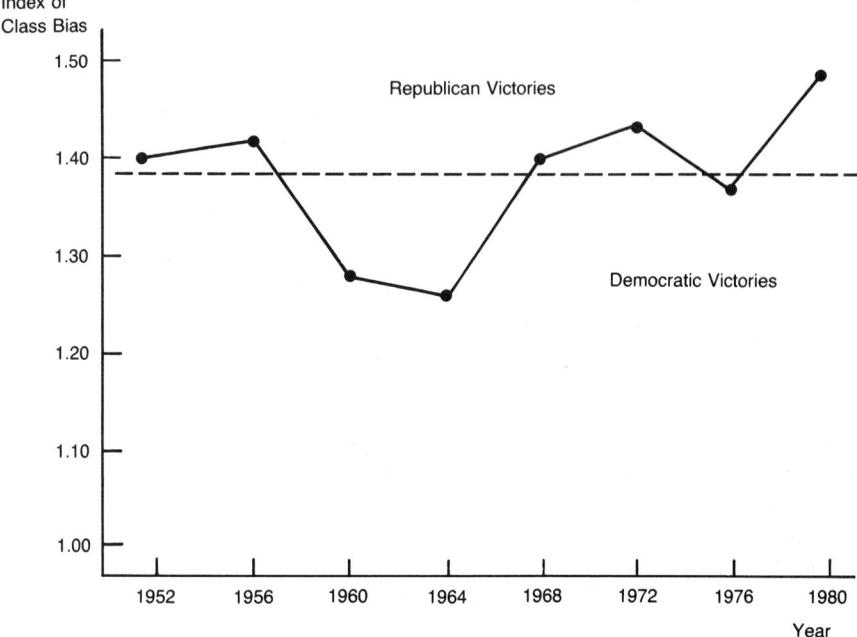

FIGURE 8-3 Class Bias in U.S. Voting Turnout, 1952–1980.

SOURCES: 1952–76: Thomas E. Cavanagh, "Changes in American Voter Turnout, 1964–1976," *Political Science Quarterly*, 96 (1981), 16; 1980: estimated from data in U.S. Bureau of the Census, *Current Population Reports*, Series P-23, no. 126 (1983), p. 16.

NOTE: The index is the ratio of voting turnout among citizens whose family incomes are in the top third to turnout among citizens whose family incomes are in the bottom third.

Figure 8–4 should help you visualize the difference between the two majorities. The figure is laid out in the same way as the spatial models presented earlier, but here the diagram is based on real data. Instead of representing ideology, the horizontal axis represents income, which is the main determinant of preferences for major economic policies, including the tradeoff between unemployment and inflation, the amount of government spending for domestic purposes, and the extent of equalization achieved through taxing and spending.[36] The upper graph shows the percentage of the population who occupied each thousand-dollar interval of income in 1980.[37] The shaded lower portion of the figure represents citizens who say they voted in that year. The white space between this area and the top graph indicates the percentage at each income interval who say they did not vote.

You can easily see that voters came disproportionately from higher-income groups. As a result, the median income of voters was more than $2,300 more than the median income for the entire population.[38] Even more striking is the fact that the distribution of voters is bimodal—contrary both to the usual assumption in spatial models and to common beliefs about United States

Figure 8–4 The Income of Voters and Nonvoters in 1980.

SOURCE: U.S. Bureau of the Census, *Current Population Reports*, Series P-20, No. 370 (1982), p. 66.

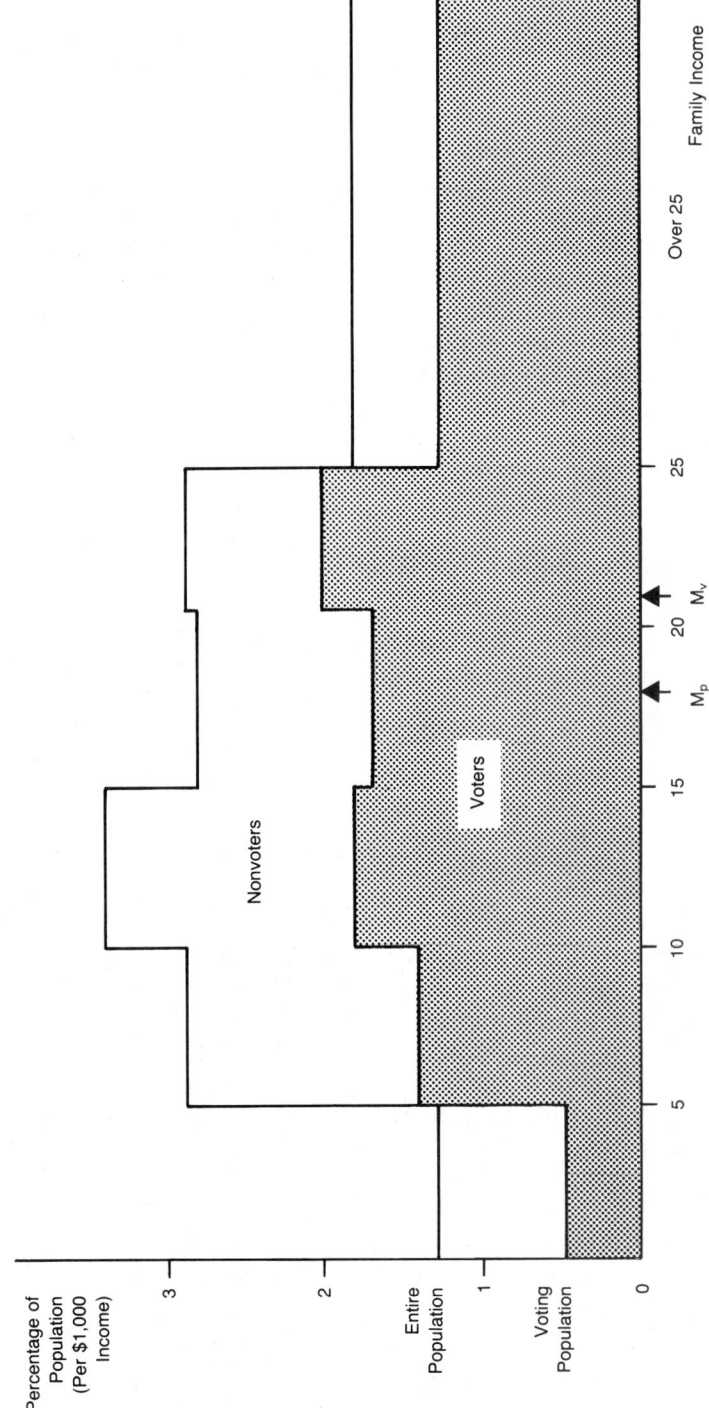

politics. As noted earlier, Downs predicts that parties will not converge if the preference distribution is bimodal and extremists are willing to abstain.[39]

In 1980 (and probably in 1984 as well), both conditions appear to have been met. (The influence of activists appears equivalent to Downs's abstention condition. Even when activists themselves faithfully vote, the extent of their enthusiasm certainly affects turnout among the less reliable voters whom they influence.) The existence of bimodality therefore helps explain why the two parties advocated strikingly different political philosophies in these two contests. The distribution of voters also makes apparent the Republicans' advantage. Democrats stayed to the left of center in part because they hoped to mobilize the larger mode at the low-income side of the *population* distribution. But their courtship of the poor was unrequited. Among *voters* in 1980, the larger mode was on the affluent side. Many commentators interpreted the Reagan victories of 1980 and 1984 as a sign that the people had turned conservative. Survey evidence indicates they did not.[40] The data in Figures 8–3 and 8–4 suggest that trends in political participation alone accounted for much of the change.[41]

Rule by Passionate Minorities

So far we have been preoccupied with whether majority preferences will prevail in elections. This is a natural concern, because, of all the institutions of government, elections involve the broadest participation, so we might expect that the influence of majorities depends mainly on votes. Nevertheless, elections also enable minorities to rule over some issues. How can this happen? Vote-seeking politicians will heed the demands of a minority if they believe its members are willing in larger numbers than their opponents to vote according to candidates' stands on a single issue, regardless of their positions or performance in any other area.

An example of a passionate minority in United States politics is the anti-abortion (or "pro-life") movement that sprang up after 1973, when the Supreme Court struck down state laws that had outlawed abortion except when necessary to save the mother's life. In 1976 (and annually thereafter), the movement persuaded Congress to pass the Hyde amendment, which severely restricted the use of federal money to pay for abortions. In 1980 pro-lifers defeated four of six pro-choice senators they had targetted.[42] In view of such success, one might think that the pro-life movement had overwhelming popular support; but instead polls during this period indicated that 50 to 90 percent of Americans approved of permitting abortions under a much wider range of circumstances than the pro-lifers were willing to tolerate.[43] The power of the anti-abortion movement depended on its supporters' willingness to make abortion the only issue on which they based their votes, an attitude that a pro-life activist justified in these words: "Anybody that would go for taking the life of little ones is not going to look out for my interests in anything else either."[44]

In contrast, to the electorate as a whole in 1976, abortion ranked in importance nineteenth of twenty issues.[45]

Is the rule of a passionate minority good or bad from the viewpoint of democratic theory? The answer depends partly on the attitude of the less-intense majority. Sometimes the majority actually sympathizes with the minority, though they probably would not let their votes be determined solely by the minority's issue. United States support for Israel is approved by most of the public but insisted upon by Jewish Americans (who constitute 2.6 percent of the population but a larger proportion of voters). Similarly, the triumph of a passionate minority over a majority who have no preference at all is perfectly consistent with democracy. Theorists are more divided about whether a passionate minority should prevail over an opposed, but less intense, majority. Some believe that a prevailing pattern of "minorities rule" is a serious political problem in the United States.[46]

There is no question that factional pressure groups have great strength in the policymaking process generally, but how much of their influence results from voting, as opposed to nonelectoral efforts such as lobbying and litigating? It can be shown that a winning coalition-of-minorities strategy *must* exist unless the majority of voters decide on the basis of a single issue or a single ideology. Consequently, some analysts believe that elections typically give power over specific policies to narrow segments of the electorate.[47] Although there can be no doubt that winning candidates often cater to intense minorities, I am more impressed by the tendency of general elections to push politicians toward widely shared concerns and majority positions. Citizens preoccupied with particular interests achieve their greatest advantages less from elections than from the other forms of participation to which we turn in Chapters 9 and 10.

NOTES

1. Benjamin R. Barber, *Strong Democracy: Participatory Politics for a New Age* (Berkeley: University of California Press, 1984), p. 188.

2. Steven J. Brams and Peter C. Fishburn, *Approval Voting* (Boston: Birkhauser, 1983), pp. 162–63.

3. Do not conclude from this case that runoff systems *generally* stimulate less strategic voting. It is easy to think of examples where majority rule encourages much more insidious strategic behavior.

4. Of course, if Blues vote strictly according to their original preference ordering, they will turn to Clean. Such predictable behavior would obviously reduce True's personal bargaining power.

5. The description that follows is based on the list system of PR rather than on the less-common and more-complicated single-transferable-vote method. For more information about PR systems, see Vernon Bogdanor and David Butler, eds., *Democracy and Elections: Electoral Systems and Their Political Consequences* (New York: Cambridge University Press, 1983); and Arend Lijphart and Bernard Grofman, eds., *Choosing an Electoral System: Issues and Alternatives* (New York: Praeger, 1984).

6. Another objection is that pure PR enables small extremist parties to gain a foothold in the legislature. During the German Weimar Republic, PR gave Adolph Hitler's Nazi Party a few seats in the Reichstag, which enabled it to expand rapidly when the inability of the Weimar system to deal

with the Depression made Germans desperate for change. The Nazis would probably not have survived in a plurality system. This disastrous experience persuaded West Germany to require that parties win at least 5 percent of votes nationally to qualify for seats allocated by proportional representation.

7. G. Bingham Powell, Jr., *Contemporary Democracies: Participation, Stability, and Violence* (Cambridge: Harvard University Press, 1982), pp. 61–62, 70.

8. For a fascinating history of Condorcet and his criterion, see Duncan Black, *The Theory of Committees and Elections* (Cambridge: Cambridge University Press, 1958).

9. *Social Choice and Individual Values*, 2nd ed. (New York: John Wiley and Sons, 1963).

10. For an outstanding article that keeps straight the difference between political and logical stability, see Nicholas R. Miller, "Pluralism and Social Choice," *American Political Science Review*, 77 (1983), 734–47.

11. On the relations between their ideas, see Black, *Theory of Committees and Elections*.

12. See, for example, Samuel Merrill III, "A Comparison of Efficiency of Multicandidate Electoral Systems," *American Journal of Political Science*, 28 (1984), 23–48.

13. Black, *Theory of Committees and Elections*, p. 182.

14. For a brief history, see Brams and Fishburn, *Approval Voting*, pp. xi–xiv.

15. Ibid., chap. 3; Merrill, "A Comparison of Efficiency," passim.

16. The approval ballot seems less immune to this sort of manipulation when combined with majority runoff or other two-stage decision procedures. Brams and Fishburn, *Approval Voting*, pp. 40–71; Samuel Merrill III and Jack Nagel, "The Effect of Approval Balloting on Strategic Voting Unde Alternative Decision Rules", American Political Science Review (forthcoming). In addition, approval plurality might encourage proliferation of parties. For this reason, I advocate its use only in elections not currently dominated by two parties—specifically, primaries and nonpartisan elections.

17. For similar conclusions based on more technical and comprehensive analyses, see Hannu Nurmi, "Voting Procedures: A Summary Analysis," *British Journal of Political Science*, 13 (1983), 181–208; Samuel Merrill III, "Approval Voting: A 'Best Buy' Method for Multicandidate Elections?" *Mathematics Magazine*, 52 (1979), 98–102; and Brams and Fishburn, *Approval Voting*, pp. 1–14, 171–72.

18. The advocate is Steven J. Brams. For an account of the first (albeit unofficial) use of the approval ballot in American politics, see Jack Nagel, "A Debut for Approval Voting," *PS*, 17 (Winter 1984), 62–65.

19. Sometimes every vote counts even in a fairly large election. I once worked in a primary for a state legislative seat that ended in a flat tie. The election board called for a rematch, from which one candidate emerged just six votes ahead of his opponent. Having survived that cliffhanger, the winner eventually went on to become speaker of the Connecticut House of Representatives.

20. *Modern Political Economy* (Englewood Cliffs, N.J.: Prentice-Hall, 1978), pp. 137–38; emphasis in the original. As we'll see later, politicians can profitably defy *weakly* felt majority preferences.

21. For general analyses of detecting rule by anticipated reactions, see Herbert A. Simon, "Notes on the Observation and Measurement of Political Power," chap. 4 in his *Models of Man* (New York: John Wiley and Sons, 1957); and Jack H. Nagel, *The Descriptive Analysis of Power* (New Haven: Yale University Press, 1975), passim.

22. Warren E. Miller and Donald E. Stokes, "Constituency Influence in Congress," *American Political Science Review*, 57 (1963), 45–56.

23. Political scientists call this retrospective (as opposed to prospective) voting. See Morris P. Fiorina, *Retrospective Voting in American National Elections* (New Haven: Yale University Press, 1981), especially chaps. 1 and 10.

24. Calculated from U.S. Bureau of the Census, Current Population Reports, Series P-60, No. 137, *Money Income of Households, Families, and Persons in the United States: 1981* (Washington: Government Printing Office, 1983).

25. Edward R. Tufte, *Political Control of the Economy* (Princeton: Princeton University Press, 1978), chap. 3.

26. Donald Stokes, "Spatial Models of Party Competition," *American Political Science Review*, 57 (1963), 368–77.

27. *An Economic Theory of Democracy* (New York: Harper & Row, 1957). See also Frohlich and Oppenheimer, *Modern Political Economy*, pp. 120–24; and William H. Riker and Peter C. Ordeshook, *An Introduction to Positive Political Theory* (Englewood Cliffs, N.J.: Prentice-Hall, 1973), chaps. 11 and 12.

28. Downs predicts that convergence will not occur if the distribution of voters is bimodal and extremist voters are willing to abstain rather than vote for a centrist. *An Economic Theory of Democracy*, pp. 118–20. Although I have used a symmetric, unimodal distribution for the sake of simplicity, I show below that the United States electorate is actually bimodal and skewed to the right.

29. In 1950, an official committee of the American Political Science Association called for changes in the party system designed "to keep the parties apart" so that voters could be assured a real choice. APSA Committee on Political Parties, "Toward a More Responsible Two-Party System," *American Political Science Review*, 44: Supplement (1950), p. 1.

30. Black, *Theory of Committees and Elections*, p. 16. Black's result requires that all voters have "single-peaked" preferences—that is, that their rankings of policies fall off steadily on either side of their ideal points. If this condition is met, there is always a Condorcet choice, and it is the median optimum.

31. *An Economic Theory of Democracy*, p. 136. For evidence of this effect, see John F. Zipp, "Perceived Representativeness and Voting: An Assessment of the Impact of 'Choices' and 'Echoes,'" *American Political Science Review*, 79 (1985), 50–61.

32. For an early comparison of amateur and professional politicians that remains highly instructive, see James Q. Wilson, *The Amateur Democrat: Club Politics in Three Cities* (Chicago: University of Chicago Press, 1962).

33. Actually, nominees sometimes diverge from the median within their own parties because multicandidate fields allow narrowly factional candidates to win. The approval-plurality voting method is designed in part to overcome this problem.

34. Research revealed the strength of the participatory right even in the late 1960s, when liberal and radical movements received far more attention from the media. Sidney Verba and Norman Nie, *Participation in America: Political Democracy and Social Equality* (New York: Harper & Row, 1972), chap. 12.

35. Powell, *Contemporary Democracies*, pp. 186–200; Tufte, *Political Control of the Economy*, chap. 4. Powell and Tufte find similar differences between leftist and rightist governments in other democracies.

36. Tufte, *Political Control of the Economy*, pp. 83–88; Douglas A. Hibbs, Jr., "Political Parties and Macroeconomic Policy," *American Political Science Review*, 71 (1977), 1467–87.

37. I have spread out the data from their original grouping by the census in intervals of $5,000. I also treat families with income over $25,000 as if they were equally dispersed across the interval between $25,000 and $40,000. A more precise depiction of the income distribution would have a long, gradually diminishing tail extending far above $40,000.

38. Specifically, I estimate the medians were $20,698 and $18,267.

39. *Economic Theory of Democracy*, pp. 118–20. For later results that partially agree with Downs under some circumstances, see Riker and Ordeshook, *Positive Political Theory*, pp. 349–50.

40. J. Merrill Shanks and Warren E. Miller, "Policy Direction and Performance Evaluation: Complementary Explanations of the Reagan Elections" (paper presented at the annual meeting of the American Political Science Association, 1985).

41. For a persuasive, well-documented argument along the same line, see Thomas Byrne Edsall, *The New Politics of Inequality* (New York: W. W. Norton & Company, 1984), chap. 5.

42. Marjorie Randon Hershey and Darrell M. West, "Single-Issue Politics: Prolife Groups and the 1980 Senate Campaign," in *Interest Group Politics*, ed. Allan J. Cigler and Burdett A. Loomis (Washington, D.C.: CQ Press, 1983), pp. 31–59.

43. Kristin Luker, *Abortion and the Politics of Motherhood* (Berkeley: University of California Press, 1984), pp. 224–28, 287. The majority of the public agreed with pro-lifers in opposing unlimited "abortion on demand"; but they disagreed in endorsing abortion to protect the life or health of the mother, to end a pregnancy begun by rape, and to prevent birth of a deformed child.

44. Hershey and West, "Single-Issue Politics," p. 40.

45. Gallup Poll data cited by Luker, *Abortion and the Politics of Motherhood*, p. 218. Of course, some pro-choice advocates were passionate about the other side of the issue, but their numbers had evidently shrunk as a result of complacency resulting from Supreme Court decisions in their favor.

46. Robert A. Dahl coined the term "minorities rule" but did not condemn the phenomenon in *A Preface to Democratic Theory* (Chicago: University of Chicago Press, 1956), chap. 5.

47. If this is so, cyclic majorities should be the prevailing pattern. See Frohlich and Oppenheimer, *Modern Political Analysis*, chap. 6.

CHAPTER 9

PRESSURE

Citizens who care deeply about a particular issue or decision soon discover that electoral activity by itself seldom gives them as much influence as they want. Elections aggregate innumerable policy concerns into a single ambiguous message. Elections are episodic, whereas policies are formed and implemented continuously. Elections equalize power by giving everyone a ballot, but people naturally seek an edge. For all these reasons, citizens resort to additional forms of political action. Depending on the type of activity (and the attitude of the observer), such efforts are variously described as citizen advocacy, lobbying, interest-group politics, or protest movements. Here, they are lumped all together under the heading "pressure" because the word best conveys the idea of people (citizens) bringing resources to bear on other people (officials whose decisions they want to shape). Although *pressure* often has an unfavorable connotation, in this chapter the word is used in a neutral or even a positive sense, as in this statement by John Gardner: "Common Cause is pursuing an old American tradition: hard-hitting pressure on politicians to bring about results desired by citizens."[1]

Observers use various schemes to sort out the confusion of pressure politics. Some arrange citizen actions on a continuum ranging from conventional tactics (letter-writing, canvassing) to illegal violence (riots, terrorism), with unconventional but legal protest (demonstrations, boycotts) and nonviolent civil disobedience as intermediate categories. Others classify pressure politics according to the goals members seek to advance. Common categories include economic interests (labor, consumers, farmers, poor people); noneconomic concerns (ecology, peace, good government); and advancement of groups, both in economic well-being and general social status (women, ethnic minorities, the elderly, homosexuals, the handicapped). Helpful though they are as a first pass, both these approaches are superficial. We can gain greater insight by examining the underlying organizational basis of citizen action.

THE ORGANIZATION OF PRESSURE

Must citizens organize to influence officials? No. When citizens have purely individual problems or grievances, they will usually act alone; the help of others will be hard to get and often unnecessary. Politicians know that responsiveness to personal petitions is a quick way to earn the gratitude and loyalty of voters. United States legislators devote a major share of their staffs' time to constituent service; and in Sweden and New Zealand, among other places, governments have appointed ombudsmen to help solve citizens' problems with the bureaucracy. Even when the cause is collective rather than private, individuals can and sometimes do take spontaneous, uncoordinated action. During the Watergate crisis, within hours after President Nixon fired the special prosecutor, Archibald Cox, in the "Saturday Night Massacre," thousands of people sent letters and telegrams of protest to the White House and Congress; and when Martin Luther King, Jr., was assassinated, in 1968, incensed blacks rioted in scores of United States cities and towns.

Movements and Organizations

Nevertheless, ordinary citizens who want to have a lasting effect on policy must almost always have help from formal associations. Organizations stimulate, coordinate, and represent citizens so that their concerted action has far more chance to succeed than equivalent effort expended separately. Most people in the United States accept this principle as a truism. A century and a half ago, Tocqueville observed the connection between mass democracy and the need for organization:

> If each citizen did not learn, in proportion as he individually becomes more feeble and consequently more incapable of preserving his freedom singlehanded, to combine with his fellow citizens for the purpose of defending it, it is clear that tyranny would unavoidably increase together with equality. . . . Americans of all ages, all conditions, and all dispositions constantly form associations.[2]

If you are still skeptical about the value of organization, consider three cases that at first glance seem to be counterexamples. The civil rights, women's, and consumer movements of the 1960s and 1970s produced remarkable changes in the United States. As the word *movement* suggests, each depended upon the contagious, grass-roots effort of thousands of individuals and small groups across the nation. Moreover, to a considerable extent, each was sparked by the initiative of a single person—Rosa Parks, the seamstress whose refusal to give up her seat to a white touched off the Montgomery bus boycott of 1957 (through which Martin Luther King, Jr., came to national attention); Betty Friedan, the former housewife whose book *The Feminine Mystique* inspired a generation of women; and Ralph Nader, the young lawyer who challenged mighty General Motors and won.

Yet, as Jo Freeman reminds us, spontaneity and structure are both essential elements of a social movement.[3] The civil rights movement would never have won its legislative triumphs had it not included five leading organizations: the venerable National Association for the Advancement of Colored People (NAACP), King's Southern Christian Leadership Conference, the youthful Student Nonviolent Coordinating Committee, the militant Congress of Racial Equality, and the establishment-oriented Urban League. Similarly, three years after publishing her book, Betty Friedan helped found and became first president of the National Organization for Women (NOW).[4] Even Ralph Nader—who for many Americans exemplifies the difference one person can make—institutionalized himself into about fifteen Washington-based organizations (all centering on his fund-raising agency, Public Citizen, Inc.) and scores of university public-interest research groups (PIRGs) and state citizen-action groups.

As these examples show, individual initiative, grass-roots movements, and formal organizations are fundamentally compatible and complementary. To be sure, there are tensions among them,[5] but properly understood they reinforce one another. Of the three, however, the most important channel for enduring, day-in and day-out influence on government is the formal organization. James Q. Wilson puts it well:

> If the causes represented by those mass efforts [movements] are to continue to be espoused, they will continue through organizational efforts or not at all. Passions can be aroused and for the moment directed; they cannot be sustained. Organization provides continuity and predictability to social processes that would otherwise be episodic and uncertain.[6]

Staff and Membership

Once an organization is formed, the crucial next step is to attract *staff*—one or more persons who will work full-time on behalf of the group.[7] Staff make an organization more effective in obvious ways. Lawyers, scientists, and communications specialists provide expert skills that members lack (or are insufficiently willing to donate). Through continuity in office, key staff persons develop organizational memory and networks of contacts that are essential to internal coherence and external influence. In relation to members, however, the work that staff do can be divided into just two categories: As *organizers,* staff inform, motivate, and coordinate in order to get members themselves to take direct, effective political action. As *agents*, staff act in place of members, doing what members themselves would presumably do if only they had the time, access, knowledge, or skill.

To the extent that staff serve as their agents, the role of members reduces to that of supplying resources needed to equip, sustain, and compensate the staff—which is to say that members, like parents of college students, send money. *Dues and financial contributions are overwhelmingly the main way that citizens participate in pressuring officials.* This is true even within organizations that encourage members to participate directly. Common Cause once estimated that 60 percent of its 252,000 members had done nothing more than contribute dues, and most of the others had only written an occasional letter to Congress. The organization identified only 11,000 members (about 4 percent) as "activists" who could be counted on to respond to staff appeals for letters to be written and telephone calls to be made to officials.[8] Although some advocates of participatory democracy sneer at dues and donations as an impoverished, if not impoverishing, form of participation, most organization members clearly find their indirect involvement advantageous. By hiring staff to serve as members' agents, organizations spread the burden of collective action across thousands of dues-payers, reducing the share of each to the small effort and limited sacrifice entailed in writing a check.

In contrast, members who engage in direct action usually pay heavier, if nonfinancial, costs. Writing letters and attending meetings can take up a lot of time. Protest marchers endure insults and sore feet. Participants in civil disobedience risk arrest, beatings, and even death.

Organizations without Individual Members

In the United States, the overwhelming majority of pressure groups have no individual members. Instead, they are made up of other organizations, usually businesses. Even groups that attempt to speak for broad, noneconomic interests are not always based on individual memberships. In a study of eighty-three Washington "public-interest" groups, Jeffrey Berry found that 30 percent had no members but were supported by foundations or other organizations.[9] Many groups that do have individual members also depend on grants or gifts from foundations, government agencies, other interest groups, or wealthy benefactors. Organizations especially rely on such subsidies at the time of their founding, before they establish a reliable membership base.[10] In this book, we are concerned only with that part of the pressure-group system that serves as a channel for individual participation, but it is important not to confuse that subset with the entire universe of lobbies.

Incentives for Member Action

When individual members do participate, whether directly or financially, political organizations must induce their support. How can this be done? The answer, of course, lies in the general analysis of motivation for collective action. (If Chapter 3 is not fresh in your mind, you should review it now.) In particular, the calculus of participation highlights three kinds of incentive that can offset participants' costs (C):

—the effect the member perceives he or she has on the collective goal, $P(B_i + B_g)$;
—the member's sense of duty or moral responsibility to contribute to the common effort, D; and
—whatever selective incentives the organization can make contingent on the member's participating, S.

If the group is large and the individuals consider only personal benefit, then the first two of these incentives usually have little or no effect. The individuals' willingness to contribute then depends on the value of the selective incentives they receive compared with the cost of their contribution ($S - C$). Let us call this quantity the *incentive balance*.[11] It measures the baseline, self-regarding "profit" or "loss" a member receives from participating. If the incentive balance shows a strong surplus, individuals will participate whether or not they care much about the group goal, whether or not they feel that their contributions make much difference in achieving it, and whether or not they have much sense of collective responsibility. Obviously, under such conditions most people find it easy to participate. On the other hand, if the incentive balance is in deficit, people who participate must care intensely about the common goal, feel unusually efficacious, or have a strong sense of duty. If the deficit is small, it may be possible to find a significant number of citizens who possess one or more of these virtues. But if the deficit is great, most people will soon give up their efforts, leaving the group either defunct or dependent on just a few diehards.

THREE TYPES OF POLITICAL ORGANIZATION

The concept of the incentive balance enables us to distinguish three principal types of political organization, which we will identify by the labels S, D, and M: *Type S* organizations supply strong, selective incentives that preserve a *surplus* incentive balance for most members, despite the substantial monetary costs they pay, which enable S-groups to support staffs and sustain stable organizations. *Type D* groups impose *deficit* incentive balances, because they offer members little in the way of selective incentives while depending on their willingness to engage in costly direct efforts. As a result, D-groups need dedicated activists, but their basic motivational disequilibrium leaves them vulnerable to early demise or frequent lapses into dormancy. In the middle, between Types S and D, are *Type M* organizations. M-groups offer weak or nonexistent selective incentives but ask only modest contributions so that most members incur only *moderate* incentive deficits that, especially among middle-class people, can be offset by a mild sense of moral responsibility.

Table 9–1 summarizes these and other characteristics of the three organizational types, and subsequent parts of this chapter explain them more fully.

Type S

Type S organizations have found means to supply selective incentives of substantial value to members. Usually this means that their services and activities have become crucial to key aspects of members' everyday lives.

Most Type S organizations are *vocational;* they are organized around the way their members earn their daily bread. By joining, members gain real economic advantages; indeed, sometimes they cannot make a living unless they join. Type S vocational organizations include labor unions (whose members are often required to belong under union shop contracts), farmers' organizations and cooperatives (which provide members with marketing services, insurance, and supplies), and professional associations (which commonly furnish journals and services to members only).[12]

Well-established *religious* organizations are a second major category within Type S. Their adherents give generously through weekly offerings and in response to special appeals. In return, members receive selective incentives that are nonmaterial but nonetheless vital. The church or synagogue offers believers not only spiritual hope but also earthly fellowship that gives warmth and meaning to their lives.

Recreational groups comprise another set of influential Type S-associations. Millions of people find it well worthwhile to pay dues to organizations that facilitate their favorite sport or hobby. Hunters and gun enthusiasts join the National Rifle Association; bird-watchers support Audubon societies; and 400,000 specialized fishermen belong to the Bass Anglers Sportsman Society (better known, naturally, as BASS).[13]

Because Type S organizations offer selective incentives that are worth a great deal to members, most can extract hefty dues or donations and still leave members with a secure incentive surplus. With large revenues per member, even relatively small S-groups can afford to hire full-time staffs. Consequently, these organizations are far more numerous nationally than Types D and M, and they organize effectively at the state and local levels as well. National S-organizations often have millions of dues-payers and budgets to match. They hire professional staff and pay them well; their top executives sometimes command six-figure salaries. With so many full-time specialists to do political work, the primary contribution Type S organizations ask from members is money. They do, however, frequently advise members on how to vote, and sometimes they seek direct participatory support, usually letter-writing.

Type D

At the opposite end of the incentive-balance spectrum lies Type D. Whether because they have not yet created a stronger organization or because

TABLE 9–1 Three Types of Pressure Groups

Characteristics of Typical Members	Type S	Type M	Type D
Selective incentives	Strong	Absent or weak, except sometimes moderate social incentives	Absent or weak, except sometimes strong social incentives
Primary means and cost of participation	Financial, often relatively large	Financial, usually modest	Direct action, often costly
Incentive balance	Surplus	Modest deficit	Deficit, often large
Role and strength of moral incentives	Secondary or absent, variable	Primary but moderate	Primary and strong

Of Staff

	Type S	Type M	Type D
Primary function	Agent	Agent	Organizer
Compensation	Comparable to private and government competitors	Usually somewhat less than private and government competitors	Often unpaid or subsistence-level
Purposive commitment	Variable	High	Intense

Of Organization

	Type S	Type M	Type D
Size range of membership	Wide: hundreds to millions	Restricted: thousands to hundreds of thousands	Active core few, but large numbers may participate sporadically
Stability	Stable	Precarious	Unstable
Congruence between policies and members' preferences	Variable, can be low	High	High
Members' primary means of control	Internal democracy, if any	Exit, unwillingness to contribute money	Exit, unwillingness to contribute effort

Examples

Type S	Type M	Type D
American Farm Bureau Federation	American Civil Liberties Union	
American Medical Association	Common Cause	Student Nonviolent Coordinating Committee
National Rifle Association	Moral Majority	Most neighborhood groups
United Auto Workers	National Association for the Advancement of Colored People	Most pro-life groups

their backers are too few or too poor, Type D groups do not generate enough member contributions to support full-time, well-compensated staff. Their key organizers are therefore likely to be dedicated but nonprofessional—unpaid volunteers or quasi-volunteers surviving on subsistence salaries. Some quasi-D-groups have more hiring power because they receive subsidies from allied organizations, wealthy benefactors, foundations, or government agencies. External sponsors, however, are notoriously fickle; many intend from the start that their donations serve only as temporary seed money.

Lacking the conventional resources of skilled permanent staff and big campaign contributions, most D-groups depend on the direct efforts of members. Moreover, without the early-warning system and preventive influence that staff can provide, these groups tend to be in a losing position from the start, so they often must ask supporters for extraordinarily strenuous efforts if they are to have any hope of overturning established policies. In return, they supply little in the way of selective incentives except, at their best, a moving spirit of solidarity. Consequently, active members incur severe incentive deficits, often in a physical or economic sense—going without sleep, repeatedly cutting classes, or forgoing income. To inspire these sacrifices, D-groups rely on purposive commitment, often fueled by righteous anger that overrides self-serving calculations and sometimes threatens to ignite violence.

Few people can sustain such intense dedication, so the most common fate of Type D groups is an early death. Some endure by lapsing into a sort of political hibernation, continuing a minimal level of activity while waiting for an issue hot enough to get sympathizers' blood moving again. Others manage to find formulas for longer active lives. One common recipe combines small scale, modest but feasible goals, social incentives, and a frequent turnover of activists to replace those who burn out. Another way to survive is encapsulation—making an activist group the center of all facets of members' lives—but this cult-like strategy often renders a group ineffective, for by cutting ties with outsiders, members lose touch with political reality. Ultimately, to thrive for a long time on a large scale, D-groups must find a way to convert themselves to Type S or M groups.

Although less durable than the others, D-groups are cheaper and easier to create. Their instability and frequent informality make an accurate count impossible, but in all probability Type D groups outnumber Types S and M combined. They are most common and most effective in local politics, where small numbers provide an insufficient base for staff but encourage (through perceptible individual effects and social incentives) voluntary citizen action. Type D organizations are less visible in everyday national politics, where they normally operate at a severe disadvantage. But conventional influence and organizational survival are not the only measures of political success. Despite their fragility, Type D groups have had a mighty impact on national politics. Passionate activists are more willing than secure staff to take the risks entailed in challenging established policies, and major social movements depend on a contagion of local initiatives sweeping from community to community. When enthusiastic masses of people ignore narrow instrumental calculations in the joyous belief that "all is possible," they sometimes accomplish historic changes.[14]

Type M

Type M organizations fall in between Types S and D, near the middle of the incentive-balance continuum. Unlike S-groups, M-groups are unable or unwilling to supply the mass of their supporters with major selective incentives, though some offer activists opportunities for enjoyable social interaction. Unlike D-groups, M-groups do not require very much of their members. Usually, they have managed to attract broad enough support to be able to afford a full-time staff while asking only modest annual dues. Thus members incur only a small incentive deficit, which among reasonably affluent citizens can be offset by a sense of civic duty and concern for the purpose to which the organization is dedicated.

Type M organizations became increasingly prominent in United States politics during the 1970s as a result of four new developments: (1) growth in the number of educated, prosperous people who had the political interest and economic ability to contribute regularly; (2) invention of computerized direct-mail technology; (3) widespread skepticism about parties and politicians in the aftermath of Vietnam and Watergate; and (4) the sophisticated organizing strategies of a new group of leaders.[15] During most of that decade, the political agenda was dominated by liberal Type M groups, including Common Cause, the Nader network, and environmental groups. In the 1980s skillful political entrepreneurs brought to the fore a new set of conservative Type M organizations, such as Jerry Falwell's Moral Majority and Terry Dolan's National Conservative Political Action Committee (NCPAC).

Some Type M organizations have longer histories. W.E.B. DuBois founded the NAACP in 1909; and the American Civil Liberties Union (ACLU) began in 1920. However, it is not easy to keep Type M organizations going. Without strong selective incentives to tie them to the group, members readily drop out when their budgets tighten or their attention shifts. In the 1960s and 1970s, waves of causes left behind residues of dead organizations, as donors switched their dollars from crusading for civil rights to opposing the war in Vietnam to protecting the environment to reforming government.[16] To survive very long, a Type M organization needs good leadership and a purpose that either remains an enduring concern for certain people or can be flexibly redefined to match the current interests of potential contributors. It also helps to establish local chapters so that social incentives can sustain an activist core.

Because it takes numerous small contributions to support even a one-person staff, M-groups are rare in state and local politics, except as chapters of national organizations. Even on a national basis, the difficulty of starting and maintaining Type M associations makes them much less common than Type S. No studies are available yet that use the typology introduced here, but we can get an idea of numbers by using some roughly comparable categories. Literally thousands of economic organizations maintain offices in Washington, D.C., but in the early 1970s Jeffrey Berry could identify only eighty-three "public-interest" organizations there, of which fewer than fifty might qualify as Type M.[17] In 1980, Jack Walker found that occupationally based groups outnumbered nonoccupational "citizen groups" by a four-to-one ratio. Walker excluded from his sample corporations, labor unions, and groups devoted to religious worship and recreation, so even if all his citizen groups are Type M, the four-to-one figure greatly understates the ratio between Type S and Type M organizations.[18]

Hybrids, Transitions, and Beginnings

Our three types are defined by locations on a continuum (the incentive balance), so we should expect that some groups will be hard to classify. For example, local chapters of the League of Women Voters offer women intellectual stimulation and social engagement through research and education projects. The resulting incentive surplus puts the league close to Type S, but it has other characteristics more like Type M (low dues) and Type D (direct involvement of many members). As more women are employed outside the home, the league may shift closer to a standard M-pattern. Another hybrid is the Sierra Club. Club membership is a bargain for outdoor enthusiasts, because dues buy a handsome magazine, reduced travel rates to scenic locations, and club-sponsored hikes, white-water trips, and wilderness outings.[19] On the other hand, many members ignore these benefits but pay dues just to support the club's political efforts on behalf of the environment. The Sierra Club thus combines Type S and Type M incentive patterns.

Few organizations begin suddenly, with enough individual members to maintain themselves in either Type S or Type M fashion. Most originate either as D-groups or with special subsidies or both. At any given time, therefore, some organizations will be found in between Type D and one of the other patterns. Thus, grass-roots advocacy groups such as ACORN (Association of Community Organizations for Reform Now) and Massachusetts Fair Share canvass for funds—a variant on the M-pattern suited to their working-class constituents, who are more likely to hand a five-dollar bill to a solicitor at the door than put a twenty-five-dollar check in the mail.[20] The American Agricultural Movement, which began in 1977 with strikes and tractorcades protesting low crop prices in the western Great Plains, by 1981 had decided to emulate the Type S Farm Bureau and Farmers Union by selling members life insurance and cooperative marketing services.[21]

MEMBERSHIP PARTICIPATION IN CONTROL OF STAFF AND POLICIES

When appraising the internal governance of political organizations, too many theorists fall into either of two camps. One group believes in the iron law of oligarchy; staff make all the decisions, they say, and any show of democracy is just a facade. Adherents of the second, more optimistic school not only believe democracy is possible but insist that all organizations must practice it by letting members directly control decisions, either through competitive internal elections or by more intensive participatory practices.

Both camps share the same excessively demanding and limited conception of the means through which ordinary members can control organizations. As we shall see, the concept of the incentive balance is a key to understanding the function and feasibility of member participation in determining the policies of political pressure groups. Consequently, the value and role of internal democracy differs markedly among our three types of organization.

Type S: Democracy as Necessary but Vulnerable

Political efforts of Type S groups usually are (or soon become) a by-product of the "business" side through which the organization furnishes members with a reliable incentive surplus.[22] Members often do not even think of these groups as political but instead see them only as a source of economic, professional, religious, or recreational benefits. When members become displeased by the political stands of an S-organization, they usually do not quit, because by leaving they would incur a personal loss. As a result, the staff of Type S associations often enjoy wide latitude to promote public policies they personally favor. S. E. Finer's comment about a British trade union applies equally well to Type S groups in the United States:

> It seems curious that when Arthur Deakin was the General Secretary of the [Transport and General Workers Union] its members were, to all appearances, staunch Rightists, and that the moment he was succeeded by Cousins . . . they all became staunch Leftists.[23]

Not all leaders of Type S organizations become free-lance political activists, and the motives of those who do run the gamut from personal advantage to political ideology, religious conviction, or sincere beliefs that certain policies best serve members' interests. But within broad limits, the need to maintain membership does not constrain the political positions that S-organizations espouse.[24]

To use Albert Hirschman's terms, because members' incentive surplus makes it hard for them to quit, the threat of their exit does not suffice to control staff. Responsiveness to members' political priorities therefore depends on "voice"—participatory attempts by members to influence organizational policies.[25]

Moreover, as we saw in Chapter 4, difficulty of exit gives members a stake in the organization that increases their willingness to participate. Therefore, internal challenges should be common in Type S organizations—if they respect members' rights. However, some incumbent leaders fight tooth and claw to protect their hefty salaries and handsome perquisites. Others do not pretend to be democratic. (When the clergy become politically active, they believe they are responding to God's will, not their parishioners'.) Many Type S associations follow the unitary model of democracy, so that their constitutions or informal norms lack "the limitations that guard against tyranny and injustice to minorities and individuals."[26] This problem was especially conspicuous in the United States labor movement until government intervention forced more unions to permit meaningful internal democracy.

In short, among Type S associations, vigorous internal democracy is at once necessary, feasible, and vulnerable. Types M and D are in quite a different position. As Type M presents a more clear-cut case, let us consider it first.

Type M: Exit as a Substitute for Participation

In Type M organizations, ease of exit creates a potent mechanism for membership control. Far from suffering a loss if they stop responding to staff appeals for money or action, their members may feel personally relieved to give up political burdens. The primary reason people belong to such groups is their desire to help achieve collective goals with which they sympathize. If the group starts pushing policies they dislike, they will simply drop out. Organizational leaders who know this work hard to keep their policies in line with the wishes of the overwhelming majority of members. To alienate even a minority will cause a painful drop in support, unless new recruits can be found to replace the disgruntled.

This is not to say that M-groups are always in perfect harmony with their supporters. Anticipating or finding out what members want is seldom easy, and staff with strong purposes of their own may deny or defy warnings that they have displeased followers. But leaders consistently too inept or too stubborn to stay in tune soon find themselves singing alone. Thus, precisely because staff must constantly strive to keep policies congruent with members' wishes, observers need not worry much about the question of representativeness in evaluating Type M pressure groups. They either represent the demands of their followers, or else they wither away. John Gardner clearly conveys the democratic quality of this sort of control by exit:

> Of course, in any voluntary citizens' organization like Common Cause, the most conclusive vote cast by the individual is his decision to join or resign. His joining

is in effect a vote for the movement; his resignation or failure to renew membership is a vote against. Thus, collectively, the members hold life-or-death control over the organization. If enough of them fail to renew their memberships, that will be the end of Common Cause.[27]

Common Cause and some other Type M organizations do observe democratic formalities by allowing members to elect boards of directors and vote on priorities. However, the value of these devices is usually not so much to ensure member control as it is to (1) legitimize the organization in a culture where democratic norms prevail; (2) tie more closely to the organization that fraction of members who enjoy participating; and (3) provide staff with feedback about member preferences. Type M groups can accomplish the last of these functions just as well by "market" surveys of members and by keeping a close watch on renewal rates.

Indeed, M-groups run serious risks if they give members direct participatory control. First, the activist minority who use the opportunity may appreciate less keenly than staff the organization's need to please the mass of less active supporters. Second, except for people who really enjoy it, participation in internal decision making either worsens members' incentive deficits or reduces the time they give to working for the group's external goals. Either way, the group is weakened as a political force.

Type D: Democracy as Motivator

Much of the argument for relying on exit to ensure member control of Type M organizations applies equally well to Type D groups. The chief difference is that members of M-groups show their displeasure by withholding money, whereas supporters of D-groups vote more with their feet by refusing to participate in meetings, demonstrations, and other forms of direct action. There are, however, two considerations that make internal democracy potentially more important for Type D.

First, more than Type M, D-groups may need internal participation to get feedback about members' desires. Organizations dependent on direct action seldom have the staff or money needed to conduct systematic surveys of supporters; and they are often too fragile to survive a temporary drop in support. Whereas a Type M organization may be able to read the message behind a declining flow of money, the Type D group that moves away from its base may collapse or be fatally discredited before it can steer back on course.

Second, the commitment-building function of internal democracy can be more important for Type D groups, which often demand sacrifices that many people will be unwilling to make unless they have participated in shaping decisions. Moreover, at its best, the process of participation creates the purposive consensus and social solidarity that sustain people through arduous and risky efforts.

The sort of participation most conducive to such commitment is direct democracy in small groups or face-to-face assemblies. Type D groups therefore often run up against the size limits we examined in Chapter 7. Thus, to the extent D-groups depend on participatory decision-making to overcome their members' incentive deficits, they have difficulty growing beyond relatively small numbers of activists. When D-groups do succeed in attracting numerous adherents, they face a dilemma. If the newcomers are simply invited to join while the decision process remains unchanged, internal direct democracy becomes less and less satisfactory as the proportion of members who can participate meaningfully becomes smaller, meetings become prolonged, and consensus becomes harder to achieve. On the other hand, if the group adapts to its success by switching to representative or referendum democracy, the special satisfactions of direct discussion will be lost and the original activists may feel less motivated to remain committed.

One solution is to establish, in effect, two classes of supporters: a core of leaders who practice direct small-group democracy within their own ranks, and a mass of followers who exercise influence through occasional votes and the implicit threat of their exit. In this way, the D-group structure becomes parallel to that of most Type M organizations, with their core staff and mass periphery of contributors. However, because D-groups typically ask more of their followers than an annual check in the mail, they generally have trouble maintaining continuous efforts once the sustaining satisfactions of participation in the group process are lost. Therefore, a better solution for successful Type D organizations may be a system of indirect representation, in which participatory small groups are maintained at every level of the organization.[28]

Monopoly and Competition

The case for relying on exit as the primary member control over Type M and D groups is strongest when there exist two or more groups working toward roughly the same political purpose. Thus, dissatisfied contributors to Moral Majority who become irked by Jerry Falwell can shift their support to Christian Voice without sacrificing their political goals. Conversely, internal democracy becomes atypically important when a Type M or Type D group achieves a dominant position in its policy area. When people believe the fate of a cause depends on one organization, competing factions sometimes wage bitter struggles for control. To survive such battles, organizations need constitutions that legitimize internal conflict and provide ways to resolve it decisively and democratically. Paralyzed by its unitary, consensus-seeking ideology, Students for a Democratic Society collapsed as a result of factional warfare in 1969.[29] In contrast, clear-cut majority votes enabled NOW to survive potentially similar crises in 1975 and 1985.[30]

Given the damage that fights inflict on a movement, disgruntled leaders or factions ought to remember that the moral and purposive incentives on which Type M and Type D groups rely are relatively cheap to supply, so they might serve their cause better by setting up a competing organization. Thus when David Brower lost a fight to control the Sierra Club, he founded Friends of the Earth, a group that became influential both in the United States and abroad. Indeed, it is quite likely that, in the United States, environmental and consumer movements have been strengthened rather than weakened by the existence within them of several partially competitive, partially complementary organizations. In any case, by making alternatives available and exit feasible, a limited proliferation of similar pressure groups serves the democratic goal of ensuring that leaders pursue policies that are reasonably consistent with the wishes of ordinary members.

EVALUATING PARTICIPATION IN PRESSURE POLITICS

Traditionally, critics have contended that the system of pressure politics—dominated by Type S organizations—benefits narrow, "special" interests at the expense of broad, "public" interests and aggravates inequality by giving political advantages to those who are already economically privileged. The next two sections consider these charges. Then we look at accomplishments and problems of the citizen-action movement of Type M and O groups that have striven to combat both failings.

Special Interests

Until the 1960s, the predominant pluralist doctrine in United States political science taught that pressure politics operated benignly. Pluralists believed that any group of citizens who really cared about an issue would organize; that multiple, accessible centers of power in government assured each active group a reasonable share of influence; and that competition among groups would prevent any one faction from gaining so much power over a policy that it could exploit everybody else. Dissenters from this complacent view contended that most pressure groups represented narrow interests, usually those of economic producers. These special interests, critics said, use governmental power to benefit themselves, forcing the general public to pay through higher prices and taxes, pollution, and unsafe products.[31] In 1965 the publication of Olson's *Logic of Collective Action* set the public-interest critique of pluralism on a convincing theoretical foundation; as the influence of that book spread, fewer and fewer informed observers any longer accepted the idea that group politics adequately represent all interests.

Early public-interest theorists hoped to fight special-interest power by strengthening the most broadly based electoral institutions: political parties and the presidency. However, just as Olson's analysis gained influence, presidential power fell into disrepute as a result of the Vietnam and Watergate misadventures of the "imperial" presidents Johnson and Nixon. Consequently, reformers seeking to create a new "civic balance" between concentrated and dispersed interests decided that rather than suppress the pressure system they would join it.[32] Defying Olson's predictions about the difficulty of organizing without selective incentives, they created or revitalized dozens of Type M organizations to advocate widely shared interests in the environment, peace, government reform, and consumer protection. Despite remarkable success, these "public-interest" groups remained vastly outnumbered by traditional Type S lobbies, which continued to work for policies that would primarily benefit their own members. Moreover, the campaign-financing reforms that Common Cause had sought backfired, opening a Pandora's box from which issued swarms of special-interest and ideological PACs. By the 1980s, public-interest groups were fighting a holding action, but they demonstrated more staying power than most observers had expected.

The resurgent conservatism of the 1980s also contained a strong public-interest component. Budget Director David Stockman and some other Reagan administration leaders worked to promote widely shared interests in tax reduction and economic growth by fighting what they considered special-interest demands on government for subsidies and protection against economic competition. Following the lead of an earlier generation of public-interest theorists, they relied on the power of a president backed by overwhelming electoral victories. However, President Reagan's budget-cutters were most successful in attacking programs intended to benefit workers and poor people, and tax reductions ended up favoring corporations, the wealthy, and the middle class. This experience confirmed the belief of many people that the pressure system is biased in favor of haves against have-nots.[33]

Class Bias

In 1960, Schattschneider commented that the "business or upper-class bias of the pressure system shows up everywhere."[34] The wave of Type M organizing during the next few decades broadened the system by encouraging participation by upper-middle- and middle-class citizens. Typical supporters of public-interest lobbies are educated and affluent. The median family income of Common Cause members is almost twice the national median.[35] Similarly, the rise of the Christian Right coincided with rapid upward mobility among evangelical Christians, whose economic advances enabled them to finance political organizations.[36] As we know from Chapter 5, voluntary participation is almost always skewed toward the affluent, and contributions as small as $15 or $25 are a "low cost" only for people with discretionary income.

In view of their class composition, it is hardly surprising that Type M groups are frequently insensitive to needs of less prosperous citizens. Environmentalists often forget that stringent pollution controls and restrictions on economic growth can cost not only corporate profits but also workers' jobs. Good-government reformers ignore the dependence of working-class political organization on patronage and other practices they find distasteful. In pursuit of their own vision of morality, religious activists deny abortions to poor people, who can least afford to support additional children.

Does all this mean that less advantaged people have no hope of advancing through pressure politics? Not entirely. Type M organizations will always remain a tool of the affluent, but Type S and Type D groups have proved effective vehicles for the disadvantaged. By harnessing powerful selective incentives, people of modest means can support influential lobbies. Since the 1930s, labor unions and farmers' associations have been among the strongest United States pressure groups. True, organized workers and farmers tend to be better off than those who are unorganized, but is not their prosperity as much the result as the cause of their organization? And poor people—driven by anger and with little to lose—may be more available than most others for Type D political action. In the 1960s and early 1970s, protest movements produced tangible progress for some of the most deprived—blacks, Hispanics, farm workers, welfare recipients, and others.

Beginning in the mid-1970s, however, both unions and the poor began to lose previous gains. Type D organizations, as we have seen, are a shaky foundation for long-term influence, especially in national politics. As for organized labor, its own loss of dynamism, increased hostility from management, and changes in the work force combined to undermine its economic and political power.[37] By the mid-1980s, the pressure system was again dominated by business and the affluent.

Lessons of Citizen Action

Despite their relative eclipse in the 1980s, earlier successes of social movements and public-interest groups compelled theorists to revise ideas about the nature of power in the United States and produced a self-conscious movement for citizen action at all levels from neighborhood to nation.[38] Experiences of this movement yield three important lessons for anyone who would use pressure politics to accomplish participatory democratic ideals.

The Primacy of Elections: Early successes prompted some citizen-action leaders to see their movement as an alternative to participation through political parties and elections. In fact the power of pressure groups ultimately depends on votes more than anything else. What else are letters to legislators but signals that their acts will sway the votes of constituents? Whether through moral suasion or disruption, protest succeeds by enlisting the mass of voters on the side of social change.[39] Even those groups whose principal resource is money acquire influence mainly by contributing to election campaigns. In the long run, interest groups win not by supplanting parties and voting, but by stimulating, influencing, and following through on electoral action.

Advocacy versus Responsibility: The commitment of many citizen activists springs from "a renewed vision of direct democracy."[40] By itself, however, participation in pressure politics advances only one of the values espoused by theorists of direct democracy: the ideal of the active life. It is by no means obvious that interest groups foster other direct-democratic goals. The individual virtues of tolerance, breadth of vision, and loyalty, and the social norms of discussion, consensus, and community all seem more likely to result from giving ordinary members true decision-making authority, rather than from encouraging them to press demands on officials. Indeed, getting together with like-minded others reinforces one-sided views and enables people to secure benefits (or avoid costs) for themselves at the expense of everyone else. There is no denying the need for pressure-group action in large representative democracies, but enthusiasts must avoid seeing in it all the virtues of a different mode of participation. Often, only group leaders are sufficiently involved in negotiating with outsiders to develop an integrative perspective; unless they transmit this broader view to followers, the latter may condemn them for "selling out." Group action is most likely to foster democratic values among ordinary citizens when the membership is diverse (as in some neighborhoods) or if (as in elections) political necessity forces everyone to work closely with a varied coalition.

The Virtue of Balance: Organizers of citizen action seek to promote such diverse interests that contradictions within the movement are inevitable. During the battle over the New York City school system in the 1960s, community-control advocates were opposed chiefly by the teachers union—itself a favorite cause of activists just a few years earlier. Similarly, at one session of a conference on participation, rural organizers discussed strategies for mobilizing poor farmers; at the very next panel, consumer lobbyists recounted their efforts to defeat milk price supports—which are the great political achievement of organized dairy farmers (few of whom consider themselves rich). *Any* strongly defended particular interest can hurt the broader "public" interest, and today's "deprived group," if well organized, becomes tomorrow's "vested interest." Sophisticated citizen action leaders understand this. Yet, their own sacrifices create in organizers and activists a strong need to invest unique virtue in the cause or group for which they advocate. It takes mental and spiritual toughness to sustain wholehearted effort while knowing that, in a democracy, real virtue lies not in achieving the triumph of any one interest but rather in strengthening the weak to create a balanced pluralism in which all have a fair chance.

NOTES

1. *In Common Cause* (New York: W. W. Norton & Company, 1972), p. 15.

2. Alexis de Tocqueville, *Democracy in America,* trans. Phillips Bradley (New York: Vintage Books, 1945), vol. II, pp. 114–15.

3. Jo Freeman, ed., *Social Movements of the Sixties and Seventies* (New York: Longman, 1983), pp. ix–30.

4. Jo Freeman, *The Politics of Women's Liberation: A Case Study of an Emerging Social Movement and Its Relation to the Policy Process* (New York: David McKay Co., 1975).

5. For a good account of strains between social movement and organized lobbies, see Anne N. Costain and W. Douglas Costain, "The Women's Lobby: Impact of a Movement on Congress," in *Interest Group Politics*, ed. Allan J. Cigler and Burdett A. Loomis (Washington, D.C.: CQ Press, 1983), pp. 191–216.

6. *Political Organizations* (New York: Basic Books, 1973), p. 7.

7. For the sake of simplicity, I use "staff" broadly to include leaders and organizers as well as specialists and subordinates. Many authors emphasize the role of "political entrepreneurs"—founders who attract support in return for services and benefits. While I recognize that for some purposes it is essential to distinguish the function of entrepreneurs, here I lump them with staff.

8. Andrew S. McFarland, *Common Cause: Lobbying in the Public Interest* (Chatham, N.J.: Chatham House Publishers, Inc., 1984), p. 62. The fact that they are a small proportion of members does not negate the importance of activists, who are crucial to the Common Cause "insider-outsider" (staff-member) lobbying strategy.

9. *Lobbying for the People: The Political Behavior of Public Interest Groups* (Princeton: Princeton University Press, 1977), pp. 27–28.

10. Jack Walker, "Origins and Maintenance of Interest Groups in America," *American Political Science Review*, 77 (1983), 390–406.

11. The notion of incentive balance is a specialized descendent of Barnard's axiom that to maintain themselves, all organizations must balance contributions with inducements. Chester I. Barnard, *The Functions of the Executive* (Cambridge: Harvard University Press, 1938). See also Peter B. Clark and James Q. Wilson, "Incentive Systems: A Theory of Organizations," *Administrative Science Quarterly*, 6 (1961), 219–66; and Wilson, *Political Organizations*, chaps. 1–3. Clark and Wilson's concept of *purposive* incentives corresponds roughly to the two terms not included in the incentive balance.

12. For more information about the incentives used by unions, farm groups, and professional associations, see Mancur Olson, Jr., *The Logic of Collective Action: Public Goods and the Theory of Groups* (Cambridge: Harvard University Press, 1965), chaps. III and VI; Wilson, *Political Organizations;* and Terry M. Moe, *The Organization of Interests: Incentives and the Internal Dynamics of Interest Groups* (Chicago: University of Chicago Press, 1980), chaps. 7 and 8.

Many vocational organizations in the United States also maintain political action committees (PACs), through which they channel campaign contributions to friendly politicians. When a vocational association (or, for that matter, a business corporation) musters strong economic pressure to persuade its members (or employees) to donate to its PAC, then the PAC is also a Type S organization. However, due to legal restrictions, many vocational and corporate PACs are probably closer to Type M. See John R. Wright, "PACs, Contributions, and Roll Calls: An Organizational Perspective," *American Political Science Review*, 79 (1985), 400–14.

13. If you're curious about BASS, see Loomis and Cigler, eds., *Interest Group Politics*, pp. 16–17.

14. Aristide R. Zolberg, "Moments of Madness," *Politics and Society*, 2 (1972), 183–207.

15. Andrew McFarland, *Public Interest Lobbies: Decision Making on Energy* (Washington, D.C.: American Enterprise Institute for Public Policy Research, 1976), chap. 1.

16. See Anthony Downs, "Up and Down with Ecology—The 'Issue Attention Cycle,'" *The Public Interest*, no. 28 (Summer 1972), 38–50. Kay Lehman Schlozman reports that only 33 percent of "public-interest" organizations active in Washington, D.C., in 1960 were still active in politics there two decades later, compared to 79 percent of professional associations and 77 percent of unions. "What Accent the Heavenly Chorus? Political Equality and the American Pressure System," paper presented at the 1984 Annual Meeting of the American Political Science Association.

17. *Lobbying for the People.*

18. "Origin and Maintenance," p. 393.

19. McFarland, *Public Interest Lobbies*, p. 87.

20. Harry C. Boyte, *The Backyard Revolution: Understanding the New Citizen Movement* (Philadelphia: Temple University Press, 1980), chap. 2.

21. Allan J. Cigler and John Mark Hansen, "Group Formation Through Protest: The American Agricultural Movement," in *Interest Group Politics*, ed. Cigler and Loomis, pp. 84–109.

22. Olson, *Logic of Collective Action*, chap. 6; Moe, *Organization of Interests*, pp. 47–50.

23. S. E. Finer, "Groups and Political Participation," in *Participation in Politics*, ed. Geraint Parry (Totowa, N.J.: Rowman & Littlefield, 1972), p. 65.

24. The breadth of those limits depends on the magnitude of members' incentive surplus, the availability of alternative sources for the selective incentives they get from the organization, the extent of their political awareness and purposive motivation, and their ability to exercise control through internal democracy.

25. For the theory of exit and voice as alternative control mechanisms, see Albert O. Hirschman, *Exit, Voice, and Loyalty: Responses to Decline in Firms, Organizations, and States* (Cambridge: Harvard University Press, 1970). For a good analysis of control by exit, see McFarland, *Common Cause*, chap. 5.

26. Grant McConnell, *Private Power and American Democracy*, (New York: Alfred A. Knopf, 1967), p. 154.

27. *In Common Cause*, pp. 118–19.

28. See pages 97–98 above.

29. For a good brief account, see Frederick D. Miller, "The End of SDS and the Emergence of Weatherman: Demise Through Success," in *Social Movements*, ed. Freeman, pp. 279–97.

30. Costain and Costain, "The Women's Lobby," pp. 201–2.

31. Major works in this tradition include E. E. Schattschneider, *The Semi-Sovereign People: A Realist's View of Democracy in America* (New York: Holt, Rinehart and Winston, 1960); Theodore J. Lowi, *The End of Liberalism*, 2nd ed. (New York: W. W. Norton & Co., 1979); and Grant McConnell, *Private Power and American Democracy*. For an excellent analytical summary, see Andrew McFarland, "Public Interest Lobbies Versus Minority Faction," in *Interest Group Politics*, ed. Cigler and Loomis, pp. 324–53.

32. On the theory of civic balance, see McFarland, *Common Cause*, pp. 38–43.

33. Stockman's own disillusionment is chronicled in William Greider's *The Education of David Stockman and Other Americans* (New York: E. P. Dutton, 1982). The strategy Greider describes nevertheless remains a brilliant example of how to suppress particular interests by keeping shared goals foremost.

34. Schattschneider, *Semi-Sovereign People*, p. 31.

35. McFarland, *Common Cause*, p. 48.

36. James L. Guth, "The Politics of the Christian Right," in *Interest Group Politics*, ed. Cigler and Loomis, pp. 60–83.

37. Thomas Byrne Edsall, *The New Politics of Inequality* (New York: W. W. Norton & Co., 1984), chap. 4.

38. McFarland, "Public Interest Lobbies versus Minority Faction;" Boyte, *The Backyard Revolution;* Stuart Langton, ed., *Citizen Participation in America: Essays on the State of the Art* (Lexington, Mass.: Lexington Books, D. C. Heath and Co., 1978); and Langton, ed., *Citizen Participation Perspectives: Proceedings of the National Conference on Citizen Participation* (Medford, Mass.: Lincoln Filene Center for Citizenship and Public Affairs, Tufts University, 1979).

39. Michael Lipsky, *Protest in City Politics: Rent Strikes, Housing and the Power of the Poor* (Chicago: Rand McNally, 1970).

40. Boyte, *Backyard Revolution*, p. 7.

CHAPTER 10

ADMINISTRATION

According to a traditional image of good government, elected leaders determine policies that civil servants efficiently and impartially administer. In this model, politicians are the proper targets for citizen pressure, whereas bureaucrats should avoid influences that might induce them to deviate from general policies. Perhaps this strict distinction between policy and administration made sense in a simpler era, but the scale and complexity of modern governments compel the thin layer of politicians on top to delegate discretionary power to vastly more numerous bureaucrats below. Working within the loose framework of general policies, nonelected officials write rules, draw up regulations, set standards, issue permits, establish rates, grant funds, and in dozens of other ways make decisions that vitally affect citizens' lives. In response, interest groups devote much effort to influencing administrators, and legislatures understandably impose on agencies a basic obligation to receive citizens' comments about proposed actions, either in writing or through public hearings.

More remarkably, governments sometimes surpass minimal requirements for public input by stimulating and organizing citizen participation in administration. Certain notable agencies have even given citizen involvement a central place in their ideology and practice.[1] In the United States, the idea of citizen participation in administration is most identified with a succession of federally funded urban programs—Urban Renewal, which began in the

1950s, the War on Poverty of the 1960s, Model Cities in the late 1960s and early 1970s, and community development block grants (CDBGs) in the 1970s and 1980s. Of these, the most controversial was the War on Poverty, with its famous requirement for "maximum feasible participation" of the poor in community action programs (CAPs). However, the origins of citizen involvement in public administration in the United States are rural. Beginning early in the twentieth century, county agents of the Department of Agriculture's Cooperative Extension Service spread new farming methods by organizing local committees; in the 1930s, the Tennessee Valley Authority promoted a new philosophy of "democratic administration."[2] More recently, strong efforts to involve citizens have been made by agencies that oversee natural resources, including the Corps of Engineers (which manages waterways) and the Forest Service.

Despite the conflict that surrounded urban participation programs in the 1960s, during the next decade "almost all new, major federal legislative programs contain[ed] citizen-participation requirements."[3] A 1978 study of federal grant programs showed that 155 operated under such mandates, of which 81 percent were enacted after 1970.[4] Government requirements nourished the growth of an emerging citizen-participation profession composed of agency citizen-involvement specialists, advocacy group staff, academics, and consultants. This network suffered when the Reagan administration curtailed or downplayed participation requirements in many programs,[5] but numerous agencies and localities continued to exceed the minimum standards demanded by law or the administration.

Our task here, however, is not to trace the ups and downs of political and administrative fashion but rather to examine more timeless issues concerning why, when, and how authorities should or should not involve citizens in government programs. Let us begin by noticing several different ways citizens participate in administration.

TYPES OF CITIZEN INVOLVEMENT

Administrative participation assumes "a bewildering variety of forms,"[6] ranging from old standbys such as the public hearing to exotic variations such as the Samoan circle (a leaderless meeting designed to facilitate free exchange of ideas early in a planning process).[7] Fundamentally, however, all citizen participation in administration boils down to four broad types of activity: doing, advising, deciding, and supporting.

Doing

Ordinary citizens can accomplish many of the civic tasks that we might otherwise hire government employees to do for us. Thus, the first way to involve citizens in administration is to ask them to do the work—the direct, physical production of public goods and services. It is easy to overlook how much citizens already do for themselves in most communities, whether through official citizen-involvement programs, as part of voluntary community service projects, or informally just by being good neighbors. As Matthew Crenson observes, "The importance of these unofficially produced benefits probably becomes most evident when citizens stop producing them. It is then that neighborhoods fall into disorder and decay."[8]

Sometimes citizen production of public services is so reliable or well organized that it entirely takes the place of an agency, as when volunteer fire fighters enable a town to avoid hiring a fire department. In other cases, participation enables an agency to do its job better without paying additional employees, as when citizen watchdogs help enforce environmental laws by alerting inspectors about suspected violations. Because direct participation in performing public tasks completely or partially substitutes for bureaucracy, public employees often resist plans to use volunteers unless they are assured their jobs will be protected. Consequently, involving citizens in doing public work meets less opposition when a government takes on new responsibilities or when it does not yet perform certain functions. Thus the remarkable neighbors' associations in Spanish cities sprang up when rapid urbanization left municipalities unable to provide adequate roads, schools, libraries, and other services.[9]

Perhaps because job security is less an issue for them, Communist regimes strongly encourage citizens to become involved in administrative work. Before the Russian Revolution, Lenin saw such participation as a way to fulfill Marx's prophecy of the withering away of the state:

> Under socialism . . . the mass of the population will rise to taking an independent part, not only in voting and elections, but also in the everyday administration of the state. Under socialism all will govern in turn and will soon become accustomed to no one governing.[10]

Though it can hardly be said that no one governs in contemporary Communist systems, they have certainly enlisted the masses in everyday administration. Over seven million *druzhinniki* (volunteer civil guards) help prevent crime and preserve conformity in the Soviet Union; in Cuba, Committees for Defense of the Revolution promote recreation, education, and public health; and in China, mass movements have built impressive public works, attacked diseases, and spread the use of birth control.[11]

Advising

In the United States, most government efforts to involve citizens are intended to elicit from them advice about actions over which a public agency retains decision-making power. Citizens can communicate with administrators in a great variety of ways—individually (through suggestion boxes, hotlines, ombudsmen) or collectively (via trade associations, advocacy groups, demonstrations); in writing (letters, formal comments) or orally (public testimony, informal conversation); on a one-shot basis (the angry consumer who protests a utility rate increase) or in a continuing relationship (the member of a citizen panel). The people who express their views may be self-selected (as at an open hearing), a random sample of an affected population (as in a systematic survey of opinion), or an elite chosen by the agency for their unusual interest and influence (as in most advisory committees).

Ideally, an agency's purpose in seeking public advice should be either to make better decisions by gathering ideas and information from citizens or to make politically more acceptable decisions by learning people's fears and wants. All too often, however, agencies receiving public input seem merely to be allowing grievants to blow off steam while going through the motions of satisfying a legal requirement. An unfavorable image is especially associated with that most common citizen-involvement device, the public hearing. Many are rigidly controlled, no doubt because when tempers (and the meeting room) get hot, hearings can easily degenerate into shouting matches. Bored officials listen dutifully to a parade of speakers, of whom the articulate are predictable, and the unpredictable, eccentric. Only when television lights come on do administrators make a zealous show of taking notes. Not surprisingly, a study of local hearings on the use of federal revenue-sharing funds detected little measurable impact on decisions, even though half a million citizens a year participated in such meetings during the 1970s.[12] Although this depressing picture may be generally representative, it is not hard to find exceptional hearings that are genuinely effective in changing official actions.[13] Moreover, plenty of other advisory devices besides hearings are available (or inventable) for administrators who really want to listen to citizens.

Deciding

If administrators' tendency to ignore advice frustrates participants, the logical next step is to take authority away from officials and give it to citizens. A venerable prototype for such delegation of powers is the jury, through which citizens participate in the administration of justice. Although strictly circumscribed by law and judges' instructions, some juries ultimately determine whether defendants will live or die. Power just as fateful, if more indirect, was formerly wielded by draft boards of local citizens, who decided which young men would be sent to fight in World War II, Korea, and Vietnam.

The difference between advisory and decision-making citizens' groups is not always clear-cut, because some advisory bodies exercise great de facto power. For example, during the first three years of the CDBG process in Buffalo, the city government funded 90 percent of the priority projects of its district advisory committees. Similarly, in Cambridge, Massachusetts, the allocation of CDBG money was once based on a play money "vote" by 400 people who attended an open meeting.[14] Nevertheless, it is important that officials not mislead citizens about who ultimately will decide, because "if expectations are created of greater authority than actually exists, the sense of betrayal is often greater than if there had been clearly defined limits in the first place."[15]

Why should governments want to bestow power on special groups of active citizens? Besides general participatory values described in Chapter 2, reasons include two arguments aimed at social change and three focused on administrative advantage:

> —In large political units, participatory boards may restore to a population democratic powers that members of smaller jurisdictions take for granted. Thus, in the battle over community control of schools and services in New York City, advocates of decentralization could point out that the Bedford-Stuyvesant ghetto contained 450,000 people whose needs "had been lost in the midst of the city's eight million."[16]
>
> —More generally, delegation of administrative authority can be used as an attempt to empower any group that fares badly in normal political or economic processes. Usually, groups singled out for help are minorities, such as "the poor," but sometimes participation is designed to advance broader interests. An example is the provision in the 1974 Health Planning Act that mandated consumer majorities on governing boards of local health systems agencies.[17]
>
> —By delegating decisions, remote administrators recognize citizens' superior knowledge of their own conditions and needs. Residents of a neighborhood understand best where a new park will be most useful, which buildings should be fixed up, and which elderly neighbor needs a downstairs bathroom. As one grass-roots speaker put it at a CDBG hearing, "If you're gonna give a person a grant, give 'em what they *need*—not what you think they *ought* to need. Otherwise it ain't gonna do them no good."
>
> —When governments must make tough choices in allocating benefits or, especially, in sharing hardships, people usually accept more readily the results of a participatory process.[18] And if anyone remains disgruntled, their anger will be aimed at fellow citizens rather than at authorities.
>
> —When popular cooperation is essential in implementation, a program has a better chance to succeed if people have participated in planning what should be done.[19] The cooperation needed may be active, as when authorities seek mass labor to build a dam in a poor country; or merely passive noninterference, as when urban officials try to prevent vandalism by graffiti "artists."

Despite these arguments, the practice of delegating government authority to citizen groups remains controversial. Critics often allege that administrators' stated reasons conceal hidden motives, including the desire to stimulate a fourth type of citizen involvement.

Supporting

Whether citizens participate by doing, advising, or deciding, they frequently become advocates for the program in which they are involved. This is so both because participation generally induces commitment and because activists often gain influence over the use of agency resources. Understanding this, smart bureaucrats use citizen participation to create allies who will support them in their constant battles for authority and appropriations. The classic success story, which inspired many later attempts of the same sort, was the creation of farm bureaus by county extension agents:

> By 1921 . . . the fundamental fact of the situation was plain and should not have been missed by any reasonably alert political observer: what the county agents had organized with the aid of public resources and at the direction of the United States Department of Agriculture was not merely an array of local organizations of farmers devoted to education, but the most powerful private pressure group agriculture has ever produced, the American Farm Bureau Federation.[20]

Of course, the strategy of creating citizen support groups does not always succeed. Participatory organizing during the War on Poverty did much to empower the poor but failed to create a constituency able to ensure the long-term survival of the Office of Economic Opportunity. Nevertheless, the principle remains valid: citizens activated and organized for administrative purposes commonly become part of the pressure system, symbiotically helping to sustain the agencies that first showed them the power of participation.

THREE IMAGES OF CITIZEN INVOLVEMENT

Efforts to involve citizens in administering government programs inspire widely varying evaluations. Some critics contend that public participation enables special interest groups to capture control of resources that ought to serve the people as a whole. Other observers charge that manipulative bureaucrats use public involvement to co-opt potential opponents. Both these arguments assume that participants and officials ought to be adversaries; they differ only according to which side is seen as dominant. A third, more optimistic image holds that by sharing power in a genuinely cooperative process, the two sides can coproduce public services. These three categories—capture, co-optation, and coproduction—do not exhaust the possibilities, and they are as much ideological as analytic. Nevertheless, as key ideal types, they help crystallize much of the debate over participation in administration.

Capture

Whether by formally delegating decision-making power or by consistently heeding "advice," agencies sometimes yield to participants effective control over chunks of public authority. Most people who use the word *capture* condemn such devolution of power.[21] Reasons for opposition include at least two major arguments.

One indictment contends that the intensive democracy of participatory administration conflicts with the extensive democracy of elective representation. For some observers, this clash raises basic issues of legitimacy, a view clearly conveyed by Daniel Patrick Moynihan's comments on a controversy of the 1960s:

> *Complete* community control . . . took the form of denying the legitimacy of those institutions of electoral representation that had developed over the years—indeed, the centuries—and which nominally *did* provide community control. Of a sudden the city councilman was not enough, the state assemblyman not enough, the Congressman not enough, the mayor and the governor and the President but tools of the power structure. . . . The institutions of representative government, imperfect as they may be, have the singular virtue of defining who speaks for the community in certain set circumstances.[22]

In the administrative doctrine that follows from this theory of legitimacy, bureaucrats should respond to elected officials and the laws they write through a strict, "clear line of authority within the bureaucracy alone," avoiding the blurring of authority that results when citizens' groups intrude in the process.[23] From this perspective, procedural ambiguity is undesirable because it brings about substantive policies that respond to narrow interests at the expense of broad public values. For example, McConnell (writing in the mid-1960s) argued that participatory advantages enabled ranchers to overgraze livestock on public lands, and irrigation users to flood scenic canyons behind dams.[24]

The second line of attack contends that handing over public power to decentralized constituencies interferes with egalitarian goals. For reasons explained in Chapter 5, educated, affluent citizens are relatively more active in citizen-involvement programs. Moreover, agencies find it to their own advantage to favor elites, whose political clout makes them formidable friends or foes. Thus, according to classic studies, participatory administration of American rural-development programs redounded to the benefit of big rather than small farmers.[25] However, in the urban programs of the 1960s and 1970s, reformers tried to use participation to make government serve the poor. Whatever success their strategy achieved depended on vigorous federal insistence on participation by poor and minority people. Therefore, this experience refines rather than refutes the egalitarian critique of participatory administration, which is premised on the belief that "protection of the weak . . . requires central authority and commitment."[26]

Co-optation

The term *co-optation* has a confusing history. The primary dictionary definition of *co-opt*—"to add (a person or persons) to a group by vote of those already members"—does not indicate whether the people co-opted genuinely share in the benefits of membership or are merely exploited by the original members. When Philip Selznick introduced the word into the study of citizen-involvement programs, he used it to cover both possibilities. After studying the history of the Tennessee Valley Authority in the 1930s and 1940s, Selznick concluded that an organization resorts to co-optation "as a means of averting threats to its stability or existence," but in doing so, it might share either the substance of power or only its burdens. In the first case, he argued, co-optation would be informal, as the agency appeases interests strong enough to insist on real concessions and savvy enough to avoid too conspicuous a role. In the second case, co-optation would be formal, as the agency tries to legitimize itself by giving "window-dressing" functions to groups who lack the resources or skill to insist on real policy control.[27]

It is debatable whether Selznick was right in identifying formal with symbolic participation and informal with effective participation. A later study of the TVA concludes that "over time voluntary associations which had been formally coopted into an organization may gain real power to influence actions and decisions. . . ."[28] In any case, his distinction was neglected during the decades after he wrote. As *co-optation* passed into everyday political rhetoric, the word became associated only with the more pejorative of his two meanings.[29] Among activists suspicious of government, to say that individuals or groups have been "co-opted" is an insult. It implies that people who ought to be critical of authorities have surrendered their independence. Thus in the late 1970s, when urban policy gave priority to funding neighborhood groups, organizers faced a dilemma about "whether a group can 'accept federal money and stay clean,' and how to avoid co-optation without naively sacrificing access to needed resources."[30]

Coproduction

The images of capture and co-optation are alike in three important ways:

—both are preoccupied with power;
—both assume that power is zero-sum—participants can gain influence only at the expense of officials (or the broader public) and vice versa;
—and both derive from what Robert Dahl calls the "lump of power" fallacy—all the real power must be in the hands of one side or the other.[31]

Are these impoverished notions the best tools we have for understanding public involvement in administration? Can we not find a more inspiring image—one that admits participants and officials can genuinely share power or, better yet, that *both* sides can gain influence by working together?[32]

Fortunately, such possibilities have become crystallized in the concept of *coproduction*. The idea applied originally to human services, where authorities often try to influence citizens in ways that are virtually impossible without their cooperation.[33] (Thus teachers and students "coproduce" education.) When municipal budgets came under pressure in the early 1980s, the term spread to "harder" functions such as police, fire, and sanitation. Researchers and administrators realized that citizen action can improve the efficiency of official service providers, as when residents sort trash for recycling or patrol streets as eyes and ears of the police. When applied to service delivery, *coproduction* for the most part denotes participation as doing; but scholars soon extended the term to more complex functions such as neighborhood planning, in which doing, advising, and deciding are intertwined.

So far, there is no concise, widely recognized definition of the word, but most writers who use it would probably agree that coproduction ideally entails the following qualities:[34]

> —Citizen involvement is voluntary (rather than legally compelled), positive (aimed at improving the situation), and active.
> —Citizens and authorities both accept the legitimacy of each other's role in planning and producing services.
> —Their relationship is basically cooperative, but differences are freely expressed.
> —In making decisions that affect both sides, officials may or may not retain ultimate authority, but influence is genuinely shared, usually through an interactive, face-to-face process of give-and-take discussion and negotiation.

Because coproduction is such an appealing ideal, it is worth our while to pay closer attention to what is needed to make it succeed.

CONDITIONS FAVORING SUCCESSFUL COPRODUCTION

The conditions identified below are restrictive enough to explain why truly cooperative relations between agencies and citizens are relatively rare.[35] Several depend, however, on perceptions and attitudes of officials or participants, and others are alterable by their strategies; so we can hope that relationships that are now exceptional will become more prevalent in the future.

Interests Not Strictly Opposed

Neither authorities nor citizens will voluntarily persist with a power-sharing process unless they gain from it. If advances for citizens always come at the expense of agency goals, officials will want to revert to unilateral decision making. If citizens learn that participation earns them no better outcomes, they will lapse into cynical apathy or active hostility. In other words, coproduction requires "win-win" situations—where the underlying conflict among interests is not too severe, so cooperative problem-solving efforts have a good chance of helping everyone.

The early identification of coproduction with citizen involvement in delivery of uncontroversial services made it easy to overlook how much good relations between citizens and officials depend on low conflict. In everyone's favorite example, the neighborhood watch, who (other than criminals) opposes safer streets? In such unitary situations, people are less jealous about power. They readily defer to whoever seems to know best how to reach the common goal—usually, in this case, the police, but sometimes a citizen with a bright idea.

When more controversial matters are at stake, cooperative processes sometimes succeed in finding a generally advantageous solution, but they may also fail to get past bedrock differences. The severity of underlying conflict over a given decision depends not only on what options are technically possible but also on the detailed structure of each party's preferences. Consider a government that wants to involve citizens in planning a nuclear power plant. If opponents worry only that the proposed plant will cost them inconvenience and economic losses, an open planning process can find ways to satisfy them with minor adjustments in the site plan and a financial compensation package. If opponents have anxieties about safety, officials may still be able to win them over by modifying blueprints and drawing up a credible evacuation plan. But if resistance is rooted in a deep-seated belief that nuclear energy irremediably threatens cancer and catastrophe, then authorities can satisfy participants only by abandoning the basic plan. Can they do so without suffering too great a loss of their own? Perhaps. If their real goal is merely to assure an adequate energy supply, opponents might be able to show how to do this through conservation and alternative sources. But if the government is unalterably committed to nuclear power—whether from pride, sunk costs, or conviction—then even the most ideal participatory process cannot stop the collision of wills.

To be sure, if both sides handle themselves with candor and good will, an open, face-to-face process may mitigate some of the hostility the clash would normally generate; but if feelings are intense on both sides, it will take remarkable self-restraint to prevent a quick switch to battle tactics.

Conflicts that threaten to prevent coproduction from reaching a generally acceptable outcome need not occur only between agencies and citizens. The public consists of a variety of interests, and sometimes participatory planning catches an agency in the crossfire of these interests. For example, the Corps of Engineers once proposed to clean up rivers near Akron and Cleveland by tunneling wastewater to a distant rural area, where it would be sprayed (as fertilizer) onto farms. During an elaborate public-involvement process, farmers mobilized in opposition, inspired less by anger at the corps than at the city folk who couldn't handle their own sludge. Fortunately, another option was found that satisfied both sides—the sludge was used to reclaim strip-mined land elsewhere in Ohio. Thus coproduction succeeded because the conflict of interests was less than absolute.[36]

Independent Power of Citizens

Partnership between officials and citizens is seldom a love match. Agencies embrace coproduction not out of spontaneous good will but because they believe strategies based on unilateral power will fail. Janice Perlman reports that in Madrid—where coproduction between planners and local "commissions of participation" has reached an advanced level—"the administration had to be pressured to take the grass-roots partner seriously and . . . each cooperative effort was the result of many months, even years of conflict." As Perlman observes, the continuing success of coproduction "rests fragilely upon the ongoing underlying threat of conflict and the ability—real or perceived—to produce it."[37]

To make threats credible, citizen groups must avoid co-optation and excessive dependence on authorities. Thus, Marilyn Gittell's study of public education policy in Atlanta, Boston, and Los Angeles found that community organizations mandated by government were less influential than citizen-initiated groups, which spoke up more vigorously for the needs of their communities. Gittell concludes that government should not mandate or maintain community organizations but that it can usefully encourage and support self-initiated groups, provided its help is small enough that the groups remain basically independent.[38] The wisdom of her advice is apparent. Even if benevolent officials are willing to underwrite their own critics, neither their continued good will nor their survival in office can be guaranteed. In short, citizens who want to work as equal partners with officials must first learn how to create and sustain effective pressure groups.

Plurality of Citizen Interests

If independence on the part of citizen organizations avoids the Scylla of co-optation, the best defense against the Charybdis of capture occurs when an agency must deal with more than one citizen group. Confronted by a strong, homogeneous constituency, an agency's course of least resistance is to reach an accommodation—opening the door to cozy access for that clientele but shutting out other elements of the public. In contrast, when two or more strong interests clash, administrators can more easily pursue an open, inclusive strategy of citizen involvement. For example, United States resource-management agencies traditionally had well-developed systems for seeking the advice of user groups (ranchers, loggers, shippers, etc.), but only when environmentalists effectively challenged user interests did agencies adopt a truly public participation process.

The emergence of conflicting interests led some officials to adopt a new vision of their own role. James Creighton and others who helped shape the Corps of Engineers citizen-involvement program suggest that instead of being either humble servants of a clientele or haughty interpreters of "*the* public interest" administrators should see themselves as managers of open decision-making processes designed to resolve conflicts among competing publics.[39] This doctrine proposes too passive a role for authorities, one based on an uncritical understanding of pluralism. As we saw in Chapter 3, some affected but latent interests will be inadequately represented in even the most contentious process. Administrators must therefore not only mediate among people who participate but also advocate for those who do not.

The principle of multiple interests may appear contradicted by public-involvement programs in which an agency attempts to set up a single representative group with which it will deal. Administrators like to simplify their relations with citizens, and if authority is delegated to one group, permitting rival groups may be logically untenable. But there is great risk that any one organization will be dominated by a single faction or interest. Government bears a responsibility to insist that any group on which it bestows special privileges must follow procedures that are fair and open to all eligible citizens. Efforts to preserve internal democracy or to adjudicate between squabbling pretenders to legitimacy can cost officials so much time and trouble that they may do better to work with a plurality of groups from the beginning.[40]

Citizen Access to Expertise

The technical prowess of full-time, professional officials poses perhaps the toughest barrier to citizen influence over administrative decisions. Of course, it is easy (especially for officials themselves) to exaggerate their superiority. Ordinary people possess expertise of their own. They can identify problems and sometimes get close to solutions. But on the whole, the advantage of authorities' knowledge remains undeniable.

Consequently, citizens cannot hope to work with agencies on anything approaching an equal basis unless a way can be found to arm them with information and expertise. Fortunately, determined citizens groups and enlightened governments have devised methods that at least partially redress the imbalance:

> —*Informing the Public.* Officials who want to educate rather than obfuscate can find imaginative ways to communicate technical ideas. During debates over nuclear power, Austria made available to all citizens a plain-language dictionary of scientific terms; Sweden financed "study circles" on energy policy in which 80,000 citizens participated.[41]
>
> —*Creating Citizen Experts.* Citizens who invest enough effort and time can acquire the knowledge of experts without sharing their biases and self-interest. To resolve a heated dispute over recombinant-DNA research, the city manager of Cambridge, Massachusetts, appointed a citizen panel. After a crash course in molecular biology, its seven members produced a report that, according to one observer, "showed that a broadly representative group of nonscientists could tackle a monumentally complex science policy issue and arrive at a solution widely regarded as intelligent and responsible."[42]
>
> —*Assigning Experts to Serve Citizens:* In a variety of ways, governments can pay experts who work independent of traditional agencies. Adversary experts can staff a separate bureau within government, as many states have done in setting up consumer advocate's offices. Some agencies make funds available to citizen groups so that they can hire expert witnesses and consultants to help them in

official proceedings. The ultimate commitment is to give groups of citizens permanent staff at public expense. Thus, residents' associations in Spanish shantytowns won the right to hire their own architects, planners, and engineers; and Dutch neighborhood groups give orders to "external experts" whose salaries are paid by the national government.[43]

—*Developing Experts Independent of Government:* Citizens are best equipped for controversy if they can secure help from experts without risking the possible fickleness of government assistance. They can benefit from the knowledge of committed volunteers, such as the dissenting scientists who played a large part in stimulating the movement against nuclear energy. Or, like many public-interest groups, they can make the hiring of full-time expert staff a central part of a strategy for long-term influence.

Supportive Attitudes and Practices

No matter how favorable other conditions are, coproduction stands little chance of success unless authorities are willing to adopt appropriate expectations and behavioral styles in working with the public. Officials must invite participation at early stages of decision making rather than leave citizens no choice but to react angrily to plans already cast (often literally) in concrete. They must recognize that people's values and emotions can contribute as much to good policy as experts' facts and techniques. They must adjust their methods, replacing adversarial formats such as hearings with new, interactive ways to exchange ideas. To guard against the danger of overselling themselves on public involvement, officials must remember that some conflict remains inevitable and that participation is no panacea. To justify substantive concessions and slower decision processes, authorities must sustain themselves with faith that coproduction will bring about wiser policies that can be implemented with the assistance of citizens, rather than against their resistance.

NOTES

1. I follow Stuart Langton in distinguishing *citizen action* (participation initiated outside government) from *citizen involvement* (participation initiated by government agencies). *Citizen Participation in America: Essays on the State of the Art* (Lexington, Mass.: Lexington Books, D. C. Heath and Co., 1978), pp. 1–2.

2. Donald E. Voth and William S. Bonner, "Citizen Participation in Rural Development: Concepts, Principles, and Resource Materials" (Mississippi State, Miss.: Southern Rural Development Center, 1978). For an eloquent statement of the TVA doctrine by its chairman, see David E. Lilienthal, *TVA: Democracy on the March* (New York: Harper & Row, 1944).

3. Langton, *Citizen Participation in America*, p. 3.

4. Mary Grisez Kweit and Robert W. Kweit, *Implementing Citizen Participation in a Bureaucratic Society: A Contingency Approach* (New York: Praeger, 1981), p. 6.

5. Jeffrey M. Berry, "Maximum Feasible Dismantlement," *Citizen Participation*, 3, no. 2 (November/December 1981), 3–5.

6. Kweit and Kweit, *Implementing Citizen Participation*, p. 3.

7. For these and other methods, see James Creighton, Jerry Delli Priscoli, and C. Mark Dunning, *Public Involvement Techniques: A Reader of Ten Years Experience at the Institute for Water*

Resources (Fort Belvoir, Va.: U.S. Army Corps of Engineers, 1983), pp. 244–371; and Judy B. Rosener, "A Cafeteria of Techniques and Critiques," *Public Management*, 57 (December 1975), 16–19.

8. *Neighborhood Politics* (Cambridge: Harvard University Press, 1983), p. ix. Crenson's book contains numerous examples of the unofficial production of public goods by neighborhood activists in Baltimore.

9. Cyrus Zirakzadeh, "The Asociaciones de Vecinos in the Basque Region of Spain, 1964–1980: A Study in Neighborhood Politics" (paper presented at the annual meeting of the American Political Science Association, 1985).

10. Quoted by Andras Hegedus, *Socialism and Bureaucracy* (New York: St. Martin's Press, 1976), p. 20.

11. Theodore H. Friedgut, *Political Participation in the USSR* (Princeton: Princeton University Press, 1979); Richard R. Fagen, *The Transformation of Political Culture in Cuba* (Stanford: Stanford University Press, 1969); James R. Townsend, *Political Participation in Communist China* (Berkeley: University of California Press, 1969). As the discussion of mobilization in Chapter 1 implies, I classify such efforts as true participation only to the extent they are voluntary.

12. Richard L. Cole and David A. Caputo, "The Public Hearing as an Effective Citizen Participation Mechanism: A Case Study of the General Revenue Sharing Program," *American Political Science Review*, 78 (1984), 404–16.

13. For examples, see page 57 above and Daniel A. Mazmanian and Jeanne Nienaber, *Can Organizations Change?: Environmental Protection, Citizen Participation, and the Corps of Engineers* (Washington: The Brookings Institution, 1979), chaps. 4, 5, 6.

14. Lawrence Johnson & Associates, Inc., *Citizen Participation in Community Development: A Catalog of Local Approaches* (Washington: Government Printing Office, 1978), pp. 31, 109.

15. Creighton et al., *Public Involvement Techniques*, p. 300.

16. Adam Walinsky, quoted by Sherry R. Arnstein, "A Ladder of Citizen Participation," *Journal of the American Institute of Planners*, 35 (1969), 216–24.

17. Theodore R. Marmor and James A. Morone, "Representing Consumer Interests: Imbalanced Markets, Health Planning, and the HSAs," *Milbank Memorial Fund Quarterly/Health and Society*, 58 (1980), 125–65.

18. For vivid illustrations of this principle in the distribution of land and taxes in revolutionary China, see William Hinton, *Fanshen: A Documentary of Revolution in a Chinese Village* (New York: Monthly Review Press, 1966).

19. John Clayton Thomas, "Citizen Participation and Public Management: Counselling a Troubled Marriage" (paper presented at the annual meeting of the American Political Science Association, 1985). See also page 14 above on the participation hypothesis.

20. Grant McConnell, *Private Power and American Democracy* (New York: Alfred A. Knopf, 1967), p. 76.

21. The term originated in the study of interest-group influence over regulatory agencies. For application to public-involvement programs, see Paul J. Culhane, *Public Lands Politics: Interest Group Influence on the Forest Service and the Bureau of Land Management* (Baltimore: Johns Hopkins University Press, 1981).

22. *Maximum Feasible Misunderstanding: Community Action in the War on Poverty* (New York: The Free Press, 1970), p. 182.

23. Voth and Bonner, "Citizen Participation in Rural Development," p. 13; see also Kweit and Kweit, *Implementing Citizen Participation*.

24. *Private Power and American Democracy*. Culhane reports, however, that by the early 1960s the Bureau of Land Management had freed itself from capture by rancher-dominated grazing advisory boards. *Public Lands Politics*, pp. 247–50.

25. McConnell, *Private Power and American Democracy;* and Philip Selznick, *TVA and the Grass Roots: A Study in the Sociology of Formal Organization* (New York: Harper Torchbooks, 1966; originally 1949).

26. John D. Montgomery, "When Local Participation Helps," *Journal of Policy Analysis and Management*, 3 (1983), 90–105. See also pages 61–62 above on the principle of stratification.

27. *TVA and the Grassroots*, pp. 13–16, 259–61.

28. Richard A. Couto, "Old and New Grass Roots: Time, TVA, and Cooptation" (paper presented at the annual meeting of the American Political Science Association, 1984), p. 10.

29. Even scholars had to bow to prevailing usage. Couto, for example, retains "formal cooptation" but replaces "informal cooptation" with "accommodation." Ibid.

30. Janice Perlman, "Grassroots Empowerment and Government Response," *Social Policy*, 10, no. 2 (1979), 16–21.

31. *Modern Political Analysis*, 4th ed. (Englewood Cliffs, N. J.: Prentice-Hall, Inc., 1984), 20–21.

32. In her well-known article, "A Ladder of Citizen Participation," Sherry Arnstein does admit that power can be shared; but she implicitly assumes it is a zero-sum value, as is evident from the eight steps by which she depicts citizens ascending from impotence to dominance: manipulation, therapy, informing, consultation, placation, partnership, delegated power, and citizen control. For an explanation of how power can be a non-zero-sum quantity, see my *Descriptive Analysis of Power* (New Haven: Yale University Press, 1975), ch. 10.

33. Gordon P. Whitaker, "Coproduction: Citizen Participation in Service Delivery," *Public Administration Review*, 40 (1980), 240–46.

34. This list draws on Jeffrey Brudney and Robert England, "Toward a Definition of the Coproduction Concept," *Public Administration Review*, 43 (1983), 59–65; and Lawrence Susskind, Michael Elliott, and Associates, *Paternalism, Conflict, and Coproduction: Learning from Citizen Action and Citizen Participation in Western Europe* (New York: Plenum, 1983), pp. 6, 13–14, 296–98.

35. This section applies not only to coproduction as defined above but also to power-sharing arrangements in which officials and citizens collaboratively decide about services that citizens will not directly help produce (e.g., the building of a highway or power plant).

36. Mazmanian and Nienaber, *Can Organizations Change?* pp. 119–31.

37. "Citizen Action and Participation in Madrid," in Susskind et al., *Paternalism, Conflict, and Coproduction*, p. 230. According to one definition of *conflict*, the ability of citizens to disrupt officials' plans actually *reduces* the conflict of interest between them by making the outcome worse if they can't agree. Therefore, the independent power of citizens to punish authorities can be viewed as one way to satisfy the condition that their interests not be strictly opposed. See Robert Axelrod, *Conflict of Interest* (Chicago: Markham, 1970).

38. "The Consequences of Mandating Citizen Participation," *Policy Studies Review*, 3 (1983), 90–95.

39. *Public Involvement Techniques*, p. 40.

40. For a case in point, see Martha Derthick, "Defeat at Fort Lincoln," *The Public Interest*, no. 20 (Summer 1970), 3–39.

41. Dorothy Nelkin, *Technological Decisions and Democracy: European Experiments in Public Participation* (Beverly Hills: Sage Publications, 1977), pp. 81, 60–65.

42. Diana Dutton, "The Impact of Public Participation in Biomedical Policy: Evidence from Four Case Studies," in *Citizen Participation in Science Policy*, ed. James C. Petersen (Amherst: University of Massachusetts Press, 1984), p. 148.

43. Susskind et al., *Paternalism, Conflict, and Coproduction*, pp. 213, 291.

CHAPTER 11

WORKPLACES

In recent decades, the most vigorous movement toward greater participation has occurred not in politics but at work. This development has been worldwide and unrestricted by conventional boundaries of ideology, culture, or wealth. Much of the inspiration comes from Yugoslavia, whose independent Communist regime made participation the foundation of its own legitimacy. In capitalist nations of Europe, public and private initiatives led to pathbreaking developments in West Germany, Sweden, Norway, and Spain. Proposals for national policies promoting workplace democracy have been major political issues in France, Italy, and Great Britain. Japan and Israel introduced widely studied participatory institutions. In the Third World, significant (if not always lasting) experiments have occurred in Algeria, Chile, China, and Peru. Although U.S. research stimulated much of the early interest in democratic management, the United States has lagged behind many other countries in adopting national policies favoring economic democracy. By the 1980s, however, the need to restore the country's competitiveness in world markets brought about a strong shift toward participatory management in United States corporations.

VARIETIES OF WORKPLACE PARTICIPATION

The variety of ways employees can be involved in workplace decisions are distinguishable along three chief dimensions:[1]

—The *organizational level* at which workers participate. Do they have a say in decisions only in their immediate work groups, or are they represented at higher echelons up to or including the corporate board?
—The *scope* of decisions that workers influence at each level. Is their involvement narrowly restricted, or, at the other extreme, are they entitled to help shape any and all policies?
—The *degree of control* workers exercise over policies within the scope of their influence. Are they merely consulted by managers, do they share power with managers, or do they possess the ultimate authority to decide?

The discussion that follows is organized according to organizational levels, as we look first at workers' influence over enterprisewide decisions, then at workgroup participation, and finally at everything in between. At each level, the models of participation that we examine differ chiefly in the scope and degree of employee influence.

Representation on Boards

At the level of the entire enterprise (firm or corporation), democratization takes two main forms: codetermination and complete workers' control.

Codetermination. Shortly after World War II, British occupation authorities in Germany's Ruhr Valley granted a German union request that worker representatives get half the seats on supervisory boards of iron, steel, and coal firms in that region. Thus was born the system of codetermination, which since has spread far beyond its Ruhr origins. In 1952, the new government of the Federal Republic of Germany extended codetermination to almost all West German firms; however, except in the original trio of industries, worker representatives were limited to about one-third of board members. In 1976, after twenty-five years of struggle, the German labor federation (DGB) won legislation mandating equal representation for employees and shareholders on the boards of all firms with more than 2,000 employees; but shareholder representatives retained the power to break tie votes.[2]

Favorable appraisals of the West German experience led the European Economic Community to endorse codetermination, and variations on the idea have been instituted by Austria, Sweden, Denmark, Norway, and Luxembourg.[3] In Great Britain, an official commission chaired by Lord Bullock recommended codetermination legislation,[4] but the Labour government of Prime Minister Callaghan did not enact it before falling from power in 1979. In the United States, a first step toward codetermination was taken in 1980, when in return for wage concessions, shareholders of Chrysler Corporation elected Douglas Fraser, the United Auto Workers president, to their board of directors.

If shareholder representatives vote as a bloc, any codetermination plan that gives workers less than a majority of the board denies them real power over policies of the firm. For this reason among others, critics on the left often denounce codetermination as a tokenist scheme to co-opt union leaders.

Indeed, the German word for codetermination (*Mitbestimmung*) means only "having a voice," and a voice—plus access to information—may be all that workers can expect from codetermination alone. However, the psychological value of those rights should not be too lightly dismissed. One Chrysler board member reported that when Fraser described the human impact of plant closings, "you could feel the shock go through the board room."[5] Nevertheless, most supporters of workplace democracy look to measures that go beyond codetermination.

Workers' Control. Under workers' control, the collectivity of all members of the enterprise has final authority over all decisions. In 1950, Yugoslavia decided to put workers in charge of every significant economic enterprise in what was then a poor, backward, and war-devastated country. In smaller units, Yugoslav workers exercise some powers directly through assemblies; and in all enterprises, crucial matters such as mergers and plant relocations are decided by referendum. Normally, however, workers delegate their authority to an elected council of about thirty members. The council in turn chooses a management board (composed mostly of its own members) and a professional director who is responsible for the economic efficiency of the enterprise.[6]

Although Yugoslavia's continually evolving experiment has attracted intense interest from around the world, no other nation has yet established so complete and lasting a system of workers' control. Nevertheless, within capitalist economies, it is possible to organize individual firms according to similar principles. In the United States, for example, conventional corporations can be restructured to create *workers' cooperative corporations,* in which rights to vote and receive profits are vested in (and only in) the people who work in the company.[7]

Limitations of Board-Level Influence. Besides providing a limited degree of power, German codetermination is doubly indirect. Workers themselves vote only for members of plant-level councils, who in turn elect employee representatives on the firm's supervisory board. The supervisory board then assigns operating authority to a management board that includes no worker representatives. Even in worker-controlled enterprises, professional managers are usually entrusted with day-to-day administrative responsibility. To be sure, they must take care not to displease the workers' councils who hire and fire them, but on many issues, managers' superior expertise enables them to dominate the councils. In short, by itself board-level representation gives employees a kind of economic democracy almost as remote and intermittent as electoral democracy in government, whereas employees probably care most about what occurs at the lowest level of organization—the shopfloor.[8]

Shopfloor Participation

Basic work groups offer a nearly ideal opportunity for intensive participation. Small numbers permit committee-style discussion, workers' great interest in decisions combines with group pressure to motivate involvement, and participants' intimate knowledge of their own jobs solves the problem of competence. These and other advantages have made employee participation at the shopfloor level the most popular form of workplace democratization. Just as West Germany and Yugoslavia pioneered, respectively, partial and complete worker control at the enterprise level, so also Japan and Norway established leading patterns for partial and complete worker influence at the shopfloor.

Quality-Control Circles. Beginning in the late 1950s and partly inspired, ironically, by United States researchers, Japanese industry developed the remarkably successful innovation known as quality-control (QC) circles.[9] QC circles usually consist of a natural working group of about five to ten employees who volunteer to meet weekly for an hour or two under the leadership of a supervisor. Each circle is always on the lookout for problems of quality, productivity, cost, or safety in its area of the factory. After identifying such a problem, the group gathers data, conducts statistical analyses, and brainstorms for alternatives. Once the QC circle decides on a solution, it has considerable authority to implement changes in the production process. Successful innovations are recognized by prizes, publicity, and conventions. By 1978, nearly five million Japanese workers participated in QC-circle activity. By permitting "every employee to be a planner and an engineer as well as a worker," the QC circle movement played a major role in Japan's attainment of a reputation for world leadership in product quality.[10]

As United States corporations struggled to compete with the Japanese, QC circles became so popular in the United States factories that one observer commented, "they are in danger of becoming the management fad of the eighties."[11] However, gimmicky imitation of QC circles will fail unless managers recognize that their success depends on deeper changes in the spirit of industrial relations. Supervisors must act more as workers' representatives than as agents of management; companies must invest substantially to train their employees in analytic methods and group dynamics; managers must believe that ordinary workers are competent to solve technical problems; and employees must become committed to the success of their firms.

Autonomous Work Groups. Although changes introduced by QC circles can have a strong impact on daily work routines, the activity itself involves only a self-selected minority of workers who give a small fraction of their time to studying a limited set of issues. More drastic steps toward shopfloor democracy began in Norway. In 1962, Einar Thorsrud, a psychologist, started a series of experiments intended to set in motion a continually intensifying process of industrial democratization. Inspired and helped by researchers from Britain's Tavistock Institute, and with the tripartite support of the Norwegian government, Trade Union Council, and Employers' Association, Thorsrud's Industrial Democracy Project reorganized basic work processes in the metals, paper, fertilizer, and shipping industries. The building block of Thorsrud's system was at first the autonomous work group, a unit of fifteen to forty workers who manage themselves without day-to-day supervision. All members are trained to do several jobs, which they share or rotate. The goal of the system is to create teamwork, commitment, and a sense of responsibility based upon self-control.[12]

Although glowing reports testify to the success of some autonomous work groups, not all experiments with the concept turn out well. Some of the failures appear to be due to typical problems of direct democracy discussed in Chapter 6—inability to resolve conflict, inadequate appreciation of the need for leaders, and inattention to the problem of interdependence.[13] Originally, the groups were to have no formal supervisors, only elected "contact persons" who would coordinate with other groups. Often, however, workers themselves asked for the return of supervisors, "but with less dictatorial behavior."[14] After learning to appreciate more the possible functions of first-level managers, Thorsrud shifted to the term "*semi*-autonomous work groups."

Intermediate Levels

In large firms, the span between corporate board and shopfloor encompasses major divisions and numerous organizational levels. If workers participate only at the highest or lowest levels (or even both), they will have no say in many key decisions. Workplace democratization therefore requires that employees have a voice (usually through representatives) at intermediate steps in the hierarchy. Among the more notable responses to this problem are BOALs, works councils, and parallel structures.

BOALs. In an effort to involve workers more closely in decisions, Yugoslavia in the mid-1970s decentralized its economic system. Replacing the enterprise or firm as the primary unit was the Basic Organization of Associated Labor, or BOAL. Smaller firms might be identical with a single BOAL, but larger enterprises are now established by agreements between two or more BOALs. Each BOAL has its own workers' council, but most are also small enough to decide some matters through direct assembly democracy.[15]

Works Councils. Soon after World War II, many European countries set up plant-level works councils (not to be confused with the workers' councils that have ultimate authority in Yugoslav enterprises). Intended mainly to ensure labor peace, the works councils consist of representatives from management and labor. In most countries, they have been judged a failure, largely because of their lack of decision-making power.[16]

Parallel Structures. Beginning in the early 1970s, United States unions and management jointly undertook a number of influential experiments designed to improve the quality of work life. The first QWL ("quill") system was instituted by the United Auto Workers and Harman International Industries, a Tennessee firm that produces most of the auto mirrors made in the United States.[17] Soon afterward, the UAW and General Motors set up a national committee to promote QWL programs in the giant corporation's far-flung plants. Encouraged by remarkable successes and learning from a few failures, by 1981 the UAW and GM had set up QWL committees in 74 of their 155 bargaining units.[18]

QWL programs usually begin with the establishment of joint labor-management committees parallel to the existing hierarchy. Ideally, labor representatives should be directly or indirectly elected by the workers. Because they lack formal authority, QWL groups might seem to be an American version of the works council, but they have enjoyed greater success whenever management and labor are jointly determined to improve productivity and work life by decentralizing authority and responsibility. Like QC circles, QWL "action groups" study problems and propose solutions, but unlike typical QC circles, QWL groups have purview over many issues affecting employees' well-being, not just productivity, cost, and quality. (QWL committees do not, however, deal with adversarial issues such as wages and individual grievances; these remain functions of the union.) QWL programs are especially interested in proposing changes in decision-making structures. They sometimes recommend autonomous work groups, but they are not confined to any one participatory device, and their general attitude is pragmatic and flexible.[19]

Self-Management

The strongest advocates of workplace democratization want complete workers' self-management, in which the "objective is to integrate fully worker participation at all levels of decision making."[20] Like Neal Herrick, they believe that "representative and participatory democracy can be mutually supportive."[21] There is much evidence in favor of this position. Thus, in QWL systems, higher-level committees help bring about shopfloor democracy. Indeed, participation at lower levels must remain limited and precarious unless it is backed up by worker influence at higher levels. For example, works councils are more effective in West Germany than elsewhere, apparently because codetermination gives employees power in supervisory boards.[22] Nevertheless, some people who favor employee involvement at one level are lukewarm or hostile toward it at other levels. To understand why, let us inquire about the motives of different groups who support workplace participation.

REASONS FOR WORKPLACE PARTICIPATION

The vitality of the movement for workplace democracy results largely from its widely varied supporters—idealistic theorists and hard-headed pragmatists, corporate executives and union leaders, capitalists and socialists. The goals that attract these different groups are not always incompatible, but most advocates are distinguishable by the emphasis they put on one or another of the following benefits: intensified democracy, increased productivity, or improved well-being of workers.

To Intensify Democracy

"The aim of organizational democracy," says Carole Pateman, "is democracy."[23] Political theorists like Pateman are attracted to workplace democratization because they believe it is the most promising way to create a more ideally democratic society. Thinkers in this tradition make four principal arguments: (1) workplaces are a superior site for intensive participation; (2) workers' control helps equalize power in society; (3) a democratic economy offers a more stable base for democratic government; and (4) participatory workplaces are schools for participatory citizenship.

The Participatory Superiority of Workplaces. Many writers who are convinced of the developmental and intrinsic virtues of participation believe that trying to involve people in government offers little hope of achieving the widespread intensive activity they want. The huge size of most political democracies induces citizens to be active superficially, intermittently, or not at all. In addition, despite the great power governments ultimately wield, their immediate jurisdictions usually include only a fraction of the outcomes that really matter in citizens' daily lives. Rather than forsake their vision, participationists transfer "the ideal of the polis . . . to the workplace."[24] Compared with political units, many places of employment are small; even the largest corporations can be divided into small work groups. Thus, in workplaces participation can often take the ideal form of face-to-face direct democracy in committees and assemblies. Moreover, workplaces supply the motivation needed for intensive involvement. At stake are the workers' incomes, the way they spend the largest part of their waking hours, their close friendships, and a major source of their self-esteem.

Power Equalization. Some theorists offer a more abstract but closely parallel argument. They point out that even if all citizens exercised equal power over government policies (which of course they don't), power in society as a whole would remain highly concentrated so long as hierarchical workplaces enable relatively few people to control so many vital decisions. Therefore, to justify extending democratic norms from politics to economics, power equalizers try to redefine as "political" the decisions controlled by corporate "governments." Only by allowing everyone to share power at work, they say, can a nation approach the democratic ideal of distributing power as equally as possible among all members.[25]

A Stronger Foundation for Political Democracy. Theorists have long believed that democratic government is most secure if it rests on a base of broadly distributed wealth and economic authority. Economic inequality undermines political equality wherever the rich are able to convert their material resources into political power. On the other hand, when the poor majority take advantage of their numerical strength, they may curtail both economic and political liberty as they struggle to equalize wealth, especially if (as in conventional socialism) they concentrate authority in the hands of bureaucrats. Robert Dahl proposes that a self-managed economy offers a way to escape this old dilemma. Compared with capitalist corporations, he argues, self-managed firms will lessen material inequality by reducing salary differentials and sharing profits. Compared with state socialism, self-management requires dispersed economic authority, as numerous firms must enjoy the freedom of action that we associate with a market economy. Thus, Dahl concludes, a self-managed economy should provide a more "appropriate social and economic foundation" for a stable, free, and egalitarian democratic order.[26]

Educative Effects. Many participatory democrats also believe that workplace democracy will "spill over" to strengthen governmental democracy in a more psychological way. Workers who develop political skill and confidence on the job, they predict, will not remain passive as citizens.[27] The evidence available so far supports this hope. Elden reports that his own research and ten other studies link work democratization to a stronger sense of efficacy and increased participation in unions, voluntary organizations, or government.[28] However, socialists and others who yearn for more far-reaching developmental effects may be headed for disappointment. Greenberg found that worker-owners in United States plywood factories are individualistic, competitive, and conservative in their political attitudes. He speculates that the need to survive in a market economy prevents them from extending to society as a whole the egalitarian cooperation they practice within their own firms.[29] Nevertheless, for people whose priority is to invigorate democracy rather than to aim it toward socialist policies, evidence that influence on the job helps workers feel more efficacious offers enough reason for optimism about the developmental value of workplace democracy.

To Increase Productivity

Although it is understandable that political theorists focus on democracy as an end in itself, their teachings probably have limited practical impact. They inspire a few activists and will perhaps have a long-term effect on public opinion. In a few nations (mostly Scandinavian) governmental policies show concern for democracy per se, but to most movers and shakers, the democratic theorists' case for workplace participation will seem idealistic, abstract, and speculative. Leaders of business and government are more impressed by arguments that participation promotes economic efficiency.

Over several decades, industrial psychologists and other management reformers have built a strong case in favor of that claim. By promoting commitment, they contend, participation induces employees to work harder and more carefully. Enlisting workers' minds as well as their bodies taps a new fund of expertise and a fount of creativity. Involvement in decisions makes members of a firm more willing to accept the rapid innovation necessary to survive in competitive markets. The greater satisfaction of workers who control their own job conditions reduces costly turnover and absenteeism. When labor and management work together, they avoid strikes and disruptive conflicts.

Empirical evidence linking participation and productivity is even more impressive, whether one considers nations or firms. Many observers give codetermination part of the credit for West Germany's postwar "economic miracle." In the twelve years after Yugoslavia established the world's first labor-managed economy, its per capita income grew at an annual rate of 8 percent, the fastest in the world except for Japan's 8.6 percent—and as we have seen, some of Japan's success can be attributed to its own participatory practices. During the same period (1952 to 1964), the United States economy grew at only about 2 percent a year.[30] Nor did the disparity change much after the more participatory economies completed their initial recoveries from wartime devastation. During the 1970s, Yugoslavia's per capita income rose 56 percent, and Japan's 45 percent, whereas the United States continued to lag at 24 percent.[31]

Within traditional capitalist economies, islands of workplace democracy show comparable gains. Worker-owned scavenger firms in the San Francisco area provide trash collection for "probably the lowest charge of any major city in the United States," even though their members earn 47 percent more than employees of conventional firms and 83 percent more than collectors who work for city governments.[32] Worker-owned plywood firms in the Pacific Northwest justify their unusually high pay scales by achieving productivity 25 to 60 percent above the industry average.[33] In the Basque region of Spain, the Mondragon system of workers' cooperatives grew from one co-op in 1956 to eighty-seven in the early 1980s, with a total of 18,000 worker-members and $1.7 billion in annual sales. Not one Mondragon co-op has ever failed.[34] Democratizing efforts short of workers' control have also paid off for numerous companies. A 1984 survey found that United States high-technology firms offering stock ownership to a majority of employees increased sales, on average, four times as much as companies that deny their employees ownership opportunities.[35] Studies of QWL and participatory management experiments in the 1970s report positive results in over 80 percent of 160 cases.[36]

It would be naive to expect that democratization inevitably produces wondrous economic gains. Participation is a process for transforming social systems, not a new machine that can be plugged in at will. Its success therefore depends on intangibles such as commitment, trust, communication, education, and leadership. Nevertheless, the accumulating evidence linking participation and productivity is so favorable that desire for competitive economic advan-

To Improve Workers' Well-Being

When participation is presented mainly as a way to boost productivity, workers suspect it is merely a sugar-coated scheme to intensify their exploitation. This fear can be laid to rest only by combining participation with worker ownership or other plans that give all employees a share in the surplus their efforts create. Except for this problem, however, workers and their advocates are increasingly attracted to democratization because it can improve the quality of work life and protect jobs.

Quality of Work Life. Critics of conventional organization have long denounced the strict separation of roles that reserves intellectual functions for managers while treating workers as though they were robots. This system has condemned generations of employees to boredom, frustration, alienation, and lack of personal fulfillment. The remedy, psychologists argue, lies in shopfloor democracy combined with related reforms such as job enlargement, but for a long time unions agreed with managers that dehumanization at work was the price of mass prosperity. By the early 1970s, however, it became evident that younger, better-educated workers would not tolerate a system that gave them so little control over their lives. Enlightened labor leaders in Scandinavia and in the United States became strong supporters of QWL systems, provided that they could depict job satisfaction, rather than productivity, as the primary goal. Workers almost always found the new arrangements better than the old. The words of a Norwegian welder explain why:

> I stood here for eight years welding together metal plates, always on the same spot and with never any change. I hardly knew what the plates were being used for. I never thought about the job and never asked anybody—I just did what I was told. The work was a vacuum. . . . Now it's much better. There is variation in the work. We discuss production and plan the whole thing ourselves—everybody is interested in seeing that it runs smoothly. You jump in where you're needed and then you get help from the others another time. But the most important thing is that you feel freer.[37]

Job Protection. When foreign or other competitors cut into a firm's sales, its workers and unions become more willing to cut costs and improve product quality by cooperating in QC circles and QWL programs. When faced with the drastic threat of plant closure, employees are increasingly turning to worker ownership rather than see their factories shut down by bankrupt owners, callous conglomerates, or corporate raiders. During the 1970s and 1980s, such employee buyouts occurred at some rather sizable firms: Dan River Textiles, Hyatt Roller Bearing, Rath Packing, South Bend

Lathe, Vermont Asbestos, and Weirton Steel. In some cases, hasty planning or legal restrictions resulted in majority employee ownership without any change toward participatory management or board-level workers' control. Subsequently, workers sometimes found themselves in severe clashes, including strikes, against the management of their own firms. Nevertheless, the assumption behind these buyouts appears well-founded. Firms that workers both own and control strive hard and often successfully to preserve jobs—for example, by sharing reduced wages or working hours to prevent laying off or dismissing members. Whether an economy composed largely of self-managed firms would do as well in mainaining overall employment is less certain. Vanek believes that such an economy "effectively does guarantee full employment";[38] other economists contend that the incentive for each firm to maximize profit per worker-owner would induce them to minimize admission of new members.

How Goals Affect Attitudes Toward Different Types of Participation

As a rule, shopfloor participation offers the most effective way to advance the goals of intensive participatory democracy, citizen education, productivity, and job satisfaction. Conversely, equalization of power and wealth and job protection depend on worker influence at higher levels, especially on boards. This bifurcation does not bother democratic theorists, who cheerfully endorse democratization up and down the hierarchy. However, key groups with tangible stakes in the process take more restrictive positions.

Workers have reasons to want influence at all hierarchical levels, but action on their behalf is taken mainly by labor unions, whose own interests make them wary of some forms of participation. West German, Swedish, and British unions have all strongly backed codetermination—a system union officials find easy to embrace, because they usually expect to become the workers' representatives. (Indeed, the Bullock Plan would have required that "employees representatives . . . be based on a single channel of representation through trade union machinery."[39]) Progressive unionists have also supported shopfloor democratization, provided they are involved in the process through effective QWL committees. In a few cases, labor leaders in the United States have assisted employee buyout schemes. However, unions inevitably feel ambivalent about workers' control. After all, what role is left for unions when workers are their own employers?[40]

If unions feel uncertain about workers' control, imagine how threatening the prospect must be to employers. As Gunn observes, the logic of capitalism induces owners and managers to insist on retaining control over "those decisions that most directly affect profit."[41] They are therefore inclined to oppose participation above the shopfloor level, except for plans that give workers a merely consultative role. In West Germany, employers' associations filed legal challenges against the 1976 extension of codetermination; their counterparts in Britain opposed the Bullock Plan.[42] Although employee stock ownership has become popular among United States corporations, most plans confine employees to a small percentage of outstanding stock and restrict their ability to vote the shares they own. Any legislative move toward widespread workers' control in the United States would surely arouse strenuous resistance from owners and managers. Advocates of workplace democracy must therefore eventually address fundamental issues of ownership and economic structure.

IDEOLOGY AND THE FUTURE OF WORKPLACE DEMOCRACY

During most of the twentieth century, the lines of debate and warfare alike were drawn by two grand dichotomies: Should the political order be democratic or dictatorial? Should the economic order be capitalist or socialist? Fascists and communists gave similar answers to the first question but disagreed about the second. Within most democracies, conflict centered on the economic issue, as bourgeois and socialist parties competed for power. Political theorists carried on their own version of the ideological struggle. Those on the left contended that capitalism generates too much inequality and insecurity to be compatible with genuine democracy; conservatives countered that socialism, by setting up a government monopoly of economic power, destroys the pluralism on which free political competition depends.

In the first two decades after World War II, controversy over basic economic issues abated. Socialists had traditionally wanted government to do two things: take ownership of major industries away from capitalists, and substitute planning for markets in allocating key resources. The performance of socialism in the Soviet Union and Eastern Europe persuaded many democratic socialists that bureaucratic ownership was not so humane nor central planning so efficient as they had expected. Economic conflict in the democracies continued to be defined by the two polarities of public versus private ownership and planning versus market, but accumulating experience showed that middle paths were possible. Government could take over some industries without destroying capitalism; it could regulate the economy without dismantling the market. At the end of this period of calm consensus and modest aspirations, the renewed vision of workplace democracy brought revived idealism and an appreciation of more complicated possibilities.

The New Complexity of Political Economy

How does democratization of work relate to the traditional ideological battle? Some theorists believe it is a refreshingly new and independent issue. Ronald Mason, for example, predicts that "workplace democracy contains the seeds of a new world order that is neither socialist nor capitalist in nature."[43] For others, the old struggle does not so easily fade away. In 1975, Ronald

Reagan described employee stock ownership as capitalism's "best tool of all in its struggle with socialism. . . . Could there be a better answer to the stupidity of Karl Marx than millions of workers individually sharing in the ownership of the means of production?"[44] On the other side, Christopher Gunn reaches what may appear to be the opposite conclusion: "Can a fully democratic and self-managed workplace be the dominant form of production under capitalism? The answer is clearly no."[45]

Conventional concepts of capitalism and socialism are inadequate for understanding the requirements and implications of workplace democratization. The innovative Yugoslavs demonstrated as much when, in establishing the first worker-managed economy, they also split apart the traditional socialist fusion of collective ownership and central planning. The free market, they decided, was both more efficient and more compatible with a system of collectively owned but worker-controlled enterprises.

Thus, whereas the world was formerly divided along just two ideological dimensions (as in Figure 11–1), the political-economic debates of our time revolve about four questions: (1) Should major industries be individually or collectively owned? (2) Should economic resources be allocated principally by competitive markets or by central planning? (3) Should people elect governments in free, competitive elections, or should the state be controlled by an exclusive, hegemonic group?[46] (4) Should the management of workplaces be predominantly hierarchical or participatory? If we dichotomize the answers to these questions, as in Figure 11–2, sixteen political-economic orders emerge.

FIGURE 11–1 The Early Structure of Ideological Conflict

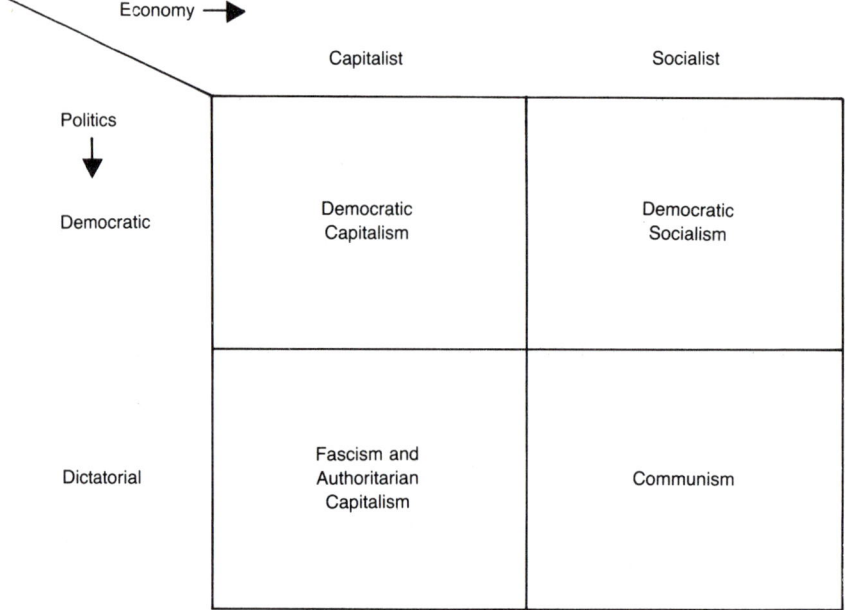

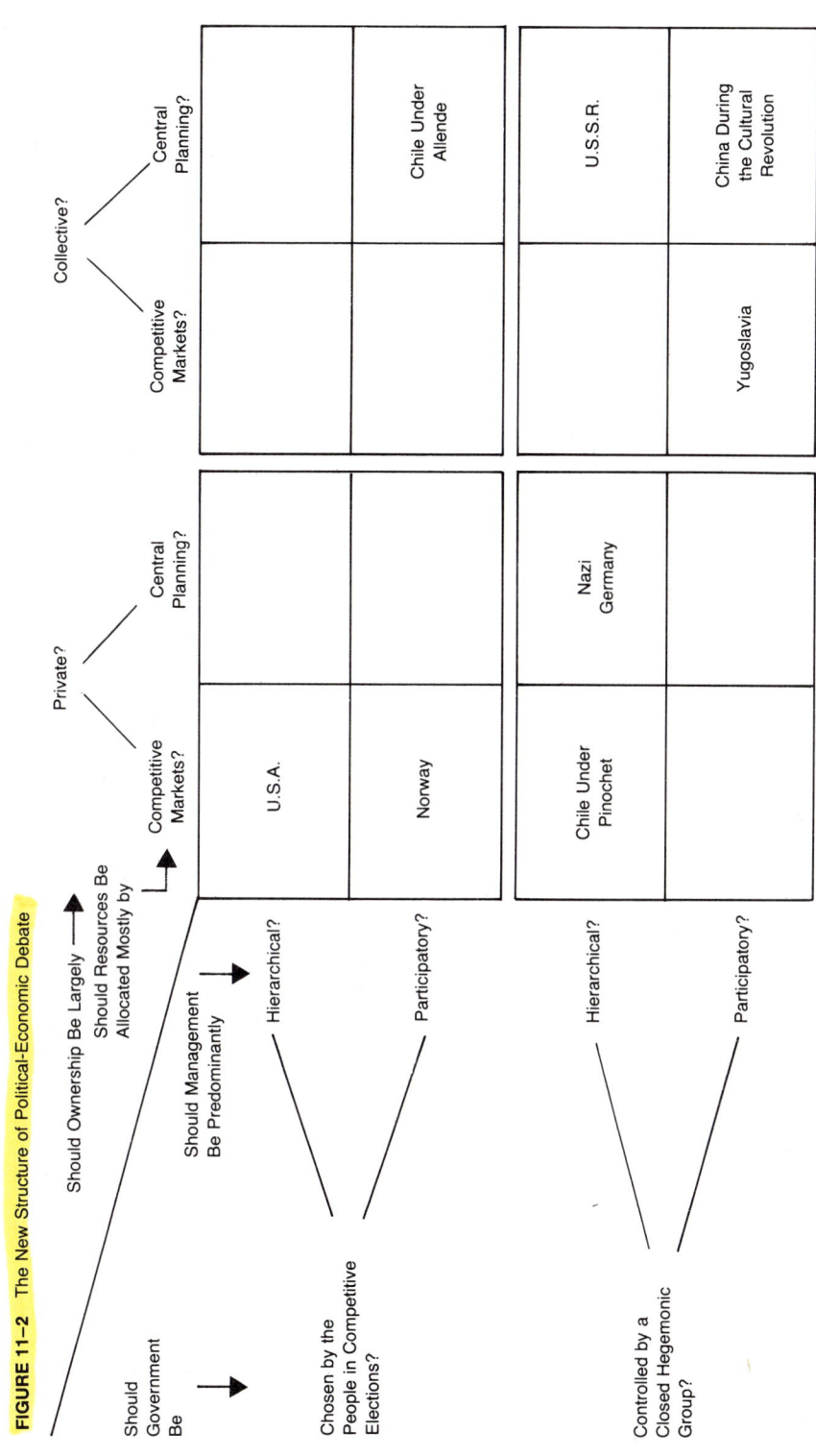

FIGURE 11-2 The New Structure of Political-Economic Debate

Even this diverse picture simplifies reality, because each dimension would be better represented as a continuum of possibilities. Nevertheless, the figure includes a few regimes of the present or past that in practice or aspiration reasonably well illustrate certain combinations.

The variety of systems that include a commitment to participatory management might lead one to think that the organization of work is independent of the other three dimensions. Let us take a closer look at each to see whether such a conclusion is justified.

Ownership

The relationship of workplace democracy to ownership of the means of production is equally troublesome for traditional capitalists and socialists. Corporate reformers always run up against the fear that participatory management will inspire workers to invade owners' privileges. On the other hand, state-owned enterprises usually turn out to be no less hierarchical than their capitalist counterparts. One response is to embrace a third option: ownership of each enterprise by its workers, ideally in such a way that every worker is an owner and all owners are workers. Worker ownership of this sort may indeed be a necessary condition for complete self-management, but dogmatic insistence on it would require radical and improbable restructuring of capitalist and socialist economies alike.[47]

More feasible intermediate possibilities become evident once we recognize that "ownership" really means a bundle of rights and powers, some of which can be retained by private shareholders or the state while others are assigned to, or shared with, workers. Of these, the most important for encouraging participation is the right to control a firm's profit or surplus—the difference between revenues and costs (including wages). On the basis of much evidence (as well as common sense), Paul Bernstein concludes that an essential condition for successful, lasting democratization is the guaranteed return to all employees of a share of the surplus they have produced.[48] Clearly, participatory schemes that induce workers to contribute ideas and effort will soon leave them angry and disillusioned if all productivity gains are siphoned off by greedy owners or an impersonal state.

Pure worker ownership is one way to ensure that workers get to keep (or control) the surplus, but less radical gains-sharing devices have also proved effective in reinforcing participation. More than 500 United States firms (most with fewer than 1,000 employees) use Scanlon Plans. Named for Joseph Scanlon, a unionist and accountant who invented the idea in the late 1930s, a *Scanlon Plan* combines a union-management agreement, a network of committees to encourage worker suggestions, and a formula that guarantees that all employees (including executives) will share a fixed portion (usually 75 percent) of any gains in profit above a "normal" base.[49] In Japan, major firms pay all employees a semi-annual *bonus* based only on the performance of the firm as a whole. Typically, the bonus amounts to about a third of the employee's total compensation.⁵⁰ United States corporations try to encourage similar identification of employees with the company by instituting *Employee Stock Ownership Plans* (ESOPs). With the aid of tax advantages written into law by a powerful supporter, Senator Russell Long, the number of firms with ESOPs reached almost seven thousand by the end of 1984; more than 10 million employees were eligible to join the plans.⁵¹ ESOPs are no magic carpet to workplace democracy: they usually distribute stock unequally among employees; most involve only a small fraction of outstanding stock; many do not give employee stock-owners full voting rights; and some are just cynical devices to improve corporate finances at workers' expense. Nevertheless, a suitably comprehensive and generous ESOP can provide the necessary material reinforcement for a system of participatory management; in a small but growing number of cases, ESOPs are the vehicle by which employees acquire control of the firms in which they work.

Just as stockholders must share ownership or some of its privileges to democratize corporations, so also must socialist states surrender some of their powers if they want participatory workplaces. In Yugoslavia, the development of self-management was accompanied by the invention of "social ownership," which Bernstein describes as "the complete absence of ownership by anyone [because] the discrete functions associated with ownership are so dispersed among several different parties that no single party can be located as 'owner' nor, theoretically, can a single party exert enough rights to act alone as owner."⁵² Significantly, the functions assigned to workers' councils include the right to allocate (to wages, collective consumption, or investment) a substantial share of enterprise profits.

In socialist countries, the decentralized "ownership" required by a participatory economy exacts a heavy ideological price. First, the ability of enterprises and work groups to retain a share of profits replaces moral with group-based but nonetheless material incentives. Second, because natural advantages and good luck will always enable some enterprises to prosper while others lag behind, decentralized control of surpluses generates more economic inequality than centralized state ownership. Conversely, under capitalism, the need to combine participatory management with gains-sharing fosters a new social solidarity within firms and creates pressure toward wider dispersion of wealth than would otherwise exist.

Markets versus Planning

Some forms of workplace democratization also encourage convergence in the way socialist and capitalist economies allocate economic resources. Whether a nation relies on the market or on central planning seems irrelevant to participation at the shopfloor level. The scope of decisions assignable to basic production groups probably differs little between the two contexts. In

China under Maoist rule, the economy was centrally controlled, but small-group participation was encouraged in both agriculture and industry. Similarly, as we have seen, firms have taken significant steps toward shopfloor participation in numerous market economies, including Japan, Sweden, Norway, and the United States.

For nonsocialist advocates of workplace democracy, the issue of plan or market also poses no problem for worker influence at higher levels. To be sure, they often urge that governments intervene to promote self-management through legal, financial, and educational assistance. However, such theorists usually take for granted the allocative efficiency of markets; and they assume that self-managed firms will not only function but thrive in market settings, because of the competitive advantages they derive from committed and productive members.

In contrast, among participatory socialists, the debate over plan versus market is a persistent and troublesome source of conflict.[53] Historically, the dominant tendency in socialist thought blames private ownership and the market jointly for the capitalist evils of unemployment, inequality, materialism, and selfishness. Humanists within this tradition hope that participation will develop in workers a sense of solidarity, equality, and social responsibility. They fear that the pressure of market competition produces a "group capitalist" mentality, in which generous sentiments extend no further than the bounds of one's own firm. Even within the firm, they argue, the need to bid for scarce skills generates material inequality, and excessive pressure for efficiency leads to the dominance of managers and experts.[54]

Opposed to this position are three arguments about autonomy, motivation, and efficiency. First, if enterprises do not enjoy substantial autonomy over production, prices, and wages, what scope is left for genuine workers' control? True, the market can be as tough a master as any planning bureau, but it operates by setting conditions to which firms must adjust, leaving them considerable discretion about how they do it and a greater feeling of freedom compared with the sense of external control that exists whenever human authorities issue direct commands. Second, if—as in the egalitarian ideal that inspires many supporters of planning—the gains produced by each enterprise are to be shared with the whole society, how will the problem of collective action be solved? A system that decentralizes decisions and rewards to small units (such as the Yugoslav BOALs) avoids placing utopian demands on human nature. Third, even if it were possible to sustain workers' participation under central planning, is not the complexity of economywide resource allocation beyond the capacity of any government to conduct efficiently?

Perhaps the most telling judgment about this debate is given by the evolving practice of socialist countries themselves. After an initial period of central planning in the 1950s, Yugoslavia decentralized, creating the first market-socialist economy. The Yugoslav system was bitterly condemned by China under Mao, but after his death, in 1976, the Chinese instituted their own version of market socialism. By the mid-1980s, there were indications that even the Soviet Union would allow its enterprises more autonomy. Yugoslavia's history shows that we should not expect such trends to continue without periodic oscillations.[55] Nevertheless, pressure to satisfy consumer desires appears to be creating a powerful long-term movement toward the market—a system eminently compatible with workers' self-management if not with theorists' dreams of workers' self-transcendence.

Political Democracy

The fact that workplace participation has flourished in communist countries such as Yugoslavia and China should induce humility in anyone who wants to believe that one type of regime possesses a monopoly on democratic virtue. Obviously, electoral democracy in national politics can coexist with hierarchy at work; and hegemonic polities can promote democratic workplaces. Nevertheless, political theorists continue to assert that democratic customs in one sphere will spread to the other. Are they merely indulging in the wistful fallacy that all good things must go together? Perhaps not entirely. No one can deny that in the West the example of democratic government inspires a persistent tendency toward more egalitarian and participatory practices at work. Conversely, articulate voices in Yugoslavia have called on the League of Communists to relinquish its hegemony, and if free political competition is introduced in that country, the veterans of workers' councils should be well prepared to assume the full powers of democratic citizenship.

The Shape of Things to Come

It is exhilarating to take a leap beyond what we already know, despite the fact that people who venture to predict the future run the risk of falling flat on their faces. In that reckless spirit, let us speculate how, barring catastrophe, the nations of the world will develop along the four dimensions that now distinguish them.

Economists' long-standing belief that markets allocate resources more efficiently than central planning now seems dominant among governmental leaders as well. No capitalist democracy places much reliance on command-style planning, and communist nations are moving toward market socialism. To be sure, primary reliance on markets does not entail that governments adopt a laissez-faire policy. To different degrees and with varying means, they will intervene to minimize unemployment and inflation, to achieve welfare and equity goals, and to ensure that firms take into account social costs and benefits. But entrusting basic decisions on production and pricing to decentralized, competitive units appears to offer the best way to encourage a responsive, innovative, and adaptive economy.

If, as much evidence suggests, workplace democratization leads to greater productivity and improved product quality, both natural selection and social learning should promote the dominance of participatory firms within competitive economies. Whether fully self-managed enterprises will enjoy a comparable edge over firms that are only partially democratized is not yet clear; in any case, the trend for some time to come should be toward more power-sharing at work.

Because democratized management succeeds enduringly only when workers share in the gains produced by their participation, we can expect that ownership rights in capitalist economies will become more dispersed and more collectivized than they are now. At the same time, socialist economies will move toward more decentralized organization and less egalitarian sharing of income. It would be rash to expect total convergence, but the two types of economy should become less sharply distinct from one another.

Finally, if the developmental effects of participation indeed spill over from workplaces to politics and if participatory market economies furnish a strong social foundation for democratic government, then we may also look for more widespread, stable, and intensified political democracy.

In short, the political economy of the future will blend market allocation, dispersed collective ownership, participatory management, and political democracy. In light of the fact that this combination currently exists nowhere, to predict its dominance may seem utopian, especially as there is nothing inevitable about social evolution. Advances always depend on people who have the wisdom and courage to pursue a better path, even against resistance from those who would defend accustomed privileges. Nevertheless, if there is any credibility to the argument of this chapter, we may look toward the twenty-first century with curious optimism.

NOTES

1. Paul Bernstein, *Workplace Democratization: Its Internal Dynamics* (Kent, Ohio: Kent State University Press, 1976), chap. 4.

2. David Jenkins, *Job Power: Blue and White Collar Democracy* (Baltimore: Penguin Books, 1974), chap. 8; Jutta A. Helm, "Codetermination in West Germany: What Difference Has It Made?" (paper presented at the annual meeting of the American Political Science Association, 1984).

3. Ronald M. Mason, *Participatory and Workplace Democracy: A Theoretical Development in Critique of Liberalism* (Carbondale: Southern Illinois University Press, 1982), p. 160.

4. *Report of the Committee of Inquiry on Industrial Democracy* (London: Her Majesty's Stationery Office, 1977).

5. John Simmons and William Mares, *Working Together* (New York: Alfred A. Knopf, 1983), p. 250.

6. See Branko Horvat, Mihailo Markovic, and Rudi Supek, eds., *Self-Governing Socialism: A Reader* (White Plains, N.Y.: International Arts and Sciences Press, 1975), vol. 1, pp. 256–70; and vol. 2, pp. 64–111.

7. David Ellerman, "On the Legal Structure of Workers' Cooperatives," in *Workplace Democracy and Social Change*, ed. Frank Lindenfeld and Joyce Rothschild-Whitt (Boston: Porter Sargent, 1982), pp. 299–313.

8. Although the widely used term *shopfloor* connotes an industrial setting, most of the principles discussed below apply equally to participation in white-collar organizations.

9. The account in this section is drawn from Robert E. Cole, *Work, Mobility, and Participation: A Comparative Study of American and Japanese Industry* (Berkeley: University of California Press, 1979), pp. 132–43; and William G. Ouchi, *Theory Z: How American Business Can Meet the Japanese Challenge* (Reading, Mass.: Addison-Wesley Publishing Co., 1981), pp. 223–29.

10. Ouchi, *Theory Z*, p. 228.

11. Ibid., p. 223.

12. Jenkins, *Job Power*, chap. 13; Einar Thorsrud, "Democratization of Work as a Process of Change Towards Non-Bureaucratic Types of Organization," in *European Contributions to Organization Theory*, eds. Geert Hofstede and Sami Kassem (Amsterdam: Van Goram, 1976), pp. 244–71.

13. Most of these failings are evident in an unsuccessful Los Angeles experiment described by John F. Witte, *Democracy, Authority, and Alienation in Work: Workers' Participation in an American Corporation* (Chicago: University of Chicago Press, 1980), chaps. 7 and 8.

14. Simmons and Mares, *Working Together*, p. 226.

15. Ellen Turkish Comisso, *Workers' Control Under Plan and Market: Implications of Yugoslav Self-Management* (New Haven: Yale University Press, 1979).

16. Jenkins, *Job Power*, pp. 68–72.

17. Daniel Zwerdling, *Democracy at Work* (Washington: Association for Self-Management, 1978), pp. 41–52.

18. Simmons and Mares, *Working Together*, chap. 4.

19. This description draws on Simmons and Mares, *Working Together*, chap. 4; Neal Q. Herrick, *Improving Government: Experiments with Quality of Working Life Systems* (New York: Praeger, 1983), pp. xxi–xxviii; and Herrick, "Parallel Organizations in Unionized Settings: Implications for Organizational Research," *Human Relations*, 38 (1985), 963–81.

20. Mason, *Participatory and Workplace Democracy*, p. 172. For the distinction between (top-level) workers' control and full-fledged workers' self-management, see Christopher Eaton Gunn, *Workers' Self-Management in the United States* (Ithaca, N.Y.: Cornell University Press, 1984), p. 20.

21. "Parallel Organizations," p. 978.

22. Jenkins, *Job Power*, p. 70; Helm, "Codetermination in West Germany," p. 9.

23. "A Contribution to the Political Theory of Organizational Democracy," in *Organizational Democracy: Participation and Self-Management*, ed. G. David Garson and Michael P. Smith (Beverly Hills: Sage Publications, 1976), p. 22.

24. Robert A. Dahl, *A Preface to Economic Democracy* (Berkeley: University of California Press, 1985), p. 94.

25. Peter Bachrach, *The Theory of Democratic Elitism: A Critique* (Boston: Little, Brown & Co., 1967); and Mason, *Participatory and Workplace Democracy*.

26. *Preface to Economic Democracy*, p. 160 and passim.

27. See especially Carole Pateman, *Participation and Democratic Theory* (Cambridge: Cambridge University Press, 1970); and Mason, *Participatory and Workplace Democracy*.

28. J. Maxwell Elden, "Political Efficacy at Work: The Connection Between More Autonomous Forms of Workplace Organization and a More Participatory Politics," *American Political Science Review*, 75 (1981), 43–58.

29. Edward S. Greenberg, "Industrial Self-Management and Political Attitudes," *American Political Science Review*, 75 (1981), 29–42. Eaton offers another explanation of Greenberg's findings: The plywood co-ops' practice of hiring some workers who do not share in ownership may inhibit them from developing fully democratic, cooperative internal relations, which in turn might account for worker-owners' bourgeois outlook. Eaton's theory offers hope that full self-management (every worker an owner) would produce the more generous mentality Greenberg seeks. *Workers' Self-Management*, pp. 121, 129–31.

30. Jaroslav Vanek, *The Participatory Economy: An Evolutionary Hypothesis and a Strategy for Development* (Ithaca, N.Y.: Cornell University Press, 1971), pp. 46–47.

31. U.S. Bureau of the Census, *Statistical Abstract of the United States, 1982–83* (Washington: Government Printing Office, 1982), p. 865. West Germany, which has not been a leader in shopfloor participation, grew 28 percent during the 1970s.

32. Raymond Russell, "The Rewards of Participation in the Worker-Owned Firm," in *Workplace Democracy and Social Change*, eds. Lindenfeld and Rothschild-Whitt, pp. 114–16.

33. Paul Bernstein, "Run Your Own Business: Worker-Owned Plywood Firms," *Working Papers for a New Society*, 2 (Summer 1974), 27.

34. Simmons and Mares, *Working Together*, pp. 136–41.

35. "Corporate Growth and Employee Ownership," *Employee Ownership*, 5 (February 1985), 1–2.

36. Simmons and Mares, *Working Together*, p. 287, app. I.

37. Jenkins, *Job Power*, p. 252. Copyright © 1973 by David Jenkins. Reprinted by permission of Doubleday & Co., Inc.

38. *The Participatory Economy*, p. 28.

39. Bullock Report, p. 111.

40. For an answer, see Simmons and Mares, *Working Together*, chap. 14.

41. *Workers' Self-Management*, p. 20.

42. Helm, "Codetermination in West Germany," p. 2; Bullock Report, pp. 167–95.

43. ==*Participatory and Workplace Democracy*==, p. 201. See also Dahl, *Preface to Economic Democracy*, pp. 150–52.

44. Quoted in Simmons and Mares, *Working Together*, pp. 127–28.

45. *Workers' Self-Management*, p. 205.

46. For an elaboration of this distinction, see Robert A. Dahl, *Modern Political Analysis*, 4th ed. (Englewood Cliffs, N.J.: Prentice-Hall, 1984), pp. 74–93.

47. Moreover, the experience of several employee-owned firms in the United States shows that worker ownership is not a *sufficient* condition for self-management. Just as state ownership "by the whole people" can operate hierarchically, so also ownership by all the workers does not produce participatory management unless an effort is made to use workers' control at the top to transform relations down the line.

48. *Workplace Democratization*, chap. 5.

49. Simmons and Mares, *Working Together*, pp. 35–36; Jenkins, *Job Power*, pp. 222–24.

50. Ouchi, *Theory Z*, p. 20. Martin Weitzman proposes a similar system for the United States in *The Share Economy* (Cambridge: Harvard University Press, 1984). Cole strangely neglects the bonus system in downplaying the role that material incentives play in motivating participation in Japanese QC circles; see *Work, Mobility, and Participation*, pp. 211–12.

51. *Employee Ownership*, 5, no. 2 (April 1985), 5.

52. *Workplace Democratization*, p. 120.

53. See Comisso, *Workers' Control Under Plan and Market*, for an enlightening discussion.

54. For arguments along these lines, see Juan G. Espinosa and Andrew S. Zimbalist, *Economic Democracy: Workers' Participation in Chilean Industry, 1970–1973* (New York: Academic Press, 1978), especially chap. 2.

55. Markets result in economic insecurity and inequality, which produce political forces in favor of government intervention; Comisso, *Workers' Control Under Plan and Market*.

EPILOGUE

If you want to follow up particular ideas, the footnotes in the preceding chapters offer a detailed guide to further reading; of the many items cited there, some are especially worth singling out. These are works I would recommend for anyone planning a course for a class or a program of self-study.

In her influential *Participation and Democratic Theory* (Cambridge: Cambridge University Press, 1970), Carole Pateman helped revive interest in the participatory tradition of political theory and its relation to workplace democratization. Perhaps the most vigorous contemporary advocate of participatory democracy is the eloquent Benjamin Barber, who proposes a provocative agenda for political reform in *Strong Democracy: Participatory Politics for a New Age* (Berkeley: University of California Press, 1984). On the other side, Samuel P. Huntington presents a clear call for less participation in his essay "The United States," which can be found in *The Crisis of Democracy: Report on the Governability of Democracies to the Trilateral Commission* by Michel J. Crozier, Huntington, and Joji Watanuki (New York: New York University Press, 1975). Key earlier expressions of "democratic elitism" are assembled in Peter Bachrach, ed., *Political Elites in a Democracy* (New York: Atherton, 1971); Bachrach himself argues for invigorated participation in *The Theory of Democratic Elitism: A Critique* (Boston: Little, Brown & Co., 1967). Participatory enthusiasts would do well to ponder the advice of two eminent political theorists who offer wisdom as well as analysis: Robert A. Dahl, *After the Revolution? Authority in a*

Good Society (New Haven: Yale University Press, 1970); and Michael Walzer, *Political Action: A Guide to Movement Politics* (Chicago: Quadrangle, 1971).

In understanding the motivation to participate, two classic works by economists are indispensable: Mancur Olson, Jr., *The Logic of Collective Action: Public Goods and the Theory of Groups* (Cambridge: Harvard University Press, 1965); and Albert O. Hirschman, *Exit, Voice, and Loyalty: Responses to Decline in Firms, Organizations, and States* (Cambridge: Harvard University Press, 1970). Good sources for later thinking on collective action are Norman Frohlich and Joe A. Oppenheimer, *Modern Political Economy* (Englewood Cliffs, N.J.: Prentice-Hall, 1978); and Russell Hardin, *Collective Action* (Baltimore: Johns Hopkins University Press, 1982). For a broad comparative perspective on systemic determinants of participation, two valuable works are Samuel P. Huntington and Joan Nelson, *No Easy Choice: Political Participation in Developing Countries* (Cambridge: Harvard University Press, 1976); and G. Bingham Powell, *Contemporary Democracies: Participation, Stability, and Violence* (Cambridge: Harvard University Press, 1982).

All students of participation owe a great debt to the research of Sidney Verba and his colleagues. Verba's early book *Small Groups and Political Behavior: A Study of Leadership* (Princeton: Princeton University Press, 1961) is still the best introduction to that subject for people interested in politics. In *The Civic Culture: Political Attitudes and Democracy in Five Nations* (Boston: Little, Brown & Co., 1965), Gabriel Almond and Verba showed how norms and attitudes affecting participation can differ among cultures. The themes of equality and organizational influence come to the fore in *Participation in America: Political Democracy and Social Equality* (New York: Harper & Row, 1972), written with Norman Nie; and in *Participation and Political Equality: A Seven-Nation Comparison* (New York: Cambridge University Press, 1978), written with Nie and Jae-on Kim.

Other research results on voting and conventional participation are usefully inventoried in Lester W. Milbrath and M. L. Goel, *Political Participation: How and Why Do People Get Involved in Politics?* 2nd ed. (Chicago: Rand McNally, 1977). Raymond E. Wolfinger and Steven J. Rosenstone provide the best statistical answers to their own question about the United States in *Who Votes?* (New Haven: Yale University Press, 1980). An outstanding work connecting voting behavior to policy is Thomas Byrne Edsall's *The New Politics of Inequality* (New York: W. W. Norton & Co., 1984). A good place to begin exploring the more abstract literature on voting theory is Frohlich and Oppenheimer's *Modern Political Economy*.

On the special type of voting involved in direct legislation, a fine resource is *Referendums: A Comparative Study of Practice and Theory* (Washington, D.C.: American Enterprise Institute for Public Policy Research, 1978), edited by David Butler and Austin Ranney. Studies of small-scale direct democracy offer fascinating reading. Jane J. Mansbridge's *Beyond Adversary Democracy* (New York: Basic Books, 1980) combines important theoretical analysis with insightful observation of a New England town and a participatory workplace. For an elegiac account of direct democracy in Swiss villages, see Benjamin Barber's *The Death of Communal Liberty: A History of Freedom in a Swiss Mountain Canton* (Princeton: Princeton University Press, 1974). Although not specifically focused on the topic, there exist no better sources for understanding the dramatic power and human complexity of participation than William Hinton's splendid *Fanshen: A Documentary of Revolution in a Chinese Village* (New York: Monthly Review Press, 1966) and its sequel *Shenfan: The Continuing Revolution in a Chinese Village* (New York: Random House, 1983).

Participatory movements that attempted (and sometimes accomplished) a United States version of revolutionary change are described in Jo Freeman's fine collection, *Social Movements of the Sixties and Seventies* (New York: Longman, 1983). A more skeptical but analytically valuable treatment of protest movements and interest groups is James Q. Wilson's *Political Organizations* (New York: Basic Books, 1973). Perhaps the best critique of United States pressure-group politics is Grant McConnell's *Private Power and American Democracy* (New York: Alfred A. Knopf, 1967). Public-interest organizations that arose partly in response to indictments such as McConnell's are well described in Jeffrey Berry, *Lobbying for the People: The Political Behavior of Public Interest Groups* (Princeton: Princeton University Press, 1977) and Andrew McFarland, *Common Cause: Lobbying in the Public Interest* (Chatham, N.J.: Chatham House, 1984).

The impact of the new wave of citizen participation on public administration is reported in many studies. Three good places to start are Daniel A. Mazmanian and Jeanne Nienaber, *Can Organizations Change?: Environmental Protection, Citizen Participation, and the Corps of Engineers* (Washington, D.C.: The Brookings Institution, 1979); Lawrence Susskind, Michael Elliott, and Associates, *Paternalism, Conflict, and Coproduction: Learning from Citizen Action and Citizen Participation in Western Europe* (New York: Plenum, 1983); and James C. Petersen, ed., *Citizen Participation in Science Policy* (Amherst: University of Massachusetts Press, 1984).

Developments in the movement toward workplace democracy are charted in two excellent progress reports: David Jenkins, *Job Power: Blue and White Collar Democracy* (Baltimore: Penguin Books, 1974); and John Simmons and William Mares, *Working Together* (New York: Alfred A. Knopf, 1983). Valuable papers on the subject are assembled in Gerry Hunnius, G. David Garson, and John Case, *Workers' Control: A Reader on Labor and Social Change* (New York: Vintage Books, 1973); and Frank Lindenfeld and Joyce Rothschild-Whitt, *Workplace Democracy and Social Change* (Boston: Porter Sargent, 1982). An outstanding theoretical analysis is Paul Bernstein's *Workplace Democratization: Its Internal Dynamics* (Kent, Ohio: Kent State University Press, 1976).

To keep up with participatory practice, you may find it helpful to follow periodicals intended primarily for participants. For a general purview with special emphasis on advocacy groups and citizen involvement in administration, see *Citizen Participation* (Medford, Mass.: Lincoln Filene Center for Citizenship and Public Affairs, Tufts University). The focus of several more specialized publications is evident from their titles: *Initiative News Report* (Washington, D.C.: Initiative News Service, Inc.); *Union Democracy Review* (Brooklyn, N.Y.: Association for Union Democracy); *The Neighborhood Works* (Chicago: Center for Neighborhood Technology); *Employee Ownership* (Arlington, Va.: National Center for Employee Ownership); and *Workplace Democracy* (Amherst, Mass.: Labor Relations and Research Center, University of Massachusetts).

INDEX

Abortion, 17, 120–21, 123–24, 140 (*see also* Pro-life movement)
Abramson, Paul R., 51
Accommodation, 159 (*see also* Co-optation, informal)
ACORN (*see* Association of Community Organizations for Reform Now)
Action, 1–2 (*see also* Participation)
  as ideal of direct democracy, 70–72
  informational content of, 5
  in referendums, 94
  sequential vs. simultaneous, 5
Active life, 142
Activists, 17, 41, 57, 59, 114–17, 120, 149, 152
  in Common Cause, 128
  religious, 140
  self-selected, 66
  in Type D groups, 129, 132, 138
  in Type M groups, 137, 142, 143
Administration, citizen, participation in, 145–59 (*see also* Citizen involvement)
Adversarial issues in QWL systems, 165
Adversarial relations, 81
Adversary democracy, 71–75
Advisory committees, 148
Advocacy groups, 125, 134, 147, 184 (*see also* Pressure groups)
Affinity groups, 28
Affluent citizens, 140–41
Age, 6, 41, 61, 80
Agricultural communities, 86
Agriculture, U.S. Department of, 146, 150
Aitkin, Don, 99
Akron, Ohio, 154
Aldrich, John H., 51
Algeria, 91, 95, 160
Alinsky, Saul, 14, 21
Allegiance, 38-39
Allende, Salvador, 47, 173
Almond, Gabriel, 39, 182
Alperovitz, Gar, 52
Altruism, 26, 32, 71 (*see also* Duty, sense of; Moral incentives)
Amateur politicians, 114
American Agricultural Movement, 134
American Civil Liberties Union, 13, 131, 133
American Farm Bureau Federation, 131, 134, 150
American Political Science Association, 123
Amicable agreement, 95 (*see also* Consensus)
Anarchy, 77, 82
Anderson, John, 102
Anticipated reactions, 109–10, 122
Anti-poverty programs, 61–62, 146, 150–51
Anti-smoking propositions, 93
Apathy, 9, 22–23, 153
Appropriate technology, 88, 98
Approval ballot, 107, 122
Approval plurality elections, 107–8, 122–23

Arendt, Hannah, 71, 82
Aristotle, 21, 68
Arkansas, 109
Arnstein, Sherry R., 158, 159
Arrow, Kenneth, 105, 122
Assemblies, 66, 70, 95, 103, 162, 166
Assembly democracy, 85–87, 90, 164
Athens, 40, 43, 47, 62, 65, 70
Atlanta, 155
At-large elections, 61
Attitudinal explanations, 42
Association of Community Organizations for Reform Now (ACORN), 134
Aubert, Jean-François, 93, 98
Audubon societies, 130
Australia, 47, 93
Austria, 6, 41, 156, 161
Authoritarian governments, 9, 46
Authoritarian leadership, 78, 95
Authorities, 7
  overload of, 17
  responsiveness of, 18, 48
  skepticism toward, 76
Authority, lines of, 151
Authority to make decisions, 6, 69
Autonomous work-groups, 163–65
Axelrod, Robert, 36, 159
Ayres, Richard E., 52

Bachrach, Peter, 20, 179, 181
Bair, Lowell, 21
Baldwin, David A., 52
Baltimore, 158
Baltzell, E. Digby, 83
Banfield, Edward C., 39, 51
Barber, Benjamin, 65, 68, 71, 72, 82, 83, 94, 96, 99, 100, 121, 181, 183
Bargaining, 81, 83
Barker, Ernest, 21
Barnard, Chester I., 143
Barry, Brian, 36
Basic Organizations of Associated Labor (BOALs), 164, 176
Basque region, 168
Bass Anglers Sportsman Society, 130, 143
Bedford-Stuyvesant, 149
Benson, H. W., 52
Berelson, Bernard, 21
Berg, Larry L., 99
Bernstein, Paul, 46, 52, 174-75, 178, 180, 183
Berry, Jeffrey, 128, 134, 143, 157, 183
Bill of Rights, 46
Bimodality of voting population, 118–20, 123
Birch, A. H., 52
Black, Duncan, 122–23
Blacks, 6, 41, 47, 63-64, 89, 125, 141 (*see also* Race, Voting Rights Act)

185

Blair Mountain, Battle of, 48–49
Blalock, Hubert M., 68
BOALs (*see* Basic Organizations of Associated Labor)
Bogdanor, Vernon, 121
Bonus system in Japan, 174–75, 180
Borda, Jean-Charles de, 106, 107
Borda method, 106–7
Boston, 155
Bottle bills, 91
Bounded communities, 45
Bowen, William G., 52
Boycotts, 125
Boyd, Richard W., 51
Boyle, Tony, 49
Boyte, Harry C., 143, 144
Braendgaard, Asger, 98
Braendgaard, Barbara, 98
Brams, Steven J., 121, 122
Brazil, 46
Brody, Richard A., 51
Brower, David, 138
Brudney, Jeffrey, 159
Buffalo, New York, 148
Bullock report, 161, 170–71, 178, 180
Bureaucracies, 90
Butler, David, 94–95, 98, 99, 121, 182

California, 91, 93, 99
Cambridge, Massachusetts, 148, 156
Campaign activities, 41, 45, 141
Campaign-financing reforms, 140
Campbell, David, 7
Campbell Steel Works, 49
Canada, 44
Canvassing, 2, 42, 109, 125
Capitalism, 89, 98, 170–72, 174–75
Capture, 150–52, 155
Caputo, David A., 158
Carter, Jimmy, 48, 110–11, 115, 117
Case, John, 67, 183
Caucuses, 54, 96, 115
Cavanagh, Thomas E., 51, 118
CDBGs (*see* Community Development Block Grants)
Centralization, 81 (*see also* Decentralization)
Chapman, John W., 52
Chile, 47, 160, 173
China, 40, 60–61 (*see also* Cultural Revolution, Chinese)
 land reform, 77, 158
 participatory decision-making in, 43
 peasants associations, 61
 political-economic system, 173
 villages, 70, 89
 women's associations, 61
 workplace participation, 176–77
Chinese communists, 15–16, 34, 61 (*see also* China)
Choice, 4
Christians, evangelical, 140
Christian Right, 140
Christian Voice, 138
Chrysler Corporation, 161–62
Cigler, Allan J., 123, 143, 144
Citizen action, 157
Citizen-action movement, 141–42 (*see also* Pressure groups, Public-interest groups)
Citizen involvement, 146–58, 184
 advising, 146–48, 153
 deciding, 146, 148–49, 153
 defined, 157
 doing, 146–47, 153
 supporting, 146, 149–50
Citizen-participation profession, 146
City planning, 82 (*see also* Planning)
Civic activities, 41
Civic balance, 139, 144
Civic virtue, 38
Civil disobedience, 125, 128
Civil liberties, 50, 73
Civil rights movement, 10, 29, 126–27 (*see also* Blacks, Race, Voting Rights Act)
Civil rights organizations, 61, 63
Civil service, 41
Clark, Peter B., 143
Class bias in voting, 92, 117–20
Class conflict, 63
Class, social (*see* Social class)
Cleveland, Ohio, 154
Clubs, 70
Codetermination, 161–62, 165, 168, 170
Coercion, 13, 28, 33, 36, 50, 64
Cole, Richard L., 158
Cole, Robert E., 179, 180
Collective action, 39–40, 182
 cost-sharing, 128
 logic of, 23–35, 65, 87
 problem of, 176
Collective goods, 23–26, 28, 35–36
Comisso, Ellen Turkish, 179, 180
Commissions of participation (Spain), 155
Commitment, 19, 35, 76
 extra-rational, 78
 result of participation, 14, 149
Committee democracy, 85–86, 166
Committees, 66, 70, 73, 95, 166
Committees for Defense of the Revolution (Cuba), 147
Common Cause, 125, 128, 131, 133, 136–37, 140, 143
Communal participation, 45
Communication, 88–89
Communist parties, 15–16, 28, 34, 47, 61, 63
Communist systems, 3, 9, 36, 40, 147, 177 (*see also* China, Cuba, Soviet Union, Yugoslavia)
Community, 78, 80, 82, 142
 identification with, 14–15
 sense of, 85
 as value of direct democracy, 71–72
Community action programs, 146 (*see also* Antipoverty programs)
Community assemblies, 84, 96–97
Community control, 74, 87, 142, 149, 151
Community Development Block Grants (CDBGs), 146, 148, 149
Community service, 6, 147
Compensation of interest-group staff, 130–33
Competence, 16, 163
Competition, 41, 138–39
Compulsory voting, 47, 60
Concurrence, 67
Conditional participation, 33–34, 36
Condorcet criterion, 104–108, 113, 117, 123
Condorcet, Marquis de, 104, 106
Condorcet paradox, 105 (*see also* Cycles, electoral)
Condorcet procedure, 104, 107
Conflict, 17–19, 21, 45, 153–57, 159
 among citizen groups, 155–56
 in direct democracies, 72–75
 and elections, 100
 and priority of equality, 66
 threat of, 155

INDEX   187

in work groups, 164
Congress, U.S., 9, 10, 48
Congress of Racial Equality, 127
Connecticut House of Representatives, 122
Connolly, William E., 20, 21
Consensus, 71–74, 80, 84–85, 138, 142
 decision-making, 54, 66
 in electoral competition, 114
 false, 73
 as product of participation, 137
 as value in direct democracy, 94–96
Conservatism
 in 1980s, 120, 140
 in referendums, 99
 in spatial models, 111–13
Conservatives, 39, 92, 123, 133
Constitution, U.S., 69
Constitutions in pressure groups, 138
Constraint, 61, 64
Consumer movement, 10, 126–27, 139–40
Contextual influences on participation, 23, 37–50
Contingent cooperation, ethic of, 33, 38 (see also Conditional participation)
Contract by convention, 36
Contributions, financial, 32
 to political campaigns, 61, 141
 to pressure groups, 128–34, 136–38, 140
Control, degree of, 161
Convergence in electoral competition, 103–4, 112–20, 123
Cook, Terrence, 96, 99
Cooperative Extension Service, 146
Co-optation, 150–52, 155
 formal, 152, 159
 informal, 152, 159
Coproduction, 150, 152–57, 159
 conditions favoring, 153–57
 defined, 153
Cornford, Francis MacDonald, 21
Corporate boards, 161–62, 164
Corporations, 128, 134, 160–69
Corps of Engineers, U.S. Army, 146, 154–55
Corruption, 76–77
Costain, Anne N., 143, 144
Costain, W. Douglas, 143, 144
Costs of organizing, 27
Costs of participation, 5, 14–17, 26–27, 32, 41, 46, 48–50, 54–55, 60, 70, 84–85, 129–34, 140
Couto, Richard A., 159
Cox, Archibald, 126
Creighton, James, 155, 157, 158, 159
Crenson, Matthew, 147, 158
Crotty, William, 51, 67
Crowds, 85–86
Crozier, Michael J., 20, 181
Cuba, 40, 147
Cultural Revolution, Chinese, 16, 73, 85, 98
Culture, political, 38–40, 182
Cycles, electoral, 105–6, 124
Cynicism, 23, 37, 80

Dahl, Robert A., 7, 20, 21, 62–65, 68, 82, 83, 85–86, 98, 124, 152, 159, 167, 179, 180, 181
Daley, Richard J., 56
Dan River Textiles, 169
Deakin, Arthur, 135
Decentralization, 84, 87–90, 137, 151
de Gaulle, Charles, 91–92

de Jouvenel, Bertrand, 84–87, 98
Delaware, 93
Delegated power, 7
Delian League, 80
Delli Priscoli, Jerry, 157
Democracy, 8, 69–82, 177–78
 ancient meaning, 6, 69
 character of, 82
 under communism, 9, 177
 direct, 69–82 (see also Direct democracy)
 intraparty, 114–17
 as majority rule, 101
 meanings of, 69–70
 and minority rule, 121
 within pressure groups, 131, 135–39, 144
 relation to participation, 2
 sanctity of, 79
 stability of, 166–67
 as system of equal power, 53
 (see also Adversary democracy, Assembly democracy, Committee democracy, Elections, Participatory democracy, Referendums, Unitary democracy, Workplace democracy)
Democratic elitism, 13, 17–20, 181
Democratic leadership, 78–79 (see also Leadership)
Democratic Party, U.S., 42, 48, 56, 57, 61, 87, 96, 104, 113, 115–18, 121
Democratic theory, 6, 65, 166–67 (see also Democracy, Values)
Demonstrations, 2, 34, 125, 137, 147–48 (see also Protest)
Denmark, 91, 161
Derthick, Martha, 159
Developing countries, 9
Developmental effects of participation, 13–14, 18, 20, 54, 70, 166–67, 170
Diminishing returns, 31
Direct democracy, 6, 66, 69–82, 84, 88, 166, 182–83
 in autonomous work groups, 164
 and citizen action, 141–42
 ideals of, 70–72
 in Type D groups, 137–38
Direct legislation, 90–96, 182 (see also Referendums)
Direct-mail technology, 133
Disadvantaged groups, 63 (see also Poor people)
Discussion, 5, 59, 66, 71–72, 138, 142
 in coproduction, 153
 protracted, 73, 80
 and referendums, 94–95
 size limits on, 84–85
 in work groups, 162–63
Diseducative effects of participation, 16–19
Diversity, 73–74, 86–87
Division of labor, 34, 163
Dolan, Terry, 133
Downs, Anthony, 111, 113–14, 120, 123, 143
Draft boards, 148
Druzhinniki, 147
DuBois, W.E.B., 133
Dues, 128 (see also Contributions, financial)
Dunning, C. Mark, 157
Dutton, Diana, 159
Duty, sense of, 23, 26, 32, 37–40, 129, 133 (see also Moral incentives)

East Berlin, 45
Eastern Europe, 171

Economic Development Administration, U.S., 49
Economic growth, 16, 168
Economic inequality, 171, 175–76, 178, 180
Economic lobbying organizations, 28, 126, 134 (*see also* Pressure groups)
Edsall, Thomas Byrne, 51, 123, 144, 182
Education, 23, 58–59, 61, 80, 117, 155
Educative effects of participation, 13, 20 (*see also* Developmental effects of participation)
Efficacious subgroups, 30
Efficacy, 18, 21, 23, 32, 36–40, 42, 167
Efficiency
  and decentralization, 88
  economic, 167
  of meetings, 86
Egalitarianism, 77 (*see also* Equality)
Egoists, rational, 26–31, 33
Eisenhower, Dwight D., 110
Elden, J. Maxwell, 167, 179
Elections, 3, 17, 100–21, 125, 142, 172–73, 177
  and citizen action, 141
  expenses of, 47
  participation in, 114–21
  presidential, 6, 22, 96, 102, 110–11, 114–15, 120
  within pressure groups, 135
  primary, 22, 54, 96, 108, 115, 122
  rules of, 101–8
  significance of, 100–101, 108–14
  state and local, 22
  (*See also* Voting, Voting turnout)
Electoral districts, 103
Electoral rules, 101–108
Eligibility, 53, 55, 68
Elites, 4
Elitist democrats, 13 (*see also* Democratic elitism)
Elitists, 9–10
Elitist theory of democracy, 16 (*see also* Democratic elitism)
Ellerman, David, 178
Elliott, Michael, 159, 183
Empathy, 13–14, 71
Employee stock ownership, 168, 170–72, 175
Employee Stock Ownership Plans (ESOPs), 49, 175
Encapsulation, 132
Energy sources, 88
England, Robert, 159
Environmental Protection Agency, U.S., 36
Environmentalists, 10, 93, 133, 139–40, 155
Equality, 6, 12–13, 53–66, 73, 78, 151, 182
  as conditional value, 65–66
  and decentralization, 89–90
  economic, 16 (*see also* Inequality, economic)
  as norm, 80
  passion for, 89
  political, 50, 97
  ways to reduce conflict between participation and, 60–64
ESOPs (*see* Employee Stock Ownership Plans)
Espinosa, Juan G., 180
Europe, 43, 48, 160, 164, 171
European Economic Community, 91–92, 161
Exit, 44–46
  ease or difficulty of, 45–46, 50, 52
  in pressure groups, 131, 135–39, 144
Expectations of cooperation, 33–34
Expertise, citizen access to, 156
Experts, 16
Expressive benefits of participation, 20 (*see also* Intrinsic benefits of participation)

Extension agents, 150
Extensive democracy, 150
Extensive participation, 5, 56, 66, 97
Extent of participation, 37, 53–58, 60, 96
  defined, 53
  and electoral rules, 101, 103–4, 108
  in U.S. referendums, 94

Facilitation, 46–47, 50
Faculty meetings, 70
Fagen, Richard R., 158
False consensus, 73
Falwell, Jerry, 133, 138
Farah, Barbara G., 67
Farm bureaus, 150
Farmers, 59, 154
Farmers organizations, 130, 141–43
Farm workers, 141
Fascist regimes, 9, 172
Fatalism, 38
Faux, Jeff, 52
Feagin, Joe R., 7
Federalism, new, 87
Federations of small groups, 28
Financial contributions (*see* Contributions, financial)
Finer, S.E., 135, 144
Finland, 94
Fiorina, Morris P., 122
Fire services, 152
Fischer, Frank, 83
Fishburn, Peter C., 121, 122
Fisher, Marc, 51
Follett, Mary Parker, 73, 82, 97, 99
Force, 47–49 (*see also* Violence)
Ford, Gerald, R., 110
Forest Service, U.S., 146
Foundations, 128, 132
France, 91–92, 95, 102–3, 160
Fraser, Douglas, 161–62
Freeman, Jo, 36, 75, 83, 127, 142, 143, 144, 183
Free riders, 24, 33
Friedan, Betty, 127
Friedgut, Theodore H., 158
Friendship, 72, 86
Friends of Clark Park, 30
Friends of the Earth, 139
Frohlich, Norman, 35, 36, 109, 122, 123, 124, 182
Full Employment and Balanced Growth Act, 65

Gains-sharing, 174–75
Gallup Poll, 124
Game theory, 25
Gamson, William A., 52
Gang of Four, 98
Gardner, John, 125, 136, 142
Garson, G. David, 67, 179, 183
General Motors Corporation, 127, 165
Geneva, 65
Gittell, Marilyn, 155, 159
Goel, M.L., 35, 51, 67, 182
Goldwater, Barry, 58, 113, 115
Goodhart, Philip, 98
Grazing lands, 59
Great Britain (*see* United Kingdom)
Greece, 40, 43, 46, 79
Greenberg, Edward S., 167, 179
Greenstone, J. David, 67
Greider, William, 144

Grofman, Bernard, 121
Group pressure, 50, 163 (*see also* Social incentives)
Guevara, Ernesto Che, 40, 51
Gunn, Christopher Eaton, 170, 172, 179, 180
Guth, James L., 144

Handgun Control, Inc., 24
Hansen, John Mark, 143
Hapgood, David, 7, 20
Hardin, Russell, 35, 36, 182
Harman International Industries, 164–65
Harris, Evelyn L.K., 52
Hart, Gary, 96
Hayden, Tom, 9
Hays, Brooks, 109–10
Health Planning Act of 1974, 149
Health Systems Agencies, 149
Hearings, public, 60, 145–46, 148
Hegedus, Andras, 158
Hegemony, 80–81, 172–74, 180
Helm, Jutta A., 178, 179, 180
Herrick, Neal Q., 165, 179
Hershey, Marjorie Randon, 123, 124
Hess, Karl, 88, 98
Hibbs, Douglas A., Jr., 123
Hierarchy, 62, 80, 97, 164, 172–73
Hindrance, 46–48
Hinton, William, 21, 60, 67, 77, 82, 83, 158, 183
Hirschman, Albert, 44–45, 51, 52, 135, 144, 182
Hispanics, 141
Hitler, Adolph, 9, 93, 121
Hoffman, Paul J., 67
Hofstede, Geert, 179
Holman, CB, 99
Home and School Association, 31
Homosexuals, 63, 126
Horvat, Branko, 178
Hotlines, 147
Hough, Jerry F., 7
Human nature, 31
Human services, 152
Humphrey-Hawkins bill, 65
Hunnius, Gerry, 67, 183
Huntington, Samuel P., 7, 11, 15–16, 20, 21, 46, 51, 83, 181–82
Hyatt Roller Bearing, 169
Hyde Amendment, 120

Idaho, 91
Ideological appeals, 103
Ideology, 57–58, 63–64, 87, 171–78
Imperceptibility of individual effects, 24, 29–30, 32, 132
Implementation, 149
Incentive balance, 129–34, 143–44
Incentive deficit, 129 (*see also* Incentive balance)
Incentives (*see* Incentive balance, Material incentives, Moral incentives, Motivation, Selective incentives, Social incentives)
Incentive surplus, 129 (*see also* Incentive balance)
Income, 58–59, 61
  distribution of, 98
  median 110–11, 118–19, 123
  and preferences for economic policies, 118
  and voting in the U.S., 42, 117–20
  (*see also* Social class)
India, 6, 41

Indirect elections, 84, 97–98, 138
Individual attributes, 37
Individual choices, 38
Indoctrination, 40
Industrial Democracy Project, 163
Inequality, economic, 171, 175–76, 178, 180 (*see also* Social class)
Inflation, 17, 118
Influence, 2, 4–7 (*see also* Power)
Information costs, 59
Initiative, 3
Initiative industry, 99
Initiative, popular, 90–96 (*see also* Direct legislation, Referendums)
Insincere voting, 102, 104, 107–8
Instability:
  electoral, 122
  of social choices, 105 (*see also* Cycles, electoral)
  under PR, 103
Instrumental benefits of participation, 11–14, 54, 70
Intensity of participation, 37
  defined, 53–54
  and referendums, 92, 94
  (*see also* Intensive democracy, Intensive participation)
Intensity problem, 65
Intensive democracy
  in administration of programs, 150
  through workplace participation, 166–67, 170
  (*see also* Participatory democracy)
Intensive particiation, 5, 43, 68, 70, 89–90, 96–97
  decision-making by, 56
  enthusiasts of, 100
  and extent of participation, 54, 57
  and influence, 117
  in pressure groups, 135
  and social class, 58
  in work groups, 162
Interdependence, 79–82, 83, 88, 164
Interest groups, 7, 41, 65, 125, 145, 183 (*see also* Pressure groups)
Intermediate goals, 30
Intrinsic benefits of participation, 14–15, 20, 54, 70, 166
Involvement, psychological, 3
Iranian oil embargo, 111
Ireland, 91
Irrigation users, 151
Irwin, Galen, 67
Israel, 44, 103, 121, 160
Issues in elections, 111–21
Italy, 39, 91, 103, 160

Japan, 41, 160, 163, 168, 174, 176
Jefferson, Thomas, 96, 99
Jenkins, David, 52, 178, 179, 180, 183
Jennings, M. Kent, 67
Jewish Americans, 121
Job protection, 169–70
Johnson-Humphrey Administration, 56
Johnson, Lawrence, 158
Johnson, Lyndon, 47, 110, 113, 139
Juries, 55, 62, 64, 148
Jurisdiction of politics, 43

Kanter, Rosabeth Moss, 77, 83
Kapp, Ernst, 68
Kassem, Sami, 179

INDEX

Kaufman, Arnold, 9, 13, 18, 20, 21
Kaufman, Herbert, 7
Kaufman, Hugh B., 36
Kelley, Stanley, Jr., 52
Kendall, Willmoore, 21
Kent State University, 47
Kibbutz, 44, 70, 76
Kilminster, Neal T., 36
Kim, Jae-on, 7, 51, 59, 64, 67, 68, 182
King, Anthony, 51
King, Martin Luther, Jr., 126–27
Kitto, H.D.F., 39, 43, 51, 83
Koch, Adrienne, 99
Korean War, 110, 148
Krebs, Frank J., 52
Kweit, Mary Grisez, 157–58
Kweit, Robert W., 157–58

Labor, U.S. Department of, 49
Labor-management committees, 165
Labor unions, 2, 8, 22, 28, 34–35, 40, 42, 48–49, 63, 70, 73, 81–82, 130, 134–36, 141, 143, 167, 170
Lafferty, William M., 20, 49, 52
Laissez-faire leadership, 78
Landsgemeinden, Swiss, 70
Langton, Stuart, 144, 157
Latent groups, 27, 31, 57, 156
Lazarsfeld, Paul, 21
Leaders, 16, 83
  adulation of, 77–78
  exploitation of, 76–78
  rejection of, 75–76, 78
  in work groups, 164
Leadership, 9, 75–79
League of Communists, Yugoslav, 177
League of Women Voters, 134
Legislatures, 86–95
Legitimacy, 17, 27, 80
Lengle, James I., 67
Lenin, V.I., 147
Letter-writing, 2, 5, 125, 130, 141, 148
Lewin, Kurt, 9, 14, 20, 78, 83
Liberalism
  in referendums, 99
  in spatial models, 111–13
Liberty, 12–13, 50
Lijphart, Arend, 121
Likert, Rensis, 97, 99
Lilienthal, David E., 157
Lindblom, Charles E., 68, 83
Lindenfeld, Frank, 52, 178, 179, 183
Lindsay, A.D., 20
Linking-pins, 97
Lippitt, Ronald, 78, 83
Lipsky, Michael, 144
Little Rock, Arkansas, 109–10
Lively, Jack, 15, 18, 21, 74, 82
Lobbying, 125 (*see also* Pressure–group system)
Lobbying groups, 35, 128 (*see also* Pressure groups)
Local government, 70, 73, 132
Logan County, West Virginia, 48
Long, Russell, 175
Loomis, Burdett A., 123, 143, 144
Los Angeles, 61, 155, 179
Lot, selection by, 62–63
Lowi, Theodore J., 144
Lucas, J.R., 65, 68
Luker, Kristin, 123, 124
"Lump of power" fallacy, 152
Luxembourg, 161

McCarthy, Joseph, 9
McClosky, Herbert, 7, 57, 67
McConnell, Grant, 67, 82, 87, 98, 144, 151, 158, 183
McFarland, Andrew S., 143, 144, 183
McGovern, George, 58, 113, 115
Machines, political, 28, 41, 56, 114
McKeesport Steel Casting Company, 49
McPhee, William, 21
McRobie, George, 98
Madison, James, 89, 107
Madrid, 155
Magleby, David, 93, 99
Majority rule, 54, 71, 75, 101–5, 107–8, 111, 113, 121
Malaya, 61
Management, 97 (*see also* Participatory management)
Manipulation of elections, 106–8
Mansbridge, Jane J., 15, 20, 21, 66, 67, 68, 72–74, 78, 82, 83, 95, 182
Mao Zedong (Mao Tse-tung), 16, 33–34, 36, 176
March, James G., 35
Mares, William, 178, 179, 180, 183
Market allocation of resources, 81, 172–73, 175–78, 180
Market economies, 73, 167
Market socialism, 176–77
Market surveys, 137
Markovic, Mihailo, 178
Marmor, Theodore R., 158
Marrow, Alfred J., 20
Marx, Karl, 82, 147, 172
Mason, Ronald, 171, 178, 179, 180
Massachusetts, 43
Massachusetts Fair Share, 134
Material incentives, 175, 180 (*see also* Selective incentives)
"Maximum feasible participation", 10, 146
Mazmanian, Daniel A., 158–159, 183
Median income, 110–11, 118–19, 123
Median voter, 112–13, 115–19, 123
Meetings, 2, 16, 31, 84–87, 137–38 (*see also* Assemblies, Committees, Town meetings)
Mencken, H.L., 16, 21
Merrill, Samuel III, 122
Mexico, 39
Michels, Robert, 85, 98
Milbrath, Lester W., 35, 51, 67, 182
Milk price supports, 142
Mill, John Stuart, 12, 14, 20, 21, 74
Miller, Frederick D., 144
Miller, Nicholas R., 122
Miller, Warren E., 67, 122, 123
Miners for Democracy, 49
Minorities, 149
Minorities, permanent, 75
Minorities rule, 121, 124
Minority parties, 103
Minority rule, 73
Mishler, William, 52
Mobilization, 3–4, 158
Model Cities program, 146
Moe, Terry M., 36, 143
Mondale, Walter, 96, 117
Mondragon cooperatives, 168
Money (*see* Contributions, financial)
Montgomery bus boycott, 127
Montgomery, John D., 158
Moral incentives, 31–36, 129, 131, 138, 175 (*see also* Altruism; Duty, sense of)
Moral Majority, 131, 133, 138

Morone, James A., 158
Motivation, 1, 22–36, 182 (*see also* Incentive balance, Material incentives, Moral incentives, Selective incentives, Social incentives)
Moynihan, Daniel Patrick, 151, 158
Mulder, Mark, 59, 67
Mutual adjustment, 81

NAACP, *see* National Association for the Advancement of Colored People
Nader organizations, 127, 133
Nader, Ralph, 50, 52, 127
Nagel, Jack H., 7, 122, 159
Naisbitt, John, 99
Napoleon, 93
National Association for the Advancement of Colored People (NAACP), 127, 133
National Conservative Political Action Committee (NCPAC), 133
National Farmers Union, 134
Nationalist movements, 63
National Organization for Women (NOW), 127, 138
National Rifle Association (NRA), 24, 130–31
Nazi Germany, 173
NCPAC, *see* National Conservative Political Action Committee
Nee, Victor, 98
Neighborhood action, 87
Neighborhood councils, 62
Neighborhood democracy, 10
Neighborhood government, 74
Neighborhood groups, 82, 97, 131, 157
Neighborhood organizers, 47
Neighborhoods, 73, 82, 142, 147, 152, 158
Neighborhood watch, 153
Nelkin, Dorothy, 159
Netherlands, 41, 60, 64, 103, 157
New England, 79, 183
New Haven, Connecticut, 56
New Jersey, 43, 104
New Left, 28
Newspapers, 88
New York City, 43, 142, 149
New Zealand, 126
Nie, Norman H., 7, 40, 45, 51, 52, 59, 64, 67, 68, 123, 182
Nienaber, Jeanne, 158, 159, 183
Nigeria, 41
Nilson, Sten Sparre, 99
Nixon, Richard M., 110, 115, 126, 139
Nominations, 105, 115, 117
Nonexcludability, 23
Nongovernmental elections, 108, 122
Nonpartisan elections, 108, 122
Norms, social, 33, 36, 38–40, 46, 59, 72, 80–81, 182
Norway, 8, 49, 91, 95, 160–61, 163–64, 169, 173, 176
Norwegian Employers Association, 163
Norwegian Trade Union Council, 163
NRA, *see* National Rifle Association
Nuclear-freeze resolutions, 91
Nuclear power, 16, 93, 154, 156–57
Nurmi, Hannu, 122

Office of Economic Opportunity, 10, 150
O'Hara, Rosemary, 67
Ohio, 47, 154
Oligarchy, iron law of, 135

Olson, Mancur, 23–36, 50, 65, 68, 76, 83, 87, 139, 143, 144, 182
Ombudsmen, 126, 147
OPEC, 111
Oppenheimer, Joe A., 35, 36, 109, 122, 124, 182
Opportunity costs, 31
Ordeshook, Peter C., 26, 31, 32, 35, 123
Ordinary members, 2
Oregon, 91
Organization, effects of on participation, 40–42, 50, 63–64, 127, 182
Organizational levels, 161, 164–65, 170
Organization theory, 7
Organizers, 34–35, 127–28, 131–32
Ouchi, William G., 179, 180
Outcomes:
  defined, 2
  importance of, 37, 44, 79–80, 86
Ownership, 174–75, 178
  collective, 173, 178
  government, 171–72, 174
  social, 175
  (*see also* Employee stock ownership, Worker ownership)

Pacific Northwest, 168
Pairwise choice, 104, 107
Paradox of participatory democracy, 18
Parallel structures, 164 (*see also* QWL systems)
Parenti, Michael, 83
Paris Commune, 98
Parks, Rosa, 127
Participant culture, 38–40
Participation
  amount of, 5
  calculus of (*see* Calculus of participation)
  case for, 11–15
  as control over staff, 131, 135–39
  costs of (*see* Costs of participation)
  decision-making, 19
  defined, 1
  demand-asserting, 19, 142
  extent, 5 (*see also* Extensive democracy, Extensive participation, Extent of participation)
  intensity, 5 (*see also* Intensive democracy, Intensive participation, Intensity of participation)
  measurement of, 5–6
  mobilized, 3 (*see also* Mobilization)
  nonconflictful, 45
  perspectives for evaluating, 10–12, 19–20
  power of, 11, 114
  public policies concerning, 46–50
  quality of, 84–85
  theory of, 5
  as umbrella term, 19
Participation hypothesis, 14, 21, 158
Participatory democracy, 13, 50, 56, 58, 73, 77–78, 82, 98, 181
  and decentralization, 88
  educative effects of, 40
  ideals of, 141
  as panacea, 10
  and referendums, 94
  as slogan, 9
  in workplaces, 165, 170
Participatory democrats, 17–20, 50, 54, 89, 128
Participatory management, 160, 168, 170, 172–74, 178, 180
Particularized contacting, 4, 5, 7, 45

Passionate majorities, 109–10, 113
Passionate minorities, 114, 120–21
Pateman, Carole, 40, 51, 166, 179, 181
Patronage, 12, 26, 41, 56, 140 (*see also* Machines, political)
Payoff matrix, 24–25
Peace, 110
Peace groups, 29, 140
Peasants, 63
Peck, James, 98
Peden, William, 99
Peisistratus, 20
Pennock, J. Roland, 52
Pennsylvania, 83
Perceptibility of effects, 24, 29–30, 32, 132
Pericles, 71
Perlman, Janice, 155, 159
Peru, 160
Peters, Thomas J., 83
Petersen, James C., 159, 183
Peterson, Paul E., 67
Petitions, 2
Petrocik, John R., 67
Philadelphia, 30, 43, 47, 57, 61
Pinochet, Augusto, 173
Planning, 149
  economic, 171–72, 175–78
  neighborhood, 153, 154
Plato, 16, 17, 21
Pleasure of participation, 31, 50, 55, 70
Plebiscites, 90, 92–93, 95 (*see also* Referendums)
Pluralism, 142, 155–56, 171
Plurality rule, 101–5, 111, 113
Plywood factories, worker-owned, 167–68, 179
Police services, 152–53
Policy-administration distinction, 145
Polis, 40, 166
Political action committees (PACs), 140, 143
Political business cycle, 111
Political entrepreneurs, 143
Political parties, 19, 41, 97, 139 (*see also* Communist parties; Democratic Party, U.S.; Republican Party, U.S.; Socialist parties)
Political science, 23, 139
Political scientists, 42, 100, 101
Political system, defined, 2
Politicians, 35, 109
Polity, defined, 2
Polls, 68 (*see also* Surveys)
Pollution, 29, 79
Polsby, Nelson, W., 66
Poor people, 141, 146, 149–51
Position issues, 111–17
Powell, G. Bingham, 52, 122, 123, 182
Power, 2, 26, 152
  bases of, 6
  of citizen groups, 154–55
  equalization of, 60, 166, 170
  in relation to participation, 11
  (*see also* Influence)
Power-sharing, 66, 153, 159
Pressure groups, 2, 19, 121, 125–42
  origins of, 134
  stability of, 131
  types of, 129–34
  (*see also* Interest groups)
Pressure-group system, 140–41, 150, 183
Primary democracy, 98 (*see also* Assembly democracy)
Primary elections, 22, 54, 96, 108, 115, 122
Prisoner's Dilemma, 25, 33

Privileged groups, 27
Productivity, 16, 167–70
Professional associations, 2, 3, 130, 135, 143
Pro-life movement, 120–21, 123–24, 131 (*see also* Abortion)
Proportional outcomes, rule of, 75
Proportional representation (PR), 103–4, 107, 121–22
Proposition 13, 91
Prosperity, 110–11, 115
Protest, 7, 8, 125, 128, 141, 183 (*see also* Demonstrations, Pressure groups, Type D groups)
Pseudo-participation, 3, 14, 80
Public administration, 183 (*see also* Administration, participation in; Citizen involvement)
Public Citizen, Inc., 127
Public goods, 35 (*see also* Collective goods)
Public interest, 139, 142, 155
Public-interest advocates, 29
Public-interest critique of pluralism, 139
Public-interest groups, 29, 128, 134, 140, 143, 157, 183 (*see also* Type M groups)
Purposive commitment, 131–32
Purposive incentives, 143 (*see also* Altruism; Duty, sense of; Moral incentives)

Quakerism, 83
QC (quality-control) circles, 163, 165, 169
Quebec, 47, 63
Quotas, 61–62
QWL (quality-of-worklife) systems, 164–65, 168–70

Rabushka, Alvin, 61, 67
Race, 6, 61, 63–64, 73, 80
Racial segregation, 109–10
Radicals, 39
Raetia, Republic of, 94
Rakove, Milton L., 67
Ranchers, 151
Randomization, 62–63
Random sample, 67–68
Ranney, Austin, 66–67, 94–95, 98–99, 182
Rath Packing Company, 169
Rational egoists, 26–31, 33
Rationality, 31–32, 114
Reagan administration, 10, 146
Reagan, Ronald, 58, 91, 110–11, 115, 117, 120, 140, 171–72
Recombinant DNA, 16, 156
Recreational groups, 40, 130
Referendum democracy, 138
Referendums, 6, 8, 10, 84, 90–96, 162
  adversarial nature, 95
  based on local assemblies, 96
  defined, 90
  mandatory, 93
  (*see also* Direct legislation, Initiatives, Plebiscites)
Reformers, 43, 54, 56, 83, 140
Registration, voter, 12, 48–49, 60
Regulatory agencies, 158
Reichstag, 121
Reiter, Howard L., 51
Religion, 73, 80
Religious organizations, 130, 134
Representation, systems of, 64
Representative democracy, 6–7, 69–70, 87, 138, 151

INDEX   193

definition of, 75
need for pressure groups in, 142
in workplaces, 165
(*see also* Elections, Voting)
Representativeness of participants, 96
and motivation, 54–58
and social class, 58–60
Representatives, 66, 84, 98
Repression, 22, 46
Republican Party, U.S., 31, 48, 57, 87, 113, 115–18, 120
Retaliation, 45–46, 52
Revolutionaries, 34
Rights, 13, 46
Riker, William H., 26, 31, 32, 35, 123
Ripple effects, 30
Rising expectations, 17–18
Riskin, Carl., 36
Roman Republic, 65
Rosener, Judy B., 158
Rosenstone, Steven J., 7, 48, 51, 52, 182
Rothschild-Whitt, Joyce, 52, 178, 179, 183
Rousseau, Jean Jacques, 14, 21, 64, 65, 82
Ruhr Valley, 161
Runoff elections, 54, 102, 107–8, 121
Russell, Raymond, 179
Russian Revolution, 147

Sachs, Stephen, 52
Samoan circle, 146
Sampling error, 68
Samson, 19
San Francisco, 168
Sanitation services, 152–53
Sartori, Giovanni, 82
Satisfaction, job, 169–70
Saturday Night Massacre, 126
Scaff, Lawrence A., 21
Scandinavia, 167, 169
Scanlon, Joseph, 174
Scanlon Plan, 174
Scavenger firms, 168
Schattschneider, E.E., 140, 144
Schelling, Thomas C., 35–36
Schlozman, Kay Lehman, 63, 68, 143
Schmidt, David D., 98–99
Schools, public, 52, 110, 149
Schumacher, E. F., 87, 98
Schumpeter, Joseph, 16, 21, 82
SCLU, *see* Southern Christian Leadership Conference
Scope of decisions, 161 (*see also* Jurisdiction; Outcomes, importance of)
Scott Bader Commonwealth, 62–63, 68
Selective incentives, 26, 28–29, 32–36, 41, 47–49, 55–56, 129–33, 140–41, 144
Selflessness, 32 (*see also* Altruism)
Self-sufficiency, 79–80
Seligman, Martin E. P., 21
Selznick, Philip, 83, 151, 152, 159
Semi-autonomous work groups, 164
Sen, Amartya, 36
Sennett, Richard, 82
SERL, *see* Socioeconomic resource level
SES, *see* Socioeconomic status
Sex, 6, 61, 73, 80
Shabad, Goldie, 82
Shafer, Byron E., 67
Shanghai Commune, 85
Shanks, J. Merrill, 123
Shareholder representatives, 101

Shopfloor participation, 162–65, 170, 176, 178
Sierra Club, 22, 134, 138
Simmons, John, 178–80, 183
Simon, Herbert A., 14, 122
Simplicity of elections, 104, 108
Single-peaked preferences, 123
Sirianni, Carmen, 83
Size, 50, 53, 65, 84–98
and collective action, 27–28, 35–36
limits for direct democracy, 19, 72, 86–87, 138
of pressure groups, 130–33
and random panels, 55, 63
"small" and "large", meaning of, 67
and workplace participation, 166
Small groups, 65–66, 138
Small numbers, 27–28, 30, 35–36
Smith, Michael P., 179
SNCC, *see* Student Nonviolent Coordinating Committee
Social class, 6, 58–59, 63–64, 67, 73 (*see also* Class bias in voting, Income, Status)
Social incentives, 27, 30, 33, 35–36, 132–33
Socialism, 167, 171–72, 174–75
Socialist parties, 63
Socialist societies, 89
Social movements, 127, 132–33, 141, 143
Socioeconomic resource level (SERL), 58 (*see also* Social class)
Socioeconomic status (SES), 58 (*see also* Social class, Status)
Solidarity, 81, 132, 137, 175–76
Solon, 20
South Bend Lathe, 169
Southern Christian Leadership Conference (SCLU), 127
Soviet Union, 47, 147, 171, 173, 177
Spain, 46, 147, 157, 160, 168
Sparta, 40
Spatial models, 111–20
Special interests, 55–57, 65, 68, 139–40
Special-purpose authorities, 44
Speech, unrestricted, 54
Spiro, Melford, 51, 76, 83
Spruce Hill Community Association, 31
Staff, 41, 157
as agents, 128, 131
of interest groups, 35, 127, 130–33, 135–38, 143
as organizers, 127–28, 131–32
State and local government, 10
State and local politics, 12, 133–34
Status, 58–63, 65, 92 (*see also* Income, Social Class)
Steiner, Jurg, 98
Stevenson, Adlai III, 56
Stockman, David, 140, 144
Stokes, Donald E., 122–23
Stone, Marvin, 99
Strain, system, 17, 21
Strategic voting, 102, 104, 107–8
Stratification, 61–62, 158
Strikes, 168, 170
Strong democracy, 82 (*see also* Barber, Benjamin R.)
Structure, 42–46, 83
Structureless groups, 76, 86
Structureless groups, 76, 86
Student Nonviolent Coordinating Committee (SNCC), 17, 127, 131
Students for a Democratic Society, 138
Subcultures, 39

Subordination, 80–81
Suggestion boxes, 147
Supek, Rudi, 178
Supreme Court, U.S., 120, 124
Survey research, 23, 32, 37, 42
Surveys, 63, 148
Susskind, Lawrence, 159, 183
Sweden, 44, 94–95, 126, 156, 160–61, 170, 176
Switzerland, 43, 65, 79, 88, 90–95, 99, 183

Tait, Adam, 52
Tannenbaum, Arnold S., 35
Tavistock Institute, 163
Taxes, 89, 91
Teachers union, 142
Television, 41–43, 88, 113
Tennessee, 165
Tennessee Valley Authority (TVA), 146, 152, 157
Third party candidates, 113
Third World, 160
Thomas, John Clayton, 158
Thorsrud, Einar, 163, 164, 179
Thucydides, 82
Tilly, Charles, 46, 52
Time, 15–16, 18, 74, 84–85
Tit-for-tat strategy, 36
Tocqueville, Alexis de, 18, 74, 89, 98, 126, 142
Tolerance, 13, 17, 19, 142
Town meetings, 6, 19, 55, 70
Townsend, James R., 67, 158
Trade associations, 147
Transitions, 17–18, 134
Transport and General Workers Union, 135
Truman, Harry S., 110
Trust, 33, 37–40
Tufte, Edward R., 82, 122–23
Turnout, 53, 68 (see also Voting turnout)
TVA, see Tennessee Valley Authority
Twenty-sixth Amendment, 41
Type D groups, 129–32
  democracy in, 136–39, 141
Type M groups, 129–31
  democracy in, 136–41, 143
Type S groups, 129–31
  democracy in, 135–36, 138–41, 143
Tyranny, 89

Uhlaner, Carole Jean, 51
Unconditional participation, 33–34, 36
Unemployed, 63, 65
Unions (see Labor unions)
Union shop contracts, 28, 35
Unitary and adversary methods, 95
Unitary democracy, 72–74
  assumptions of, 82
  defined, 72
  in Type S groups, 136, 138
United Auto Workers, 131, 161, 164–65
United Kingdom, 39, 91–92, 160, 170
United Mine Workers, 48–49
United States
  cities, 61
  class bias of voting, 117–20
  codetermination, 161
  Constitution, 69
  crowded fields of candidates, 108
  economic growth, 168
  educational politics, 45
  exceptionalism of, 63
  federal grant programs, 146
  federalism, 43
  grass-roots ideology, 87–88
  legislators, 126
  political culture, 39–40
  political-economic system, 173
  power in, 141
  Presidency, 139
  presidential elections, 6, 22, 96, 102, 110–11, 114–15, 120
  QC circles, 163
  referendums, 91
  resource-management agencies, 155
  rural programs, 146, 151
  school finance, 89
  separation of powers, 43
  South, 6, 89, 109–10
  tradition of November elections, 43
  unitary democracy, 73
  urban programs, 145–46, 151
  voting turnout rates, 47–48, 117–20
  workplace democracy, 49, 160, 171
United Way, 31
Universal Voter Registration Act, 48
Universities, 2, 80
University of Pennsylvania, 35, 61
Untouchables, 63
Urban League, 127
Urban Renewal, 145
User groups, 155
USSR (see Soviet Union)
Utopian communities, 2, 70, 77
Utopian goals, 36

Valence issues, 111, 113
Values, 8–21 (see also Developmental effects of participation, Equality, Instrumental benefits of participation, Intrinsic benefits of participation, Participatory democracy)
Vanek, Jaroslav, 170, 179, 180
Verba, Sidney, 7, 21, 39–40, 45, 51, 52, 59, 63–64, 67, 68, 83, 123, 182
Vermont, 59
Vermont Asbestos, 169–70
Vietnam, 9, 29, 133
Vietnam War, 44, 47, 56, 110, 133, 139, 148
Viguerie, Richard A., 99
Violence, 125, 132 (see also Force)
Virginia, 96
Vocational associations, 130, 143
Voice, 44–45, 136, 144 (see also Exit, Participation)
Voluntary action, 4, 78, 153
Volunteers, 147, 157
von Fritz, Kurt, 68
Voth, Donald C., 157, 158
Voting, 2, 45, 89–98, 100–21, 182
  and adversary democracy, 72
  compulsory, 4, 47, 60
  influence of organization on, 64
  as paramount form of participation, 100
  and social class, 59
  in Type M groups, 137
  (see also Elections, Referendums, Voting turnout)
Voting rights, 8, 89
Voting Rights Act of 1965, 41, 110
Voting turnout, 8, 12, 29, 108
  in Australia, 47

class bias in U.S., 117–20
decline in U.S., 6, 41–42
of men and women, 51
in Netherlands, 60
in PR and presidential systems, 104
and U.S. election results, 120

Wagner Act, 28
Walinsky, Adam, 158
Walker, Jack, 134, 143
Walzer, Michael, 83, 182
War on Poverty, 10, 146, 150
Washington, D. C., 134, 143
Watanuki, Joji, 20, 181
Watergate, 126, 133, 139
Waterman, Robert H., Jr., 83
Weimar Republic, 121
Weirton Steel, 170
Weissberg, Robert, 36
Weitzman, Martin, 180
Welfare recipients, 141
Wertheimer, Alan, 52
West, Darrell M., 123–24
West Germany, 8, 39, 122, 160–63, 165, 168, 170, 179
West Virginia, 48
Whistle-blowers, 29, 36
Whitaker, Gordon P., 159
White, Ralph K., 78, 83
Wildavsky, Aaron, 66
Wilson, James Q., 39, 51, 123, 127, 143, 183
Win-win situations, 153 (*see also* Conflict)
Wisconsin, 96
Witte, John F., 179
Wolfinger, Raymond E., 7, 48, 51, 52, 182
Women, 11, 41, 47, 63, 65, 134

Women's movement, 28–29, 61, 75–76, 125–26
Worker-managed economies, 98
Worker ownership, 81, 167–68, 174, 180 (*see also* Employee stock ownership)
Workers, 63
Workers' control, 161–63, 168, 170, 179
Workers' cooperative corporations, 162
Workers' councils, 47, 59, 62
Workers' self-management, 165, 167, 170, 172, 174, 176–80
Working-class political organization, 140
Workplace democracy, 5, 8, 10, 46, 49, 80, 160–61, 166–67, 171, 175–76, 181, 183
Workplace participation, 46, 89, 160–80
Workplaces, 2, 70
Works councils, 164–65
World War II, 148, 161, 171
Wright, John R., 143
Wright, Vincent, 98–99

Yablonski, Jock, 49
Yates, Douglas, 59, 67
Young, Oran R., 36
Youngstown, Ohio, 49
Yugoslavia, 8, 49, 59, 62, 89, 160–61, 163–64, 168, 172–73, 175–77

Zeal, 55, 57–58
Zero-sum conception of power, 152, 159
Zhang, Chunqiao, 85, 98
Zimbalist, Andrew S., 180
Zipp, John F., 123
Zirakzadeh, Cyrus, 158
Zolberg, Aristide, 143
Zwerdling, Daniel, 68, 179